# The
# Flying Saucer
# Reader

# The Flying Saucer Reader

## BY JAY DAVID

THE NEW AMERICAN LIBRARY

*I am most grateful
to my able research associate Elaine Crane
for her assistance in the preparation
of this book.*

First Printing

Published by The New American Library, Inc.
1301 Avenue of the Americas, New York, New York 10019
Published simultaneously in Canada
by General Publishing Company, Ltd.

Library of Congress Catalog Card Number: 67–18737

Printed in the United States of America

Acknowledgment is made to the following authors and publishers for permission to reprint the material listed:

". . . Challenged," from FLYING SAUCERS ON THE ATTACK by Harold
T. Wilkins. Copyright 1954 by Harold T. Wilkins. Reprinted by permission
of Citadel Press.

"The Killian Case," from FLYING SAUCERS: TOP SECRET by Major Donald
E. Keyhoe. Copyright © 1960, by Donald E. Keyhoe. Reprinted by permission of G. P. Putnam's Sons.

## This is a continuation of the copyright page

# Introduction

*On November 16, 1966,* The New York Times *noted that "an Air Force plan to have university experts investigate unidentified flying objects is getting good acceptance in the academic world." The interest of the intellectual community, coupled with the fact that* The New York Times *— which, until recently, was somewhat hesitant about printing UFO stories at all — devoted a number of column inches to this subject, are two examples of the growing stature of, and interest in, this phenomenon.*

*Throughout history strange aerial objects have been seen and recorded, but only in the last twenty years has "ufology" become a national pastime. In 1947, a private pilot by the name of Kenneth Arnold sighted a formation of bright objects flying at tremendous speed near Mt. Ranier in Washington. Commenting to newsmen, he said, "They flew like a saucer would if you skipped it across the water." The term "flying saucer" was thus incorporated into the English language, and the twentieth century's saucer "flap" was launched.*

*Since the late 1940's scores of books and articles have been written on this subject by people who have seen unidentified flying objects, who claim to have been contacted by people from other planets (either mentally or physically), who theorize why we must have visitors from outer space — or from the center of the earth. Others dismiss the idea of flying saucers as complete nonsense. Some assert that the Air Force is* withholding vital information on UFOs, while the Air Force denies the charge in no uncertain terms.

I have carefully considered nearly everything written on the topic and have chosen each particular item with the intention of presenting a well-rounded and comprehensive view of the entire subject — a definitive anthology, if you will.

This book takes no sides. Instead, it offers a selection of the best material published during the last dozen years. Are we being visited by intelligent life from other worlds? The evidence is here — you be the judge.

JAY DAVID
New York City

# Contents

PART ONE   *The Evidence*

*Astonishing stories of strange aerial objects are constantly being reported. What do people see? Baffling lights, luminous craft, hovering airships are most often described, but occasionally someone will hint at human-like beings aboard a particular craft. The accounts very often come from reliable witnesses, and a large percentage of these witnesses come forward reluctantly — for fear of ridicule. Farmers have seen UFOs and so have doctors, lawyers, astronomers, nurses, mechanics, policemen, and children. Amateur radio operators assert they regularly converse with beings on other planets, and scientists inform us that they receive interesting signals from outer space.*

*The following chapter includes descriptions of various sightings and contacts from Biblical times to the present day.*

*SIGHTINGS*

PART ONE  *The Evidence*

*Astonishing stories of strange aerial objects are constantly being reported. What do people see? Baffling lights, luminous craft, hovering airships are most often described, but occasionally someone will hint at human-like beings aboard a particular craft. The accounts very often come from reliable witnesses, and a large percentage of these witnesses come forward reluctantly — for fear of ridicule. Farmers have seen UFOs and so have doctors, lawyers, astronomers, nurses, mechanics, policemen, and children. Amateur radio operators assert they regularly converse with beings on other planets, and scientists inform us that they receive interesting signals from outer space.*

*The following chapter includes descriptions of various sightings and contacts from Biblical times to the present day.*

*SIGHTINGS*

# In

# Biblical Times . . .

*How long have men seen mysterious objects in the heavens? The following interpretation of the Bible, from Brinsley Le Poer Trench's book* The Sky People, *suggests that the phenomenon dates back to those ancient days.*

Moses kept the flock of Jethro, his father-in-law, and he led the flock to Mount Horeb. It was there that he had his first great contact with the Sky People. Many more were to follow.

And the angel of the Lord appeared unto him in a *flame of fire** out of the midst of a bush: and he looked, and behold, the bush burned with fire, and the bush was not consumed.

And Moses said, I will now turn aside, and see . . .
God called unto him out of the midst of the bush, and said, Moses, Moses. And he said, Here am I.

And he said, Draw not nigh hither: put off thy shoes from off thy feet, for the place whereupon thou standest is holy ground.

Exodus 3:2-5

A spaceship — flying saucer — often illuminates the neighboring countryside with its electric forcefield. The glowing light within this forcefield surrounding the ship would most certainly have caused the bush to look as if it was on fire. Moses was so curious about the phenomenon of the bush being burned with fire and not consumed that he turned to look closer at it. The Lord, seeing him about to come nearer, called out warning him not to do so.

* Italics mine.–*Author.*

**3**

If Moses had gone too near before the current had been turned down he would have suffered a severe electrical shock or even death. There are many instances in saucer reports today of the effects of a spacecraft's forcefield, some of which are related further on in this chapter. Other instances where people have been warned not to come too near are given in the Bible and these will be commented on later.

Moses was commanded by the Lord to bring the Israelites, who had been oppressed by Pharaoh, out of the land of Egypt. This he did and according to the Bible, the Israelites were led through the wilderness near the Red Sea.

> And the Lord went before them by day in a *pillar of a cloud,* to lead them the way; and by night in a *pillar of fire,* to give them light; to go by day and night:
>
> He took not away the pillar of the cloud by day, nor the pillar of fire by night, from before the people.
>
> Exodus 13:21-22.

What was the pillar of a cloud by day and the pillar of fire by night that guided and protected the Israelites? This is a wonderful description of a modern flying saucer. Many current reports received of spaceships today refer to clouds and these ships at night look brilliant, brighter than any stars.

At this period of Biblical history, the Israelites were a wandering nomadic people. They were not living in a mechanical jet age like those in the world today. How else would they describe great spaceships than by words used in their everyday language, such as pillar of cloud, thick cloud, pillar of fire, fiery chariot, and whirlwind? It is interesting to note here Jesus' prophetic statement in Mark 13:26-7.

> And then shall they see the Son of Man coming in the clouds with great power and glory.
>
> And then shall he send his angels, and shall gather together his elect from the four winds, from the uttermost part of the earth to the uttermost part of heaven.

Yes, it is quite extraordinary the number of times in the Bible the Lord appeared in a cloud.

And the Lord said unto Moses, Lo, I come unto thee in a thick cloud, that the people may hear when I speak with thee, and believe thee forever. And Moses told the words of the people unto the Lord.

Exodus 19:9.

And be ready against the third day: for the third day the Lord will come down in the sight of all the people upon Mount Sinai.

And thou shalt set bounds unto the people round about, saying, Take heed to yourselves, that ye go not up into the mount, or touch the border of it: whosoever toucheth the mount shall be surely put to death:

There shall not an hand touch it, but he shall surely be stoned, or shot through; whether it be beast or man, it shall not live: when the trumpet soundeth long, they shall come up to the mount.

Exodus 19:11-13.

In these three verses, the Lord (the Captain of the spaceship) tells Moses he will come *down* on to the top of Mount Sinai in the sight of all the people. He then warns Moses not to let the people or any animals come near the craft nor within a certain distance, until he gives a signal — an all clear. Hundreds of modern sightings have testified to the existence of a powerful electric forcefield around these craft, and people who have got too near have suffered burns. . . .

And it came to pass on the third day in the morning, that there were thunders and lightnings, and a thick cloud upon the mount, and the voice of the trumpet exceeding loud; so that all the people that was in the camp trembled.

Exodus 19:16.

And the Lord came down upon Mount Sinai, on the top of the Mount: and the Lord called Moses up to the top of the mount; and Moses went up.

Exodus 19:20.

What a wonderful description this is of a spaceship coming down on Mount Sinai. The Captain of the craft once more has thought for the people and tells Moses to warn them yet again.

> And the Lord said unto Moses, Go down, charge the people, lest they break through unto the Lord to gaze, and many of them perish.
>
> Exodus 19:21

Then the Lord, who was obviously Jehovah, gave Moses the Ten Commandments. . . .

> And the Lord said unto Moses, Come up to me into the mount, and be there: and I will give thee tables of stone, and a law, and commandments which I have written, that thou mayest teach them.
>
> And Moses rose up, and his minister Joshua: and Moses went up into the mount of God.
>
> And Moses went up into the mount, and a *cloud* * covered the mount:
>
> And the *glory of the Lord* * abode upon Mount Sinai, and the *cloud* * covered it six days: and the seventh day he called unto Moses out of the midst of the cloud.
>
> And the sight of the *glory of the Lord* * was like *devouring fire* * on the top of the mount in the eyes of the children of Israel.
>
> And Moses went into the *midst of the cloud* * and gat him up into the mount: *and Moses was in the mount forty days and forty nights.* *
>
> Exodus 24:12-13, 15-18.

Moses was invited to go up Mount Sinai to where the glory of the Lord was covered by a cloud. Notice how the sight of the glory of the Lord was like devouring fire on top of the mount seen from below by the Israelites. Compare this description with the earlier one given of the object that guided the Israelites through the wilderness — a pillar of cloud by day and a pillar of fire by night.

* Italics mine.–*Author.*

When the cloud was not covering the spaceship on Mount Sinai, it glowed like devouring fire. Then in verse 18, we read that Moses was on the mount forty days and forty nights. In the light of the foregoing description of a space craft, it seems pretty certain that Moses spent forty days and forty nights inside the ship conferring with the Lord, its Captain. . . .

# Miracle

# at Fatima . . .

*Let us jump from antiquity to the twentieth century —*
*1917. World War I divided the globe, but in a small*
*village in a corner of Europe thousands upon*
*thousands of people gathered to witness a momentous*
*event. The following description of that event is from*
Flying Saucers Through the Ages, *by Paul Thomas.*

. . . On 13 October 1917 at Fatima in Portugal — where today there is a large church — a huge crowd of curious people, thought to consist of more than 50,000, were gathered to await a wonder visible to everyone. Three little children had declared that a Lady of Light (*uma senhorita de luz*) had been appearing to them regularly for several months and that this wonder had been definitely promised by the Lady. It would take place at mid-day (local time) on this 13 October "in order that all might believe."

Thus 50,000 people from all over the country, many from the capital, Lisbon, waited in driving rain to see if the spectre would appear in a dramatic fashion before the waiting multitudes, or whether nothing would happen at all — which was much more likely.

A little before the appointed hour the rain ceased and the sky began to clear of clouds. When it was exactly mid-day, local time, the three children fell down in ecstasy, and 50,000 or more people saw something that they thought was the sun looking as if it had been "detached from the sky" and had become like "a polished silver disc, not blinding bright, with clear-cut edges." It shuddered, rocked and turned round and round giving off bright lights that changed colour. It stopped turning and then zig-zagged downwards which caused general stupor, and then returned to the sky, where "it took on its normal appearance," that is to say, it was no longer possible to look at it.

The whole thing had lasted about ten minutes.

Today Fatima has become a centre of pilgrimage which has become famous the world over — it is the rival of Lourdes in France. The basilica welcomes thousands of the faithful every year who have come to worship the Virgin Mary. Cures take place there as well as lasting conversions. It is one of the most important places for Roman Catholics in the twentieth century.

Do not let us make any mistake; all this is momentous.

It is true that the miracle of Fatima is not one of the dogmas that a Roman Catholic is compelled to accept as authentic; indeed, there are many believers who have their own opinions on the subject and on several occasions we have mentioned this subject to priests who, accepting the miracle of Lourdes as a divine manifestation, did not hesitate to consign Fatima to the realm of superstition: but it is a fact that priests who talk like this have studied the facts of the Lourdes story, while they have only learned about Fatima by hearsay.

Nevertheless Fatima is a place where the blind recover their sight, where those who weep are comforted, and where cripples walk. This in itself should lead to respect, or at least discretion, on the subject of suns which dance.

Besides it is far from our thoughts to reduce this "miracle" to the passing of an ordinary flying saucer — nothing could allow us to dismiss this affair as ordinary. . . . What advantage would be gained by making such a transposition? What would be gained by "explaining" a miracle, itself something that could not be proved, by the presence of a metallic flying saucer — which is just as difficult to prove as the other? . . . The similarity or dissimilarity in the two cases would not bring us anywhere nearer solving the mystery, it would just be one inexplicable object instead of another.

But the suggestions that we are going to put down follow a completely different train of thought, and it is here more than ever necessary to keep a clear and impartial judgement. Whether you, reader, believe in flying saucers, whether you are indifferent, or whether you are a sceptic, we ask you to follow our chain of reasoning calmly and without prejudice either way. We will see later where our reasoning will take us. It is all quite logical.

Let us first have a look at the story of Fatima from the beginning.

On 13 May 1917 — the thirteenth day of the fifth month of the third complete year of the Great War — three little shepherd children, two little girls and one boy, came back from the fields as usual; but on return they told their parents, not without a great deal of stumbling and hesitation, how a "Lady of Light," of great beauty, had appeared to them above the top of an evergreen oak. The vision had spoken: she asked them to return to the same place on the thirteenth of the following month.

All they received as a result were several vigorous blows. No one had the right to pretend to be Bernadette Soubirous, the saint of Lourdes, especially sixty years afterwards, and it was very disagreeable for the parents of a humble family to find they had children who saw visions. However the good reputation of the children was in their favour and the curiosity of the villagers was roused enough for an escort to follow the children to their rendezvous.

There those who had come were able to watch the children fall on their knees while a faint white vapour formed round them; the daylight as well as the temperature began to lose their intensity and a fresh breeze began to blow. No one saw a "beautiful Lady" but the eldest of the children, Lucia, talked as if she were speaking to someone and then listened to inaudible replies. The villagers, according to their own words, only heard a soft buzzing. . . . At the moment that Lucia said the "Lady" was disappearing something happened: the branches of the evergreen oak bent down as if pulled in the direction shown by the little girl.

It was not surprising that on 13 July several hundred people gathered at Cova da Iria, the place where the apparitions took place, to take part in a display which was just like that of the previous month. Lucia declared afterwards that the "Lady" had confided a certain number of "secrets" to her. This time the departure of the celestial visitor was accompanied by a sharp report so that a triumphal arch, put up to celebrate the occasion, was shaken on its foundations.

Reaction was not slow in forthcoming. The local governor, disbelieving, wanted to make the children swear that they had made it all up, but all to no avail. He then tried to make them disclose the "secrets" the "Lady" had given them, but met with as little success. On 13 August, while a very large crowd made its way to Cova da Iria, he decided to arrest the little promoters of public disorder and took them to the sub-prefecture of police at Ourem, and submitted them to a new interrogation, first together and then separately: he threatened to plunge them into a large pot of boiling oil if they persisted in their silence: "Your little brother has already been fried!" he said to one of the little girls, who went pale, but continued to remain silent.

While this was taking place the pilgrims assembled at Cova da Iria learned that the children would not be coming. There was first dismay and then anger — certainly the absence of the little shepherds would result in nothing happening. Nevertheless a sort of thunder-clap was heard, like the explosion of a fog-signal, *followed* by a flash of lightning. The white mist rose up from the ground and everything took place as if the children had been there. And it all lasted about ten minutes.

Four days later, the three little children, back at their normal work, suddenly saw the valley light up with the yellow glow that usually preceded the apparitions, and behold, there was the "Lady." Lucia threw herself on her knees and besought her to do something that would make those around her believe when she told what she had seen. The "Lady" — according to Lucia naturally — promised a remarkable sight for October.

But it was only August and an interview took place meanwhile on 13 September. This time 20,000 to 30,000 people were gathered round the children and already the vision was becoming more complex in a striking manner. In addition to the white vapour surrounding the children some of the people there — but not all — saw a luminous globe majestically crossing the sky, coming from the east and making for the evergreen oak. Ten minutes later, the interview over, the same globe reappeared and went off towards the sky. People pointed at it, whilst an old white-haired lady with her missal in her hand, stamped "I see nothing! I see nothing!"

It was then declared that a large number of white objects, like thin flakes of snow, fell from the sky and disintegrated as soon as they touched the ground.

These are the actual words used by those who witnessed these "atmospheric phenomena" (that is what they were called) and let us not forget that these witnesses, when they spoke, always thought that they were describing the details of an appearance by the Virgin Mary, from various things they have said.

"To my great surprise," declared one of these witnesses, "I saw clearly and distinctly a ball of light sliding slowly and majestically through space. . . . Then suddenly, with the extraordinary light that it let out, this globe disappeared before my eyes, and the priest who was at my side saw it no more either." When he asked this priest what he thought the globe was, the latter replied without any hesitation, "that it was without doubt the *craft* in which the Virgin Mary was brought down to her children. . . ."

"All those who saw this globe," another witness said, "had the impression that it was an *aeroplane of light* bringing the Mother of God to meet the shepherd children and then taking her back to Paradise. . . ."

Let us not try to understand why, in the minds of those gathered there, the Mother of God should have felt the need to use a craft or an aeroplane to come down to Earth. From what we have seen already this idea is nothing short of laughable. Let us remember that despite the absurdity of such a theory, the impression mechanically felt by those who saw the wonder was that of an "aerial vehicle" and not of a meteor or simple mass hallucination.

That everyone did not see the globe is more disturbing especially that whether or not they saw the object had no bearing on their degree of faith. Perhaps these celestial craft are only visible from certain angles. Or perhaps they are able to implant certain ideas in the minds of certain people. We just do not know. In any case, we can draw the rather disquieting conclusion that craft of this nature are able to fly over our heads without our always being able to see them ourselves.

Let us go on to the shower of white objects: "Under the wondering eyes [of those present] something like flakes of snow [sic] but round and brilliant came down very slowly towards the ground in a brilliant ray of supernatural light. As if they were drawn to Earth by the irresistible current of a river of light of dazzling brightness, a huge number of white objects like snowflakes drifted down from the sky. They became narrower as one watched them coming down, and disappeared as soon as they touched the ground."

A lady declared that she had seen these "flower petals" settle on her left shoulder; she wanted to pick them up but they had vanished.

There were similar showers of white rain at Cova da Iria, especially on 13 May 1918, the anniversary of the first appearance, and on 13 May 1924. . . .

Let us return to Fatima whilst the dawn is breaking on that celebrated 13 October, the date fixed for the appearance of the wonder which was to be the final proof of the truth of the tales of little Lucia. The "Lady of Light" had promised that after that everyone would be able to believe her. If the wonder took place the little shepherdess had told the truth and had invented nothing.

According to calculations made at the time, between 50,000 and 70,000 people gathered around Cova da Iria. Among this crowd the majority of the people were believers, but in addition were those who were just curious, the sceptics, and even anticlerical journalists who had come to jeer at the credulity of the public. One of them, editor-in-chief of the Socialist paper *O Seculo* (*The Century*) gave, as a result, a particularly valuable testimony (in a letter to a fellow-atheist, the Mayor of Santarem) as he was completely impartial.

At 10.00 the sky was covered with black clouds and the rain fell heavily; but nobody thought of going home. Photographs taken on that day graphically show the crowd covered by a forest of umbrellas. A little before the customary time of the appearance of the "Lady," and although the weather had only slightly improved, Lucia asked people to shut their umbrellas; the request, passed round from mouth to mouth, was rapidly carried out.

At 13.30, official time, but mid-day by local time, the clouds began to disperse. The children fell in ecstasy; the usual white mist formed and rose round them three times. In a few moments Lucia cried out loudly: "Look at the sun!" Surprised, the people, who had been watching the evergreen oak anxiously in the hope of seeing something or someone, turned round. The wonder that was announced then took place.

"I could see the sun," wrote one of those present, "like a disc with sharp edges luminous and brilliant, but not in any way hurtful to the eyes. I heard people comparing it to a disc of matt silver; but I did not think this was quite correct as it was of a brighter colour, vivid and rich, shimmering like a pearl. This disc did not look in the least like the Moon, which looks transparent and pure at night: it looked like *a living star*. It was different from the Moon in another way, it was not spherical, it looked like a flat and polished disc which had been cut from the pearl in a shell . . . and was clearly seen to have a ridged edge like a drawing-board."

But this silvery sun, flat and disc-shaped, could not have been very high up, for in the words of another witness "the light clouds which crossed the sky from east to west did not hide the brightness of the star and as a result one gained the impression that these clouds passed behind the Sun and not in front of it." The "star" was therefore at that moment between the clouds and the Earth.

Suddenly the Sun shuddered and rocked, and then began to turn round and round sending out bundles of light-beams which changed colour at regular intervals. The whole landscape was affected by these colours, "but *senhora,* you've turned yellow!" cried one of the witnesses, before the lady turned in succession green, blue and then crimson at the same time as everyone else. After two or three minutes, the disc seemed to hang motionless for several seconds, then it began again its gyratory movements, changing colour all the time. Finally, becoming blood-red it began to come down in a series of zig-zagging leaps, each of which brought it nearer the Earth, where the temperature rose sharply. Finally, after a final swing, much more slowly, the disc rose rapidly up to the heavens — at that moment completely bare of clouds. Then everything suddenly reverted to normal; the Sun, motionless in the sky shone with its customary dazzling light, preventing the crowd from looking at it any further.

The clothes of those who, since the morning, had been drenched by the rain were now completely dry.

The accounts and testimonies which we have just told, can be found almost exactly the same in the books devoted to the appearances at Fatima. Take, for example, *Fatima, Espérance du Monde,* by G. Renault (Editions Plon), a study composed of photographs taken at the time of the event, on 13 October 1917, as well as reproductions of articles from contemporary journals.

While the details of the "dance of the Sun" as told to us by witnesses are fresh in our mind, let us compare them with more recent sightings of "unidentified flying objects"; perhaps we shall be no longer astonished to find that they coincide exactly.

| *Fatima*<br>(extracts from officially confirmed reports) | *Flying Saucer Sightings*<br>(from Aimé Michel and Donald Keyhoe) |
|---|---|
| A disc with sharp edges, at the edge bright, luminous, and brilliant, but not tiring the eyes at all. | A luminous disc as large as the full Moon, but shining with a brighter glow was hanging motionless in the night sky. Suddenly the object began to rock. . . . (A baker from Arras, 1954.) |
| I heard people compare it with a matt silver disc, but this did not seem accurate to me as it seemed to have a brighter, more vivid and richer colour like the sheen of a pearl. | The object was lit-up by a pale light, not blinding, rather like that of neon. (The crew of a French Air Force plane, 1954.) |
| This pearly disc was moving at a dizzy speed. It was not the twinkling of a star: it turned round at an astounding speed. | It was a wheel looking as if it had been made of red-hot iron, turning round. (The crew of an air-liner of TWA in the USA in 1952.) |

It was suddenly transformed into a wheel of fire. The sun threw bundles of rays of blue, red, violet, yellow, and green light in all directions.

Shining first with an intense blue, the object soon changed to white, while a red halo appeared at its edges. The object revolved with a rapid motion. (Sighting at Dole (Jura) in 1954.) Above Phoenix (Arizona) the craft changed successively from red to green, then from yellow to blue. (1952.)

Suddenly detached from the sky, the sun seemed to rebound in the sky by a series of leaps and bounds. . . . It approached by a series of zig-zag movements.

When the craft began to come down, it began to shake like a dead leaf, like the movement of a pendulum. Then it hung in the sky turning like a top. (Lieut. J. Kilburn on board a jet aircraft, September 1952.)

As if hesitating, the sun paused before going, recalled by a mysterious order taking its place high in the heavenly vault.

The final descent was like that of a dead leaf, but after hanging for a moment like a pendulum, the craft shot upwards at an angle, and disappeared. (Le Bourget, 1952.)

The clothes of those who since the morning had been drenched by the rain were now completely dry.

After the passage of a craft giving off intense heat a log merchant from Lusigny, near Troyes, declared that despite the rain, the ground and the trees were as dry as if the sun were shining. (20 October, 1954.)

# The Washington
# National Sightings . . .

*Edward J. Ruppelt was the former head of the Air
Force Project Blue Book, a special project set up to
investigate UFO reports. The following selection is
from his book* The Report on Unidentified Flying
Objects. *In his own words, "No flying saucer report
in the history of the UFO ever won more world
acclaim than the Washington National Sightings."*

. . . When radars at the Washington National Airport and at
Andrews AFB, both close to the nation's capital, picked up UFO's,
the sightings beat the Democratic National Convention out of
headline space. They created such a furor that I had inquiries from
the office of the President of the United States and from the press in
London, Ottawa, and Mexico City. A junior-sized riot was only nar-
rowly averted in the lobby of the Roger Smith Hotel in Washington
when I refused to tell U.S. newspaper reporters what I knew about
the sightings.

Besides being the most highly publicized UFO sightings in the
Air Force annals, they were also the most monumentally fouled-up
messes that repose in the files. Although the Air Force said that the
incident had been fully investigated, the Civil Aeronautics Authority wrote a formal report on the sightings, and numerous magazine
writers studied them, the complete story has never fully been told.
The pros have been left out of the con accounts, and the cons were
nearly overlooked by the pro writers.

For a year after the twin sightings we were still putting little
pieces in the puzzle. . . .

On July 10 the crew of a National Airlines plane reported a light "too bright to be a lighted balloon and too slow to be a big meteor" while they were flying south at 2,000 feet near Quantico, Virginia, just south of Washington.

On July 13 another airliner crew reported that when they were 60 miles southwest of Washington, at 11,000 feet, they saw a light below them. It came up to their level, hovered off to the left for several minutes, and then it took off in a fast, steep climb when the pilot turned on his landing lights.

On July 14 the crew of a Pan American airliner enroute from New York to Miami reported eight UFO's near Newport News, Virginia, about 130 miles south of Washington.

Two nights later there was another sighting in exactly the same area but from the ground. At 9:00 P.M. a high-ranking civilian scientist from the National Advisory Committee for Aeronautics Laboratory at Langley AFB and another man were standing near the ocean looking south over Hampton Roads when they saw two amber-colored lights, "much too large to be aircraft lights," off to their right, silently traveling north. Just before the two lights got abreast of the two men they made a 180-degree turn and started back toward the spot where they had first been seen. As they turned, the two lights seemed to "jockey for position in the formation." About this time a third light came out of the west and joined the first two; then as the three UFO's climbed out of the area toward the south, several more lights joined the formation. The entire episode had lasted only three minutes.

The only possible solution to the sighting was that the two men had seen airplanes. We investigated this report and found that there were several B-26's from Langley AFB in the area at the time of the sighting, but none of the B-26 pilots remembered being over Hampton Roads. In fact, all of them had generally stayed well south of Norfolk until about 10:30 P.M. because of thunderstorm activity northwest of Langley. Then there were other factors — the observers heard no sound and they were away from all city noises, aircraft don't carry just one or two amber lights, and the distance between the two lights was such that had they been on an airplane the airplane would have been huge or very close to the observers. And last, but not least, the man from the National Advisory Committee for Aeronautics was a very famous aerodynamicist and of such professional stature that if he said the lights weren't airplanes they weren't. . . .

When the keg blew the best laid schemes of the mice and men at ATIC, they went the way best laid schemes are supposed to. The first one of the highly publicized Washington national sightings started, according to the CAA's logbook at the airport, at 11:40 P.M. on the night of July 19 when two radars at National Airport picked up eight unidentified targets east and south of Andrews AFB. The targets weren't airplanes because they would loaf along at 100 to 130 miles an hour, then suddenly accelerate to "fantastically high speeds" and leave the area. During the night the crews of several airliners saw mysterious lights in the same locations that the radars showed the targets; tower operators also saw the lights, and jet fighters were brought in.

But nobody bothered to tell Air Force Intelligence about the sighting. When reporters began to call intelligence and ask about the big sighting behind the headlines, INTERCEPTORS CHASE FLYING SAUCERS OVER WASHINGTON, D.C., they were told that no one had ever heard of such a sighting. In the next edition the headlines were supplemented by, AIR FORCE WON'T TALK.

Thus intelligence was notified about the first Washington national sighting.

I heard about the sighting about ten o'clock Monday morning when Colonel Donald Bower and I got off an airliner from Dayton and I bought a newspaper in the lobby of the Washington National Airport Terminal Building. I called the Pentagon from the airport and talked to Major Dewey Fournet, but all he knew was what he'd read in the papers. He told me that he had called the intelligence officer at Bolling AFB and that he was making an investigation. We would get a preliminary official report by noon.

It was about 1:00 P.M. when Major Fournet called me and said that the intelligence officer from Bolling was in his office with the preliminary report on the sightings. I found Colonel Bower, we went up to Major Fournet's office and listened to the intelligence officer's briefing.

The officer started by telling us about the location of the radars involved in the incident. Washington National Airport, which is located about three miles south of the heart of the city, had two

the technician had checked the radar and found that the targets weren't caused by a radar malfunction, ARTC had called for Air Force interceptors to come in and look around. But they didn't show, and finally ARTC called again — then again. Finally, just about daylight, an F-94 arrived, but by that time the targets were gone. The F-94 crew searched the area for a few minutes but they couldn't find anything unusual so they returned to their base.

So ended phase one of the Washington National Sightings.

The Bolling AFB intelligence officer said he would write up the complete report and forward it to ATIC.

That afternoon things bustled in the Pentagon. Down on the first floor Al Chop was doing his best to stave off the press while up on the fourth floor intelligence officers were holding some serious conferences. There was talk of temperature inversions and the false targets they could cause; but the consensus was that a good radar operator could spot inversion-caused targets, and the traffic controllers who operated the radar at Washington National Airport weren't just out of radar school. Every day the lives of thousands of people depended upon their interpretation of the radar targets they saw on their scopes. And you don't get a job like this unless you've spent a good many years watching a luminous line paint targets on a good many radarscopes. Targets caused by inversions aren't rare — in the years that these men had been working with radar they had undoubtedly seen every kind of target, real or false, that radar can detect. They had told the Bolling AFB intelligence officer that the targets they saw were caused by the radar waves' bouncing off a hard, solid object. The Air Force radar operator at Andrews backed them up; so did two veteran airline pilots who saw lights right where the radar showed a UFO to be.

Then on top of all this there were the reports from the Washington area during the previous two weeks — all good — all from airline pilots or equally reliable people.

To say the least, the sighting at Washington National was a jolt.

Besides trying to figure out what the Washington National UFO's were, we had the problem of what to tell the press. They were now beginning to put on a squeeze by threatening to call a congressman — and nothing chills blood faster in the military. They wanted some kind of an official statement and they wanted it soon. Some people in intelligence wanted to say just, "We don't know," but others held out for a more thorough investigation. I happened to be in this latter category. Many times in the past I had seen what first seemed to be a good UFO report completely fall apart under a thorough investigation. I was for stalling the press and working all night if necessary to go into every aspect of the sighting. But to go along with the theme of the Washington National Sightings — confusion — there was a lot of talk but no action and the afternoon passed with no further investigation. . . .

[The second Washington national sighting came along almost a week to the hour from the first one.]

About 10:30 P.M. on July 26 the same radar operators who had seen the UFO's the week before picked up several of the same slow-moving targets. This time the mysterious craft, if that is what they were, were spread out in an arc around Washington from Herndon, Virginia, to Andrews AFB. This time there was no hesitation in following the targets. The minute they appeared on the big 24-inch radar scope one of the controllers placed a plastic marker representing an unidentified target near each blip on the scope. When all the targets had been carefully marked, one of the controllers called the tower and the radar station at Andrews AFB — they also had the unknown targets.

By 11:30 P.M. four or five of the targets were continually being tracked at all times, so once again a call went out for jet interceptors. Once again there was some delay, but by midnight two F-94's from New Castle County AFB were airborne and headed south. The reporters and photographers were asked to leave the radar room on the pretext that classified radio frequencies and procedures were being used in vectoring the interceptors. All civilian air traffic was cleared out of the area and the jets moved in. . . .

But just as the two '94's arrived in the area the targets disappeared from the radarscopes. The two jets were vectored into the areas where the radar had shown the last target plots, but even though the visibility was excellent they could see nothing. The two airplanes stayed around a few minutes more, made a systematic search of the area, but since they still couldn't see anything or pick up anything on their radars they returned to their base.

A few minutes after the F-94's left the Washington area, the unidentified targets were back on the radarscopes in that same area.

What neither Major Fournet nor I knew at this time was that a few minutes after the targets left the radarscopes in Washington people in the area around Langley AFB near Newport News, Virginia, began to call Langley Tower to report that they were looking at weird bright lights that were "rotating and giving off alternating colors." A few minutes after the calls began to come in, the tower operators themselves saw the same or a similar light and they called for an interceptor.

An F-94 in the area was contacted and visually vectored to the light by the tower operators. The F-94 pilot saw the light and started toward it, but suddenly it went out, "like somebody turning off a light bulb." The F-94 crew continued their run and soon got a radar lock-on, but it was broken in a few seconds as the target apparently sped away. The fighter stayed in the area for several more minutes and got two more lock-ons, only to have them also broken after a few seconds.

A few minutes after the F-94 over Newport News had the last lock-on broken, the targets came back on the scopes at Washington National.

With the targets back at Washington the traffic controller again called Air Defense Command, and once again two F-94's roared south toward Washington. This time the targets stayed on the radarscopes when the airplanes arrived.

The controllers vectored the jets toward group after group of targets, but each time, before the jets could get close enough to see anything more than just a light, the targets had sped away. Then one stayed put. The pilot saw a light right where the ARTC radar said a target was located; he cut in the F-94's after-burner and went after it, but just like the light that the F-94 had chased near Langley AFB, this one also disappeared. All during the chase the radar operator in the F-94 was trying to get the target on his set but he had no luck.

After staying in the area about twenty minutes, the jets began to run low on fuel and returned to their base. Minutes later it began to get light, and when the sun came up all the targets were gone.

Early Sunday morning, in an interview with the press, the Korean veteran who piloted the F-94, Lieutenant William Patterson, said:

> I tried to make contact with the bogies below 1,000 feet, but they [the radar controllers] vectored us around. I saw several bright lights. I was at my maximum speed, but even then I had no closing speed. I ceased chasing them because I saw no chance of overtaking them. I was vectored into new objects. Later I chased a single bright light which I estimated about 10 miles away. I lost visual contact with it about 2 miles.

When Major Fournet finished telling me about the night's activity, my first question was, "How about the radar targets — could they have been caused by weather?" . . .

Dewey said that everybody in the radar room was convinced that the targets were very probably caused by solid metallic objects. There had been weather targets on the scope too, he said, but these were common to the Washington area and the controllers were paying no attention them. . . .

Prior to the Washington sightings in only a very few of the many instances in which radar had picked up UFO targets had the targets themselves supposedly been seen visually. Radar experts had continually pointed out this fact to us as an indication that maybe all of the radar targets were caused by freak weather conditions. "If people had just seen a light, or an object, near where the radar showed the UFO target to be, you would have a lot more to worry about," radar technicians had told me many times.

Now people were seeing the same targets that the radars were picking up. . . .

# The New Guinea Episode . . .

*Jacques Vallee is a mathematician-analyst connected with Northwestern University. This episode from his book,* Anatomy of a Phenomenon, *is particularly interesting because the main witness is an ordained priest.*

. . . The June 1959 New Guinea Episode is one of the great classics in UFO history. It is, however, known to few persons, although it has a perfectly official character and has remained unidentified after a number of investigations. The main witness, Rev. William Booth Gill, is an ordained priest of the Church of England and a graduate of Brisbane University. He was accompanied, mind you, by thirty-seven other witnesses when the sighting occurred and the narratives are extremely consistent and clearly reliable.

Mr. Gill had been on the staff of the Anglican Mission in Papua for thirteen years when the event took place. He had been working mainly on the northeastern coast of Papua, in the Goodenough Bay area, about ninety miles from Samarai, and his main interest had been educational work. He states very clearly, in an interview with Australian reporters, that before the sighting he thought UFOs were "a figment of imagination, or some electrical phenomenon." The interview continues as follows:

The first sighting occurred over Waimera about twenty-five miles from us. It was observed by Dr. Ken Houston at a place called Waimera, near Tagora, and that was late November of last year. At Boianai itself, where I am working, the first recorded incident was on the night of Sunday, the 21st of June.

My own observations began on the 26th of June and extended over a number of days.

We have here the indication of repeated sightings taking place, once again, over a small area. This is a new example to be added to similar concentrations of UFO activity, like the Charente area in France in 1952, the Haute-Loire area in 1954, or the northern regions of France at another period within the same wave. The states of New Jersey, Illinois, and Michigan have known similar "flaps" in recent years, and the series of incidents over Texas and the Southwest in November of 1957 is memorable. But nothing similar to the New Guinea episodes was ever reported there.

Mr. Gill states that he came out of the dining room on June 26 at 6:45 P.M., after dinner and:

. . . casually glanced at the sky with the purpose, I suppose, of seeing Venus. Well, I saw Venus but I also saw this sparkling object which was to me peculiar because it sparkled, and because it was very, very bright. . . . The whole thing was most extraordinary. The fact that we saw what appeared to be human beings on it, I think, is the important thing. It is certainly the important and exciting thing to us. They were not noticeable at first. The object came down at about, I should say, 400 feet, maybe 450 feet, perhaps less, maybe 300 feet. It is very difficult to judge at that time of night and, not having experience in measuring elevation, it is purely guesswork, but as we watched it men came out from this object, and appeared on the top of it on what seemed to be a deck on top of the huge disk. There were four men in all, occasionally two, then one, then three, then four — we noted the various times that men appeared, and then one, two, and three appeared and one and two, and then numbers one, three, four, and two and so on. And then later all those witnesses who are quite sure that our records were right . . . signed their names as witnesses of what we assume was human activity or beings of some sort on the object itself.

Another peculiar thing about it was this shaft of blue light which emanated from what appeared to be the centre of the deck. They would bend forward and appear to manipulate something on the deck, and then straighten themselves up occasionally, would turn around in our direction, but on the whole they were interested in something on the deck. Then from time to time — this light — rather like a thin spotlight emanated skywards to stay on for a second or two, and then switch off. I recorded the times that we saw that blue light come on and off — for the rest of the night. After all that activity it ascended and remained very high.

The craft looked like a disk with smaller round superstructures, then again on top of that another kind of superstructure — round rather like the bridge on a boat. Underneath it had four legs in pairs pointing downward diagonally. These appeared to be fixed, not retractable, and looked the same on the two nights — rather like tripods. On the second night the pencil beam came on again for a few seconds, twice in succession.

Mr. Gill, after stating that he was a poor mathematician, said that the dimensions of the object seemed to him to be about thirty-five to forty feet at the base and perhaps twenty feet at the top.

At the question: "Did you try to establish contact with the pilots of the craft?" he answered:

"We did. As one of the men seemed to lean over as though over a rail and look down on us, I waved one hand overhead and the figure did the same as though a skipper on a boat waving to someone on a wharf. I could not see the rail but he seemed to lean over something with arms over it. We could see him from just below waist up. Ananias, the teacher, waved both hands overhead and the two outside figures waved back with two arms over heads. Then Ananias and I both waved arms and all four figures seemed to wave back — no doubt that movement made by arms was answered by the figures."

"What was the reaction of the natives at signal?"

"Surprised and delighted. Small mission boys called out — everyone beckoned to invite the beings down but no audible responses. . . . No expressions discernible on the faces of the men — rather like players on a football field at night."

"We understand you tried to signal the beings with a torchlight?"

"Yes, we flashed the light and the object swung like a pendulum, presumably in recognition. When we flashed the torchlight towards it, it hovered, and came quite close towards the ground . . . and we actually thought it was going to land but it did not. We were all very disappointed about that."

A strip of motion-picture film of ninety-four frames was taken at Port Moresby on August 23, 1953, by T. C. Drury, deputy-director of the Civilian Aviation Department in New Guinea. It showed a disk-shaped object in flight, making ninety-degree maneuvers, after coming out of a peculiar cloud. This is a sign that the area of Port Moresby was indeed repeatedly the source of important reports. According to the former Minister for Air, the man who took the film was a "reliable, credible person." The film has been studied by the Intelligence of the Royal Australian Air Force and was also examined by experts of the United States Air Force. . . .

# The Chase
# in Rapid City,
# South Dakota . . .

*A radar sighting by a ground crew, and a visual sighting by a pilot. "The best UFO report in the Air Force files," said Captain Edward J. Ruppelt in another selection from* The Report on Unidentified Flying Objects.

. . . I first heard about the sighting about two o'clock on the morning of August 13, 1953, when Max Futch called me from ATIC. A few minutes before a wire had come in carrying a priority just under that reserved for flashing the word the U.S. has been attacked. Max had been called over to ATIC by the OD to see the report, and he thought that I should see it. I was a little hesitant to get dressed and go out to the base, so I asked Max what he thought about the report. His classic answer will go down in UFO history, "Captain," Max said in his slow, pure Louisiana drawl, "you know that for a year I've read every flying saucer report that's come in and that I never really believed in the things." Then he hesitated and added, so fast that I could hardly understand him, "But you should read *this* wire." The speed with which he uttered this last statement was in itself enough to convince me. When Max talked fast, something was important.

A half hour later I was at ATIC — just in time to get a call from the Pentagon. Someone else had gotten out of bed to read his copy of the wire.

I used the emergency orders that I always kept in my desk and caught the first airliner out of Dayton to Rapid City, South Dakota.

I didn't call the 4602nd because I wanted to investigate this one personally. I talked to everyone involved in the incident and pieced together an amazing story.

Shortly after dark on the night of the twelfth, the Air Defense Command radar station at Ellsworth AFB, just east of Rapid City, had received a call from the local Ground Observer Corps filter center. A lady spotter at Black Hawk, about 10 miles west of Ellsworth, had reported an extremely bright light low on the horizon, off to the northeast. The radar had been scanning an area to the west, working a jet fighter in some practice patrols, but when they got the report they moved the sector scan to the northeast quadrant. There was a target exactly where the lady reported the light to be. The warrant officer, who was the duty controller for the night, told me that he'd studied the target for several minutes. He knew how weather could affect radar but this target was "well defined, solid, and bright." It seemed to be moving, but very slowly. He called for an altitude reading, and the man on the height-finding radar checked his scope. He also had the target — it was at 16,000 feet.

The warrant officer picked up the phone and asked the filter center to connect him with the spotter. They did, and the two people compared notes on the UFO's position for several minutes. But right in the middle of a sentence the lady suddenly stopped and excitedly said, "It's starting to move — it's moving southwest toward Rapid."

The controller looked down at his scope and the target was beginning to pick up speed and move southwest. He yelled at two of his men to run outside and take a look. In a second or two one of them shouted back that they could both see a large bluish-white light moving toward Rapid City. The controller looked down at his scope — the target was moving toward Rapid City. As all three parties watched the light and kept up a steady cross conversation of the description, the UFO swiftly made a wide sweep around Rapid City and returned to its original position in the sky.

A master sergeant who had seen and heard the happenings told me that in all his years of duty — combat radar operations in both Europe and Korea — he'd never been so completely awed by anything. When the warrant officer had yelled down at him and asked him what he thought they should do, he'd just stood there. "After all," he told me, "what in hell could we do — they're bigger than all of us."

But the warrant officer did do something. He called to the F-84 pilot he had on combat air patrol west of the base and told him to get ready for an intercept. He brought the pilot around south of the base and gave him a course correction that would take him right into the light, which was still at 16,000 feet. By this time the pilot had it spotted. He made the turn, and when he closed to within about 3 miles of the target, it began to move. The controller saw it begin to move, the spotter saw it begin to move and the pilot saw it begin to move — all at the same time. There was now no doubt that all of them were watching the same object.

Once it began to move, the UFO picked up speed fast and started to climb, heading north, but the F-84 was right on its tail. The pilot would notice that the light was getting brighter, and he'd call the controller to tell him about it. But the controller's answer would always be the same, "Roger, we can see it on the scope."

There was always a limit as to how near the jet could get, however. The controller told me that it was just as if the UFO had some kind of an automatic warning radar linked to its power supply. When something got too close to it, it would automatically pick up speed and pull away. The separation distance always remained about 3 miles.

The chase continued on north — out of sight of the lights of Rapid City and the base — into some very black night.

When the UFO and the F-84 got about 120 miles to the north, the pilot checked his fuel; he had to come back. And when I talked to him, he said he was damn glad that he was running out of fuel because being out over some mighty desolate country alone with a UFO can cause some worry.

Both the UFO and the F-84 had gone off the scope, but in a few minutes the jet was back on, heading for home. Then 10 or 15 miles behind it was the UFO target also coming back.

While the UFO and the F-84 were returning to the base — the F-84 was planning to land — the controller received a call from the jet interceptor squadron on the base. The alert pilots at the squadron had heard the conversations on their radio and didn't believe it. "Who's nuts up there?" was the comment that passed over the wire from the pilots to the radar people. There was an F-84 on the line ready to scramble, the man on the phone said, and one of the pilots, a World War II and Korean veteran, wanted to go up and see a flying saucer. The controller said, "O.K., go."

In a minute or two the F-84 was airborne and the controller was working him toward the light. The pilot saw it right away and closed in. Again the light began to climb out, this time more toward the northeast. The pilot also began to climb, and before long the light, which at first had been about 30 degrees above his horizontal line of sight, was now below him. He nosed the '84 down to pick up speed, but it was the same old story — as soon as he'd get within 3 miles of the UFO, it would put on a burst of speed and stay out ahead.

Even though the pilot could see the light and hear the ground controller telling him that he was above it, and alternately gaining on it or dropping back, he still couldn't believe it — there must be a simple explanation. He turned off all his lights — it wasn't a reflection from any of the airplane's lights because there it was. A reflection from a ground light, maybe. He rolled the airplane — the position of the light didn't change. A star — he picked out three bright stars near the light and watched carefully. The UFO moved in relation to the three stars. Well, he thought to himself, if it's a real object out there, my radar should pick it up too; so he flipped on his radar-ranging gunsight. In a few seconds the red light on his sight blinked on — something real and solid was in front of him. Then he was scared. When I talked to him, he readily admitted that he'd been scared. He'd met MD 109's, FW 190's and ME 262's over Germany and he'd met MIG-15's over Korea but the large, bright, bluish-white light had scared him — he asked the controller if he could break off the intercept.

This time the light didn't come back.

When the UFO went off the scope it was headed toward Fargo, North Dakota, so the controller called the Fargo filter center. "Had they had any reports of unidentified lights?" he asked. They hadn't.

But in a few minutes a call came back. Spotter posts on a south-west-northeast line a few miles west of Fargo had reported a fast-moving, bright bluish-white light.

This was an unknown — the best. . . .

# UFOs
# in the Deep Freeze . . .

*Traveling even farther South, we find that UFOs
have caused quite a furor in Antarctica. These
sightings, described in* Strangers from the Skies, *by
Brad Steiger, have an added measure of value; they
were made by scientific experts at military outposts.*

. . . Although the forbidden knowledge claimed to be revealed
by Dr. Bernard's book* might stretch the bounds of credulity possessed by most people, after last summer's flurry of UFO activity in
the polar regions — especially Antarctica — military personnel
stationed in the earth's "deepfreeze" are almost willing to accept
even such a tale of an "underground world of supermen" to account for the phenomena which they observed. . . .

Not only have the scientific outposts seen the objects, but they
have attempted to photograph them. The secretary of the Argentine
navy made the following statement to the press, which was reprinted in Buenos Aires newspapers.

"The Navy garrison in the Argentine Antarctica (Deception Island) observed, on July 3, at 19:40 hours (local time) a giant lens-
shaped flying object, solid in appearance, color mostly red and
green, changing occasionally, with yellow, blue, white, and orange
shades. The object was moving on a zigzagging trajectory toward
the east but several times it changed course to the west and north
with varied speeds and no sound. It passed at an elevation of 45
degrees over the horizon, distance estimated at about 10 to 15 kilometers from the base.

* Raymond Bernard, *The Hollow Earth.*

"During the maneuvers performed by the object the witnesses were able to register its tremendous speeds and also the fact that it hovered motionless for about 15 minutes at an estimated altitude of about 5,000 meters (3.10 miles). The meteorological conditions for the area of the sighting can be considered as very good for this time of the year: clear sky, some strato-cumulus, moon in the last quarter, and perfect visibility.

"The object was witnessed by the meteorologist together with 13 members of the garrison and three Chilean sub-officers visiting the base. The observation lasted for 20 minutes and photographs of the object were taken.

"On the afternoon of the same day the same object was observed from the Argentine base on the South Orkney Islands, moving away toward the northwest, elevation 30 degrees over the horizon, distance estimated at about 10 to 15 kilometers (six to nine miles). The Chilean base also observed the object referred to above the afternoon of that same day."

The Argentine bases in the Antarctic are some of the oldest of the southern scientific outposts. Each is equipped with sensitive equipment for detecting changes in the magnetic field of the area. On July 3, 1965, all of this equipment was functioning properly, and they all registered abnormal changes in the magnetic field around the bases.

A later press release made by the secretary of the Argentine navy gave a more detailed account of the sighting, which only confirmed the object's mysterious nature. The commander of the Argentine base at Deception Island said that all seventeen men under his command had seen the object, including three Chilean sub-officers, who were visiting the base because one of them had a broken arm that needed medical attention.

An interesting passage in the report states: ". . . information from the Navy garrison at South Orkney Islands calls attention to a fact of extreme importance; during the passage of the strange object over that base, two variometers working in perfect condition registered disturbances in the magnetic field which were recorded on their tapes."

This release also explained that the probability that the photos would yield conclusive results were low, since the area was dark and the film used was of low sensitivity. It was impossible for the film to be immediately processed, as the bases were unreached in the middle of the Antarctic winter when they were taken.

On the same day, July 7, 1965, the Ministry of Defense in Santiago, Chile released the contents of their sightings to the press. The first observation occurred on June 18th and was reported by Commander Mario Jahn Barrera.

"I have to report that today at 4:00 P.M. (local time) was sighted from this base an aerial object, luminous intensity of a first magnitude star, appearing east of the island at 60 degrees elevation, changing direction to the left in a 180-degree turn to the west and then turning 90 degrees to the right; moving away to the south following an irregular trajectory at 4:20 P.M. Meteorological conditions good, dark sky. The phenomenon was observed by all in the garrison."

A report on the object which the Argentine base had sighted on July 3rd was also released.

"Sergeant Moya, in the course of meteorological observations on July 3, spotted the presence of an aerial object sighted for 20 minutes by nine members of the garrison. Red-yellow luminosity, changing colors, elevation 45 degrees, crossing the island at SW in a NW-SE direction. High velocity, oscillatory course, luminosity first magnitude star. Good conditions of visibility. Communications on the same day, at 20:30 hours (local time), with the English base revealed that on July 2, at 19:45 hours, five members of that garrison had sighted celestial object north of the island, moving in a zigzagging course, stopping in mid-air for five to ten minutes and disappearing in a vertical direction. Red-yellow color changing to green, elevation 20 degrees, and brightness first magnitude star.

"Communication with the Argentine Base, Deception Island, disclosed that, on July 3, 16 persons including three Chilean sub-officers had observed an aerial object over the northern area of the island moving in a north-northeast direction, varying speed, oscillatory course, changing yellow-green-orange color, leaving a contrail at 30 degrees elevation. Round-shaped, disappearing into cirrus clouds. Was tracked by theodolites and high-powered binoculars. Corporal Duran, from this garrison, took 10 color photographs through the theodolite. Still on the same day, at the Argentine base at Orkney Island, two meteorological observers sighted an aerial object flying at high speed on a parabolic trajectory, course E-W, white luminosity, causing disturbance in the magnetic field registered on geomagnetic instruments with patterns notably out of the normal.

"There was no previous communication between the bases listed above that could produce a psychosis of this kind of observation — which must be of great interest for scientific organizations interested."

The release of these two communiques by the Chilean Defense Ministry sent reporters scurrying to their typewriters, but soon they were back knocking at the door, hungry for more. An interview, via radio, was granted with the commanding officer of the Chilean base, Mario Jahn Barrera. The radio was handled by Commander Jose Berichevski, Chief of Public Relations for the Chilean Air Force, from the Air Force radio-operations center in Santiago.

Barrera minced no words, "It is nonsense to say that we saw a flying saucer like those from science fiction stories. What we sighted was something real, a solid object which was moving at incredible speeds, performed maneuvers, emitted a greenish light, and caused interference in the electro-magnetic instruments of the Argentine base situated close to ours, on a small island.

"Its red-yellow color changed to green and orange. It was flying at a short distance from the base at an elevation of 45 degrees, over the north of the island, and moving in a zigzagging course.

"It hovered in mid-air after performing one of its maneuvers, remaining motionless for about 20 minutes and then moving away at high speed. We observed this object through high-powered binoculars.

"I don't believe it could be an airship of terrestrial manufacture. As an officer in the Chilean Air Force, my knowledge about man-made machines gives me absolute conviction that nothing similar exists on the earth: in shape, velocity, and mobility in space. We have taken 10 color photographs which will be developed in Santiago.

"As soon as we sighted the object we tried to contact by radio the Argentine and English bases. But such contact was impossible because there was a very strong interference on the radio, on all channels. With the radio useless and under intense emotion we continued to observe the thing in space, on a clear night without winds. . . ."

# Terror at the Moreno Ranch . . .

*Flying Saucers do not limit their activities to North America. While the following tale, also from Brad Steiger's* Strangers from the Skies, *seems to lean more toward science fiction than reality, there were many witnesses who corroborated the Morenos' story.*

"Senor Moreno! Senor Moreno, wake up!"

Antonio Moreno rolled over and blinked into the darkness until his eyes reluctantly made out the form of his ranch hand standing in the doorway of the bedroom.

"What is it?" Moreno mumbled. "What's wrong?"

It was 9:30 P.M. on the evening of October 21, 1963, and seventy-two-year-old Antonio Moreno and his sixty-three-year-old wife, Teresa, had gone to bed early. Neither of them was pleased to have his sleep interrupted by an excitable young employee who was probably upset over some matter that could easily have waited until morning.

"There seems to have been an accident on the railroad tracks," the young man said.

"An accident?" Senora Moreno questioned, wrapping a housecoat around her nightgown. "But I am a very light sleeper. The railroad tracks are only a half mile away. I would surely have heard the noise if there had been an accident."

"But there is a very strange light on the tracks, and men are working at something," the young man protested. "See for yourself. You should be able to see the light from your bedroom window."

The Morenos did as their nervous employee requested and were surprised to see a brilliant light floating above a number of men, who seemed to be inspecting the railroad tracks.

"What a bright light," Senora Moreno said, narrowing her eyes as if she were looking into an arc light. "What are those men doing, Antonio?"

"It is indeed peculiar," Moreno frowned. "Why would anyone be inspecting the railroad tracks at this time of night?" Moreno's ranch was near Tranca, in Cordoba province, Argentina. The area was not so isolated that railroad crews needed to put in overtime to perform maintenance duties.

"That great light moved!" the employee shouted. "It moved at least twenty feet down the track."

Moreno put a forefinger to his lips. "Don't shout," he admonished the young man. "Senora Moreno's sister and her children are asleep in the next room. There is no need to awaken them for such a silly reason. The light is obviously on some elevated railroad flatcar."

"My curiosity is aroused," Senora Moreno said, reaching for the flashlight which she kept beside her bed. "I'm going to walk down the tracks and see what those men are doing."

Moreno started to protest, then shrugged his shoulders. He knew that it was useless to argue with his wife once she had decided upon a particular course of action.

Senora Moreno did not get very far. At the sound of the closing screendoor, the men at the tracks were seen to suddenly direct their attention toward the ranch house. Almost at once, a disc-shaped object, about 25 feet in diameter, swooped down on Senora Moreno. The startled woman retreated into the ranch house, and the entire household, alerted by her screams, watched in terror as the glowing disc hovered at about tree-top level and began to direct a beam of white light at the house.

Senora Moreno gasped in surprise and horror, and her body trembled with a "tingling sensation" when the beam of light entered a window and struck her. One of her sister's children woke with a scream as the beam moved over his body.

"We are being invaded by monsters from outer space!" the young ranch hand cried.

Senora Moreno quieted him. "Help my sister move her children to places where the light can't strike them. We must be quiet."

Peeping out through a window, Antonio Moreno was horrified to see four other saucers glide up to join the disc that was shooting the strange beams of light at their house. Only one of the new arrivals participated in the attack, however. The other three seemed contented to hover in the air about 210 feet away. Each of the objects was identical with the others — about 25 feet in diameter with a row of windowlike openings, brightly lit, running up the middle.

Members of the besieged household took refuge behind furniture and avoided the windows. Whenever anyone attempted to move, a beam of the "tingling" light would send him scurrying for cover.

"What do the things want with us?" Moreno asked no one in particular. "Why must they do this to us? And what are those shiny suits doing to the railroad tracks?"

Senora Moreno managed another peek out of a window and saw that one of the discs had begun to project a reddish-violet beam while the other maintained the white shafts of light. "The house then became like an oven," the Morenos later told a correspondent for the *Clarim* at Tranca, Argentina.

"They are trying to drive us out!" Senora Moreno's sister began to wail hysterically. "They are trying to smoke us out of our homes as if we were animals!"

"Well, we shall not be budged," Senora Moreno announced with determination.

For forty minutes, the beleaguered ranch house withstood the rising temperature engendered by the mysterious hovering saucers. At last, the ranch hand noticed that the "men" at the railroad track had begun to board the disc that had provided them with light for their inspection tour. Within seconds, the terrible beams of light were extinguished, and the discs that had surrounded the ranch house began to move away.

At the moment of the discs' departure, the Morenos' three watchdogs began to raise a terrible fuss, howling, barking, and snarling. "Where were the dogs before?" Moreno puzzled. "It was as if they were stunned."

The entire Moreno household were still "stunned" when correspondents from newspapers arrived to interview them. They told the newsmen that a "thick mist-like smoke, which smelled like sulphur, hung over the trees for several minutes after the departure of the strange aircraft."

The reporter for *Clarim* informed his readers that the smell of sulphur had still permeated the ranch house when he had conducted his interview two days later. The October 24, 1963 issues of both the Rio de Janeiro *Tribuna Da Imprensa* and the Buenos Aires *La Nacion* carried extensive accounts of the hour of terror endured by the Moreno household.

Although the tale of hovering saucers, that directed alternating "tingling" and suffocating beams of light, seems to smack more of fantastic fiction than of reality, the Morenos' story was not without corroborating testimonies and other eyewitness accounts, that tend to make the whole incident rather uncomfortable to contemplate.

A Senor Francisco Tropuano told a correspondent for the France-Press wire service that he had been only a mile away from the Moreno ranch when, at about 10:20, he saw six discs traveling across the sky in close formation. Although he knew nothing of the terrible hour that the Morenos had suffered until he read of it in the papers, Senor Tropuano had discussed his independent sighting quite freely with his friends and neighbors.

Two days before the Morenos' besiegement had been publicized, a truckdriver's encounter with the "tingling" rays of light had been reported in the Monte Maix, Argentina *El Diario* and the *O Jornal* of Rio de Janeiro, Brazil.

Eugenio Douglas, a commercial truckdriver, told correspondents that, on the evening of October 18th, on the highway approaching Monte Maix, his entire truck had become enveloped by a brilliant white light. Senor Douglas had only a few moments to speculate about the source of the light when his entire body began to tingle like "the peculiar sensation one gets when his foot goes to sleep."

Douglas lost control of his truck and drove it into a ditch. The beam seemed to "shut itself off" and the truckdriver, upon clearing his head, saw that the brilliant light had come from a glowing disc, about 25 feet in diameter, which blocked the highway. As he blinked unbelieving eyes, he was approached by "three indescribable beings" which he could only compare to "shiny metal robots."

The terrified truckdriver vaulted from the cab of his vehicle, fired four revolver shots at the approaching monsters, and began to run wildly across the open fields. When he at last stopped to catch his breath and look over his shoulder, he saw that the "indescribable beings" had boarded the disc. He was soon to learn that the "robots" had not taken kindly to being fired upon.

After the disc had become airborne, the luminous flying object made several passes over the head of the desperately running truckdriver.

"Each time the disc swooped down on me," Douglas told newsmen, "I felt a wave of terrible, suffocating heat and that prickling sensation."

Eugenio Douglas ran the entire distance to Monte Maix. When he arrived at police headquarters, he was in a near-hysterical condition. As painful evidence to support his incredible tale, his body bore several welt-like burns, which the medical examiner had to admit were "strange and unlike any that I have ever seen." *Accion* reporters from Agrega, Argentina published an interview with the doctor in which the physician conceded that he could "offer no explanation for the burns."

Saucers have often been sighted along railroad tracks, and, recently, theorists have wondered if the discs and their crews might not be more interested in the highpower lines that follow the tracks rather than in the tracks themselves. In the Exeter, New Hampshire sightings in September of 1965 the UFO's were most often reported to be hovering above highpower lines. The 25-foot diameter of the saucers is commonly reported by those who have seen the flying discs. And . . . the sighting of "robots" or "men in shiny suits" is by no means limited to the Pampas. Nor, regrettably, is the "tingling" beam of light which the discs often direct at men, livestock, and machinery.

# UFOs and
# the Sonic Boom . . .

*From most sources we gather that UFOs usually
make little or no noise. W. Gordon Allen, in*
Spacecraft from beyond Three Dimensions, *disagrees.*

. . . Now, about the aura that seems to surround a genuine
UFO appearance. . . . It is with some definiteness that we say
that one of the phenomena that occurs at the same time as a spacecraft is the so-called "sonic boom," or "skyquake." The newspaper
stories tend to report "sonic boom *thought* to be made by a jet
passing through the sound barrier." Please note that in these stories it is called a *sonic boom,* and is *thought,* and the word "jets" is
used, even in conjunction with statements by various military deny-
ing that they had any jets in the air. The implication, however, is
enough for the casual reader to pass it by as just another sound
barrier broken. But this is not the whole story. First, the most strin-
gent precautions have been taken by the military to allow no breaks
of the sonic barrier over populated areas. Secondly, these "sonic
booms" occur over much larger areas than the relatively small one
that a jet's boom would be projected over. Something is going
through the sound barrier, all right; but if you scan the sky immediately afterward with binoculars you might still be able to see the
spacecraft.

Following are some newspaper accounts of skyquakes that were
not small jets popping through the sound barrier. These were full-
sized skyquakes caused by spacecraft going through the barrier
. . . or operating just at the barrier. Here is a skyquake story as
carried by the United Press wire service in Oregon and from the
front page of the Salem *Capital Journal;* it also appeared on front

pages of all West Coast daily newspapers, and all radio-station newscasts on September 3, 1957:

PORTLAND (UP). — An explosion at 10:15 A.M. today, so loud it was heard as far north as Vancouver, Washington, and as far south as Clackamas County, was investigated today by the Air Force base here, and the investigation was being continued by McChord Field, Wash., in belief that it was caused by a plane breaking the sonic barrier. A plane was spotted at about 25,000 feet just after the explosion.

Steward Granniss, information officer with the 337th fighter group here, said that all indications were that the explosion was a sonic boom. But he said none of the airplanes based at the Portland International Airport with the 337th fighter group was capable of breaking the speed of sound.

Headquarters here asked McChord Field to investigate and 25th air division officials there said an investigation would be made to determine if any division aircraft was responsible for breaking the sonic barrier over Portland. They said if any division aircraft was responsible, necessary action would be taken to prevent a recurrence.

Grannis said Air Force regulations specifically state that planes are not to pass through the sonic barrier under 30,000 feet over land. At that or higher level little effect is felt upon the ground, he said.

In this story are all kinds of implications, and it is typical of the manner in which skyquakes are handled by the press. But to a UFO hobbyist, the skyquake is a perfect alerting signal. That day and evening his binoculars should be on the sky, and chances are very good that he will be rewarded by a glimpse of a still-hovering spacecraft.

The story can be recognized for exactly what it is. A big bang was heard over a major city of the world. The police are called and no blasts are reported. Whom to call next? "Sonic booms" are another possibility in our aviation-conscious world, and the Air Force is called. The P.I.A. officer says that it might be a sonic boom, all right (he had no way of knowing that it was over a very widespread area, a lot less localized than the boom from a jet would be), but certainly his group's planes would be technically incapable of having violated U.S. Air Force regulations. The next check is with a bigger group near McChord Field south of Seattle; the report from McChord is that "if any of our planes disturbed you good people in Portland we'll take measures."

The story is by now so garbled that everyone is happy to accept the explanation of the "sonic boom from a jet," even though it is actually denied in the story. No one has called it a SKYQUAKE and no one has hinted that it is a phenomenon that accompanies the appearance of spacecraft. But this is typical of the manner in which news stories can mislead the public while the public is perfectly willing to believe that they are being informed by the daily press. Skyquakes are skyquakes, and the explanation for them has not yet (to the author's knowledge) appeared in the daily press. Perhaps the explanation is too fantastic for the editors, but not one-half as fantastic as the search for words to indicate what skyquakes are not.

Here is another 1957 story, from the San Francisco region:

SAN FRANCISCO, July 22 (INS). — A giant shock wave that shook buildings, rattled windows and threw some persons off their feet was widely felt through the San Francisco Bay area today.

The powerful atmospheric concussion — possibly the boom from a jet plane cracking the sonic barrier — alarmed thousands of people who flooded police stations, newspapers, and radio stations with telephone calls.

The University of California's Berkeley seismological station said the mysterious blast which came at 11:02 A.M. was not caused by an earthquake as many had feared.

The Navy admitted that some of its supersonic jet planes based in the bay area were in the air at the time, but could not say whether any of these craft was responsible for the atmospheric disturbance.

Persons in San Francisco's Montgomery Street financial district said they felt buildings sway slightly under the impact of the shock.

The blast appeared to have been more intensively felt north of the Golden Gate where residents of Marin County reported that windows were shattered and some people knocked off their feet.

There was a distinct rattling of windows in various districts of San Francisco.

This was quite a blast. But it was not an earthquake, said the University of California. It was not a sonic boom, said the Air Force (because of the fact that sonic booms from jets are relatively limited in the areas they strike). Then what was it? No one has yet come up with an answer. The author believes that without much doubt it was made by a large spacecraft in the bay area on that date. At least on a clear day, like that over Portland, when there are no planes capable of breaking the barrier, there would have to be something, would there not?

There was more in the spring and summer of 1957. Here is an example from the front page of the *Evening Tribune* of San Diego (April 2, 1957):

### BLAST, SMOKE STARTLE CITY
*Sonic "boom" cited,*
*people rush to streets*

A blast rocked metropolitan San Diego and outlying areas at 1:07 this afternoon.

Police and fire department said the blast was believed to have been a sonic boom caused by a jet plane speeding through the sound barrier.

By coincidence, a cloud of dark smoke arose above the South Bay at the time of the blast.

Many residents who left their homes or ran to windows at the earth-shaking sound saw the smoke. They believed the explosion had occurred in the South Bay.

Police said a spokesman at the Naval Station, 32nd Street and Harbor Drive, attributed the smoke to fire fighting training at the Naval Station.

Mrs. George Yeager said dishes fell from shelves at her home at 1415 31st Street.

Some residents on Geneva Street near the Emerald Hills golf course ran from their homes and into the street when the blast was heard and felt.

Police said the jets were reported in the air at the time of the explosion.

Also, half-pound TNT charges were being set off at the Silver Strand as part of Navy demolition exercises. The Navy said, however, the explosions weren't powerful enough to be felt for any great distance.

Well, there is some good reporting in that story: the reporter ferreted out a great number of things that the explosion wasn't. The truth seemed to be that no one could tell the fellow just exactly what caused it. The explosion was heard all over the populated part of another of the United States' major cities. It might well have been felt over even a wider area, if there had been people to report it. Certainly it must have covered a circle forty miles in diameter, and the San Francisco blast might have been at least fifty miles in diameter.

It would seem that the Air Force, the Navy, and the Army should be concerned about these things — unless, of course, they are pretty certain that they are not Russians on the doorstep. Could it be that they are quite certain as to the causes of the blasts and therefore just go on setting off half-pound T.N.T. charges and let it go at that?

Skyquakes that could have been caused by spacecraft have been with us for a long time and will no doubt be here for a much longer time. . . .

*CONTACT*

# Visitor
# from Venus . . .

*Several people claim to have been contacted by space
visitors. Perhaps the best known of the contactees is
George Adamski, who, on November 20, 1952,
supposedly met and talked with one of the crew of
a vehicle that had just arrived from Venus. The
following description of that meeting is from* Flying
Saucers Have Landed, *by Desmond Leslie and
George Adamski.*

It was about 12:30 in the noon hour on Thursday, 20 November
1952, that I first made personal contact with a man from another
world. He came to Earth in his space craft, a flying saucer. He
called it a Scout Ship. . . .

This took place on the California desert, 10.2 miles from Desert
Center toward Parker, Arizona. . . .

It was late in August 1952 that Mr. and Mrs. A. C. Bailey, of
Winslow, Arizona, first came to Palomar Gardens and asked to
talk with me privately. I had never met them prior to that time.
During the conversation, they told me about Dr. and Mrs. George
H. Williamson, of Prescott, Arizona. These four people were as
interested in the flying saucers as I. . . .

Later the Baileys and Williamsons came up together. After
spending several days at Palomar Gardens as our guests, they
asked me to telephone them before my next attempt to establish a
contact. During their stay we had met a great deal and had become
better acquainted and they wanted to be with me if things could be
so arranged.

I promised to call them as they requested, but warned them that

I seldom planned such trips more than a day or two in advance. Thus, on the evening of 18 November I telephoned Dr. Williamson that I was leaving about midnight the next night for a destination near Blythe, California, and asked him if they would be able to meet me there early on Thursday morning, the 20th.

They could. So could the Baileys with whom Dr. Williamson kept in contact. Thus the arrangements were made and hopes were high, as they always were for these trips. . . .

It was about 11 A.M. when we arrived. . . .

The sky was beautiful and clear with little wispy clouds forming here and there, only to float away into nothingness. And although we knew most of the mountains in the background were miles away, they appeared quite close in the deceptive atmosphere of the desert.

Each of us was alert, scanning the broad expanse of sky visible in all directions, and hoping steadfastly for a bright flash somewhere out there that would indicate the presence of a space craft. . . .

Suddenly and simultaneously we all turned as one, looking toward the closest mountain ridge. . . . Riding high, and without sound, there was a gigantic cigar-shaped silvery ship, without wings or appendages of any kind. Slowly, almost as if it was drifting, it came in our direction; then seemed to stop, hovering motionless.

Excitedly, Dr. Williamson exclaimed, "Is that a space ship?"

At first glance it looked like a fuselage of a very large ship with the sun's rays reflecting brightly from its unpainted sides, at an altitude and angle where wings might not be noticeable.

Schooled in caution against over-excitement and quick conclusions, especially in regard to aircraft, Lucy replied, "No, George, I don't believe it is."

"But that baby's high! And see how big it is!" exclaimed Al.

"And Lucy! It doesn't have wings or any other appendages like our planes do!" persisted George. And turning to me, "What do you thing, Adamski?"

Before I could answer, Lucy interrupted. "You're right, George! Look! It's orange on top — the whole length!"

Excitement filled the air as the truth was quickly realised, and everybody began talking at once. Alice wanted me to get my tele-scope out of the car and take a picture of this beautiful ship so close by. Al Bailey wanted his Betty to take a movie of it while it was hovering, but she was so excited that she could not set the camera correctly. By the time she got herself calmed, the ship was already moving again.

The two pairs of binoculars which had been brought along were being passed rapidly from one to the other so all could get a good look. And it was with the binoculars that George noted a black, or dark, marking on the side as though an insignia of some kind was there. This marking was entirely different from any he had ever seen before, although he was unable to make it out in detail. A member of the Air Force during the last war, Dr. George Williamson is well acquainted with the insignias of planes of other nations as well as our own.

A never-to-be-forgotten sight. It could easily have been seen by any passing motorist. But comparatively few people have ever learned to look up. Especially is this true, and rightfully so, of car drivers travelling down an open highway. Their attention is focused on the road ahead.

Had any one of us been pointing upward, as people often do, chances are that some passing car might have stopped, and those within it could have seen this gigantic space visitor as easily as we were seeing it. But we were all cautious not to attract such atten-tion.

And in spite of all the excitement, I knew this was not the place; maybe not even the ship with which contact was to be made, if that was the plan. But I did feel this ship had a definite "something" to do with it all.

Fully aware of the curiosity created by our party here in the desert where no one would normally picnic, I did not want to be more conspicuous by setting up my telescope and camera in such an open spot. Above all else, I didn't want to make the slightest mistake that might prevent a landing and personal contact being made, if such a possibility existed. And now I felt certain that it did.

I said, "Someone take me down the road — quick! That ship has come looking for me and I don't want to keep them waiting! Maybe the saucer is already up there somewhere — afraid to come down here where too many people would see them."

Don't ask me why I said this or how I knew. I have already said that I have a habit of following my feelings, and that is the way I felt. But I cannot tell you why. For those who have an understanding of the subtler working of the mind, no explanation is necessary. For others, an explanation might necessarily be long and difficult.

Lucy quickly got into our car and started the motor. Al asked if he might go too, and climbed in beside her. Telling the others to stay where they were and to watch closely all that took place, I got into the back seat of the car.

As Lucy turned the car around and started down the highway, Al looked up and I looked out the back window and both of us saw the big ship turn also, silently moving along with the car, but high in the sky and what looked like about half-way between the highway and the mountain ridge. We both watched it closely as we rode along for about half a mile. . . .

We decided to try driving in closer and succeeded in making it safely, stopping within 200 feet of my chosen spot. Here the large ship appeared to be almost directly over the car, and as the car stopped, it stopped! . . .

I told Al and Lucy to get back to the others as quickly as possible and for all of them to watch closely for anything that might take place. . . .

Asked how long they should wait before returning for me, yet to be sure their presence would not interrupt anything that might be going on, I told Lucy to return for me in an hour, unless I signalled for them before that time. . . .

Alone with my telescope and my thoughts, I busied myself attaching the camera to the telescope and making adjustments with the eyepiece. This adjustment had become slightly distorted in the moving and setting up. All the time thoughts kept racing through my mind, possibilities of what could take place; fears that nothing would. . . .

Suddenly my reverie was broken as my attention was called to a man standing at the entrance of a ravine between two low hills, about a quarter of a mile away. He was motioning to me to come to him, and I wondered who he was and where he had come from. I was sure he had not been there before. Nor had he walked past me from the road. He could not have come from the side of the mountains on which we were. And I wondered how he had crossed over and descended any part of them without me having noticed him.

A prospector perhaps? Or someone living among these mountains? I had thought no one would be within miles of this spot when I chose it. Or could he be a rock hound, stranded way out here? But why was he motioning to me unless he needed help? So I started toward him, mentally questioning in a minor way, but still feeling the exaltation of my recent experience.

As I approached him a strange feeling came upon me and I became cautious. At the same time I looked round to reassure myself that we were both in full sight of my companions. Outwardly there was no reason for this feeling, for the man looked like any other man, and I could see he was somewhat smaller than I and considerably younger. There were only two outstanding differences that I noticed as I neared him.

1. His trousers were not like mine. They were in style much like ski trousers and with a passing thought I wondered why he wore such out here on the desert.

2. His hair was long, reaching to his shoulders, and was blowing in the wind as was mine. But this was not too strange for I have seen a number of men who wore their hair almost that long.

Although I did not understand the strange feeling that persisted, it was however a friendly feeling toward the smiling young man standing there waiting for me to reach him. And I continued walking toward him without the slightest fear.

Suddenly, as though a veil was removed from my mind, the feeling of caution left me so completely that I was no longer aware of my friends or whether they were observing me as they had been told to do. By this time we were quite close. He took four steps toward me, bringing us within arm's length of each other.

Now, for the first time I fully realised that I was in the presence of a man from space — A HUMAN BEING FROM ANOTHER WORLD! I had not seen his ship as I was walking toward him, nor did I look around for it now. I did not even think of his ship, and I was so stunned by this sudden realisation that I was speechless. My mind seemed to temporarily stop functioning.

The beauty of his form surpassed anything I had ever seen. And the pleasantness of his face freed me of all thought of my personal self.

I felt like a little child in the presence of one with great wisdom and much love, and I became very humble within myself . . . for from him was radiating a feeling of infinite understanding and kindness, with supreme humility.

To break this spell that had so overtaken me — and I am sure he recognised it for what it was — he extended his hand in a gesture toward shaking hands.

I responded in our customary manner.

But he rejected this with a smile and a slight shake of his head. Instead of grasping hands as we on Earth do, he placed the palm of his hand against the palm of my hand, just touching it but not too firmly. I took this to be the sign of friendship.

The flesh of his hand to the touch of mine was like a baby's, very delicate in texture, but firm and warm. His hands were slender, with long tapering fingers like the beautiful hands of an artistic woman. In fact, in different clothing he could easily have passed for an unusually beautiful woman; yet he definitely was a man.

He was about five feet, six inches in height and weighed — according to our standards — about 135 pounds. And I would estimate him to be about 28 years of age, although he could have been much older.

He was round faced with an extremely high forehead; large, but calm, grey-eyes, slightly aslant at the outer corners; with slightly higher cheek bones than an Occidental, but not so high as an Indian or an Oriental; a finely chiselled nose, not conspicuously large; and an average size mouth with beautiful white teeth that shone when he smiled or spoke.

As nearly as I can describe his skin the colouring would be an even, medium-coloured suntan. And it did not look to me as though he had ever had to shave, for there was no more hair on his face than on a child's.

His hair was sandy in colour and hung in beautiful waves to his shoulders, glistening more beautifully than any woman's I have ever seen. And I remember a passing thought of how Earth women would enjoy having such beautiful hair as this man had. As I said before, he wore no protection over it and it was being blown by the winds.

His clothing was a one-piece garment which I had a feeling was a uniform worn by space men as they travel, like Earth men in various types of work wear uniforms to indicate their occupations.

Its colour was chocolate brown and it was made with a rather full blouse, close-fitting high collar much like a turtle neck, only it did not turn down. The sleeves were long, slightly full and similar to a Raglan sleeve, with close-fitting bands around the wrists.

A band about eight inches in width circled his waist. And the only break in colouring of the entire garment was a strip about an inch and a half in width at the top and bottom of this waistband. This was brighter and more of a golden brown.

The trousers were rather full and held in at the ankles with bands like those on the sleeves at the wrists, in style much like a ski pant.

Actually it is very difficult to describe this garment in colouring for I know of no descriptive word in our language that would suit it perfectly.

It was definitely a woven material, very fine, and the weave was different from any of our materials. There was a sheen about the whole garment, but I could not tell whether or not this was due to a finishing process or whether it might be the kind of substance of which its thread was made. It was not like our satin, silk, or rayon, for it had more of a radiance than a sheen.

I saw no zippers, buttons, buckles, fasteners or pockets of any kind, nor did I notice seams as our garments show. It is still a mystery to me how his garment was made.

He wore no ring, watch, or other ornament of any kind. And I saw nothing to indicate, nor did I have a feeling, that he had a weapon of any kind on his person.

His shoes were ox-blood in colour. They too were made of some apparently woven material but different from his suit because these looked much like leather. It was soft and flexible because I could see the movement of his feet within them as we stood talking.

High like a man's oxford, they fitted closely around his feet, which I would say were about size 9 or 9½. However, the opening was on the outer side about half way back on the heel between the arch and the back of the heel. Two narrow straps were here, but I saw no buckles or fasteners, and I reasoned that these straps must have the quality of stretching similar to the woven inserts in some women's shoes.

The heels were slightly lower than on Earth men's shoes, and the toes were blunt. I noticed his shoes particularly because during our conversation he made it very plain to me that his shoeprints were most important. But more about that later.

Suddenly realising that time was passing and I was getting no information by just looking at him, I asked him where he came from.

He did not seem to understand my words, so I asked him again.

But his only response was a slight shake of the head and an almost apologetic expression on his face, which indicated to me that he was not understanding either my words or the meaning behind them.

I am a firm believer that people who desire to convey messages to one another can do so, even though they neither speak nor understand the other's language. This can be done through feelings, signs, and above all, by means of telepathy. I had been teaching this as fact for 30 years and now I concluded I would have to use this method if information of any kind was to pass between us. And there were a lot of things I wanted to know, if I could only think of them.

So, to convey the meaning of my first question to him, I began forming, to the best of my ability, a picture of a planet in my mind. At the same time I pointed to the sun, high in the sky.

He understood this, and his expression so indicated.

Then I circled the sun with my finger, indicating the orbit of the planet closest to the sun, and said, "Mercury," I circled it again for the second orbit, and said, "Venus." The third circle I spoke, "Earth," and indicated the earth upon which we were standing.

I repeated this procedure a second time, all the while keeping as clear a picture of a planet in my mind as I was able to perceive, and this time pointing to myself as belonging to the Earth. Then I indicated him, with a question in my eyes and my mind.

Now he understood perfectly, and smiling broadly he pointed to the sun; made one orbit, made the second, then touching himself with his left hand, he gestured several times with his right index finger toward the second orbit.

I took this to mean that the second planet was his home, so I asked, "You mean you came from Venus?"

This was the third time I had spoken the word "Venus" in relation to the second planet, and he nodded his head in the affirmative. Then he, too, spoke the word "Venus."

His voice was slightly higher pitched than an adult man's. Its tonal quality was more that of a young man before his voice completes the change from childhood to maturity. And although he had spoken but one word, there was music in his voice and I wanted to hear more of it.

Next I asked, "Why are you coming to Earth?"

This question too was accompanied with gestures and facial expressions as well as mental pictures, as were all the questions I asked of him. I repeated each question at least twice to be sure that he understood the meaning of the words I was speaking. The expressions of his face and his eyes told me clearly when he understood, or when there was still any uncertainty in his mind as to what I was trying to ask. I also repeated the answers he gave me to be sure that I was understanding him correctly.

He made me understand that their coming was friendly. Also, as he gestured, that they were concerned with radiations going out from Earth.

This I got clearly since there was a considerable amount of radiation of heat waves rising from the desert, as is often the case. Such as the waves that are often seen rising from pavements, and highways on hot days.

He pointed to them and then gestured through space.

I asked if this concern was due to the explosions of our bombs with their resultant vast radio-active clouds?

He understood this readily and nodded his head in the affirmative.

My next question was whether this was dangerous, and I pictured in my mind a scene of destruction.

To this, too, he nodded his head in the affirmative, but on his face there was no trace of resentment or judgment. His expression was one of understanding, and great compassion; as one would have toward a much loved child who had erred through ignorance and lack of understanding. This feeling appeared to remain with him during the rest of my questions on this subject.

I wanted to know if this was affecting outer space?

Again a nod of affirmation.

In this respect let me say here, it has long been known by scientists of Earth that the cosmic ray, as it is called, is more powerful in outer space than it is in the Earth's atmosphere. And if this be true, is it not just as logical to assume that the radio-active force from the bombs being tested by nations of Earth could also become more powerful in space, once leaving the Earth's atmosphere? Logical deduction supports the statement of this space man.

But I persisted and wanted to know if it was dangerous to us on Earth as well as affecting things in space?

He made me understand — by gesturing with his hands to indicate cloud formations from explosions — that after too many such explosions, Yes! His affirmative nod of the head was very positive and he even spoke the word "Yes" in this instance. The cloud formations were easy to imply with the movement of his hands and arms, but to express the explosions he said, "Boom! Boom!" Then, further to explain himself, he touched me, then a little weed growing close by, and next pointed to the Earth itself, and with a wide sweep of his hands and other gestures that too many "Booms!" would destroy all of this.

This seemed sufficiently clear, so I changed the subject and asked him if he had come directly from Venus in the ship I had photographed?

Here he turned around and pointed up behind the nearby low hill.

There, hovering just above the Earth, was the saucer I had seen earlier and thought had left. I had been so engrossed in the man that I had failed to look beyond him into the recesses of the cove to where the small craft had apparently returned and remained hovering all this time.

He was amused at my surprise and laughed a most hearty laugh.

But I didn't feel that he was laughing at me, and consequently I felt no embarrassment.

I laughed with him, and then asked if he had come directly from Venus to Earth in that?

He shook his head in the negative and made me understand that this craft had been brought into Earth's atmosphere in a larger ship.

Recalling to mind the large ship we had first seen, I asked if that was the one?

A nod of affirmation was his reply.

Now in my mind's picture I put a number of smaller craft like this one at which I was looking — inside the big ship. I could tell by his expression that he was receiving my mental pictures, and I compared this big craft with our own naval plane carriers.

A nod of his head told me this was right.

So I asked if the large craft might be called a "Mother" ship?

He seemed to understand the word "mother" for now his nod of affirmation was accompanied by an understanding smile.

Next I asked if our ships which had appeared around the "Mother" ship, and those that came down close and observed me as I was photographing his smaller craft had bothered them any?

To this he answered "yes" with a nod of his head.

Then I asked, "How does your ship operate? By what power?"

Although he was very expert in mental telepathy, I had some difficulty in getting a picture of this question in my mind. Even though I gestured with my hands as well as I could, it took me several minutes before I succeeded in getting him to understand the meaning of my question. But I did finally succeed.

He made me understand that it was being operated by the law of attraction and repulsion, by picking up a little pebble or rock and dropping it; then picking it up again and then showing motion.

I in turn, to make sure I understood, picked up two pebbles and placed them close to each other as though one was magnetic, pulling on the other, illustrating in that way as I spoke the word "magnetic." After a short time of doing this, he answered me; even repeating the word "magnetic" which I had already spoken a number of times.

Then he replied "yes."

Here I remembered about the little disks that had so often been reported. This was easy, for I indicated with my hands a small circle, then I pointed to his hovering craft and to him, while in my mind I was wondering if these little disks were piloted.

He quickly understood and shook his head in the negative. Then also making a small circle with his two hands, he raised it to his eyes and then pointed to his ship, followed by a gesture toward space, and I received his thought of the big ship.

I understood this to mean that the little disks so often reported sighted were really eyes of larger craft — either the saucers or the mother ships — remotely controlled and not piloted. As I reviewed this in my mind, he assured me I was right.

Then in my mind I saw an explosion in space with a bright flash.

As this picture formed in my mind, he laughed and made me understand that in such cases something had gone wrong with the little disks so they could not be brought back to the ship that had sent them out. Then the control had caused a cross-current, or short circuit, to take place. And an explosion resulted. But he assured me that this was always done out far enough so that there was no danger to men on Earth.

Suddenly the thought came to me to ask if he believed in God?

This he did not understand, for he was not familiar with the word "God." But I finally succeeded in getting the thought in my mind — he was watching me closely — of creating something, and then with the motion of my hand, symbolising the vast sky, the earth and all, and speaking the words "Creator of All."

After a few repetitions of this he understood my thoughts, for I am sure my gestures were not too good.

And he said, "yes."

I realised fully that he naturally wouldn't understand our names for things and to him God probably would be represented by some other word or name.

But he made me understand, by elaborating a little longer with his gestures and mental pictures, that we on Earth really know very little about this Creator. In other words, our understanding is shallow. Theirs is much broader, and they adhere to the Laws of the

Creator instead of laws of materialism as Earth men do. Pointing to himself, then up into space — which I understood meant the planet on which he lived — he conveyed the thought to me that here they live according to the Will of the Creator, not by their own personal will, as we do here on Earth.

I then asked if there were any more landings forthcoming like this one.

He answered me, saying there had been many landings before, and there will be many more.

Are space people coming only from Venus? Or are there other planets or systems from which they come? I asked, and here again I had a little difficulty in conveying my thoughts. But I finally succeeded.

To this he made me understand that people are coming Earthward from other planets in our system, and from planets of other systems beyond ours.

I had suspected this for a long time, so his reply was no surprise to me. But now I wanted to know, "Is space travelling a common practice with the people of other worlds? And is it easy?"

He spoke the word "yes" in answer to both of these questions.

I remembered reports of men being found dead in some saucers that have been found on Earth — saucers that had apparently crashed. So I asked if any of their men had ever died on coming to Earth?

He nodded his head in the affirmative, and made me understand that things had on occasion gone wrong within their ships.

I could understand this because I knew that both the big ship we had all seen first and the smaller one I had photographed were mechanical craft. And things can go wrong with any mechanical device.

But I wasn't satisfied. I had a feeling that he was trying to save my feelings, but I wanted the whole truth. So I persisted, and asked whether men of this world had been responsible for any of these deaths?

His reply to this was "yes," and by holding up his hands several times, as well as with other gestures, he tried to tell me how many.

But I could not get the numbers. I could not be sure whether he was indicating actual numbers, or whether his indications should be multiplied by tens or hundreds, or by what number according to our method of counting.

Remembering a question that had often been asked of me by people with whom I had talked, I asked why they never land in populated places?

To this he made me understand that there would be a tremendous amount of fear on the part of the people, and probably the visitors would be torn to pieces by the Earth people, if such public landings were attempted.

I understood how right he was, and within my mind wondered if there ever would be a time when such a landing would be safe. I was wondering, too, if such a time ever arrived, would they then attempt public landings.

He read my thoughts as they were passing through my mind, and assured me that such a time would arrive. And when it did, they would make landings in populated territories. But he made me understand clearly that it would not be soon.

In the beginning of our conversation, when I realised that I would have to use my hands for gestures to get this man from Venus to understand my questions, I had set my kodak on the ground. Now I picked it up and asked him if I could take a picture of him?

I am sure that he understood my desire, since he was so good at reading my mind. Also I am positive that he knew I would do him no harm because he showed no signs of fear when I picked up the kodak. Nevertheless, he did object to having his picture taken, and I did not insist.

I have heard many times that men from other worlds are walking the streets of Earth. And if this be true, I could easily understand his desire not to be photographed, because there were a few distinguishing points about his facial features. Normally these would not be noticed. But in a photograph they would be conspicuous and serve as points of identification for his brothers who have come to Earth. However, I respected his desires and felt it unwise to question further on this subject.

But I did ask him if any Earth people had been taken away in space craft.

He smiled broadly, and in a half-way manner nodded his head in the affirmative, although I felt that he was not too willing to give that information.

One more question persisted — that of a particular case I knew.

He answered this question for me, but warned me not to mention it further. In fact, I might add right here that he told me a number of things which I must not reveal at this time.

So, changing the subject again, I asked how many other planets are inhabited?

He indicated that large numbers of them throughout the universe are inhabited by human beings like us.

Then more specifically, I inquired how many in our system?

He made a large circle with his hand and covered it with a sweeping motion, as if meaning that all of them were.

I wondered whether I understood him correctly, and he made me realise quite firmly that I did.

Naturally my next attempt was to learn if people everywhere are all of the same form as we on Earth.

His response to this question was emphatic, as if he knew exactly what he was talking about, and I understood clearly that the form is very much universal. He tried to explain further, but I could not understand too clearly whether they vary in size, colouring and flesh textures on various planets, or whether there is a mixture on each planet as on Earth. Logical analysis would indicate the likelihood of the latter.

Despite the conclusions of most "orthodox" scientists it has always seemed to me a fallacy to believe that other planets are not the home of intelligent beings even as is our Earth.

All planets are apparently made out of similar substances. All revolve in the same space. Some are larger, some smaller than others, and all are in varying degrees of development — changing ceaselessly. This is true of all forms, whatever they are, wherever they be.

Reflecting telescopes will never give the full answer. For just as they reflect the light from a planet, they reflect also the particles moving in our atmosphere, and throughout space, and in the atmosphere surrounding the body they are studying.

Until finer devices are developed to filter out all the reflections from the countless moving particles everywhere present, a correct reading of any other body in space will be impossible with a reflecting telescope.

On the other hand, if and when the much-talked-of space platform becomes a reality, I believe actual facts about space will be revealed to our ever-searching scientists, and this will cause the reversal of many theories that today are accepted as facts.

Presence of space craft in our atmosphere, and personal contacts such as the one I have made, prove the old astronomical theories to be wrong. As completely wrong as man's sailing around the world proved the ancient theory of the Earth being square to be incorrect.

Since there are people on other planets, I wanted to know if they die, as Earth men die?

He smiled, and remembered a question I had asked earlier, if any of his people had died in coming to Earth?

So to clear the subject for me, he pointed to his body and nodded in the affirmative — that bodies do die. But pointing to his head, which I assumed to mean his mind, or intelligence, he shook his head in negation, this does not die. And with a motion of his hand, he gave me the impression that this — the intelligence — goes on evolving. Then pointing to himself, he indicated that once he lived here on this Earth: then pointing up into space — but now he is living out there.

I tried to learn the time involved in this type of transition but did not succeed in getting an answer from him. I did receive an impression but cannot say definitely that it is correct since so many thoughts were going through my mind. I could have allowed a slight confusion to enter.

An awareness of time began pressing upon me and there were so many questions I still had not asked him. I was trying to remember them and decide which ones were most important.

One question I wanted very much to ask him was, "Is the moon inhabited?" I believe it is, and that the people of other planets who indulge in inter-planetary travelling have bases there. My theory about other planets and the atmosphere surrounding them includes the moon.

But I forgot this one. Should I ever get another chance to talk with an inter-planetary traveller, I hope I remember to ask this question.

Nor did I ask him his name. But in a time like this, names and personalities are entirely forgotten. They mean so little and are very unimportant. Perhaps, if I should be privileged to meet him a number of times in the future I might remember to ask his name. Nor would I ask the name of any other inter-planetary traveller I should ever be permitted to contact, if it was in any way similar to this contact. In fact, I didn't even think of this point until someone later asked me about it.

He, too, must have received an impression that our visit was drawing to a close and that he must return to his waiting ship. For he kept pointing to his feet and talking in a language I surely had never before heard. It sounded like a mixture of Chinese with a tongue that I felt could have sounded like one of the ancient languages spoken here on Earth. I have no way of knowing this as fact. It was only my reaction as I listened, and his voice was indeed musical to listen to.

From his talk and his pointing to his feet, I felt there must be something very important there for me. And as he stepped to one side from the spot where he had been standing, I noticed strange markings from the print of his shoe left in the earth. He looked intently at me to see that I was understanding what he wanted me to do. And as I indicated that I did, and would comply, he stepped carefully on to another and another spot. Thus he made three sets of deep and distinct footmarkings. I believe his shoes must have been especially made for this trip and the markings heavily embossed on the soles to leave such deep imprints.

Then motioning for me to come with him, we turned and walked side-by-side toward the waiting ship.

It was a beautiful small craft, shaped more like a heavy glass bell than a saucer. Yet I could not see through it any more than one can see through the glass bricks that are popular in some of the newer office buildings and homes, which permit more light to enter than would solid walls.

It was translucent and of exquisite colour.

As we approached it, I suddenly became aware of a shadowy

form moving within the ship, but there were no definite outlines and I could not say whether it was a man or a woman.

However, that no mistake may be given here, let me say that I definitely do not believe this ship was made of glass such as we know it. It was a specially processed metal. Let me explain it in this way.

Carbon is a soft, opaque, elementary substance. Diamond is a clear hard stone which radiates prismatic colours in the presence of light — and is almost indestructible. Yet basically a diamond is carbon. Through natural processes of heat and pressure, Nature has transmuted the soft carbon into the hard diamond.

Earth scientists are working with this same principle and are having success to a limited degree.

It is my belief that the men on other planets — more versed in universal laws — have learned and are using these laws for practical purposes. I believe they know how to bring their primary elements from the opaque stage to a translucent stage, yet practically indestructible in hardness, as is the diamond. And it was of such a material that this space craft was made.

And after being so close to one of their small craft as I was to this Scout Ship, it is my firm conviction that it is this quality that makes them so elusive to our eyes and even to cameras, yet showing them on radar screens which require a density of some kind to show up. For I am told by radar operators that lights alone, or light reflections on clouds, do not show on radar screens. Neither do clouds, with the exception of rain clouds and ionised clouds.

Also it is this translucent quality, along with the power they use, that makes them often appear as different coloured lights without definite form.

The ship was hovering above the ground, about a foot or two at the far side from me, and very near to the bank of the hill. But the slope of the hill was such that the front, or that part of it closest to me, was a good six feet above the earth. The three-ball landing gear was half lowered below the edge of the flange that covered them, and I had a feeling this was a precautionary act just in case they had definitely to land. Some of the gusts of wind were pretty strong and caused the ship to wobble at times. When this took place, the sun reflecting on the surface of the ship caused beautiful prismatic rays of light to reflect out from it, as from a smoky diamond.

This was observed, too, by the six others who maintained a steady watch from a distance.

The splendour as it flashed its prismatic colours in the sunlight surpassed every idea I had ever had about space craft. A beautiful vision in actuality. The answer to many questions. A long-cherished hope realised . . . for there before me, silent in the desert stillness and hovering as if poised for flight, this ship of unearthly construction awaited our approach!

The very realisation of the experience I was having overwhelmed me . . . and I found myself speechless. No longer was I concerned with Earth alone. Rather, it was more like living in two worlds at the same time, and though I should live to be a hundred years of age, or more, I shall never forget the joy and the thrill of my first close approach to a Scout Ship from planet Venus — a sister to Earth.

Nearing the ship, I noticed a round ball at the very top that looked like a heavy lens of some kind. And it glowed. I wondered if this could be used as one end of a magnetic pole to draw their power from space as they were moving through it. In the photographs this ball looks like a large ring, and I have been asked if it was used to hold the smaller craft in place in the mother ship. I doubt this, unless it is suspended in its place in the larger ship through the force of magnetism. This could easily be.

The top of the craft was dome shaped, with a ring of gears or heavy coil built into and encircling the side wall at the base of this domed top. This, too, glowed as though power was going through it.

There were round portholes in the side wall, but not all the way round, because immediately above one of the balls of landing gear I noticed that the wall was solid. Whether this was true over the other two balls I cannot say because I did not walk around the ship. The covered portholes must have been made of a different quality or thickness of material for they were clear and transparent.

And once, for a fleeting second, I saw a beautiful face appear and look out. I felt that whoever was inside was looking for the one who was still out with me, but no word was spoken. The face disappeared so quickly that I caught only a glimpse of it, but I did notice that this person, too, had long hair like the man I had been talking with.

The lower outside portion of the saucer was made like a flange, very shiny yet not smooth as a single piece of metal would appear. It seemed to have layers of a fashion, but they couldn't be used as steps because they were in reverse to what steps should be. I have no idea of the reason for such construction, but it must have had a purpose.

I was absorbed in observing every detail of this strange and beautiful craft as we neared it, and I wondered just how they were managing to keep it in the hovering state as I saw it.

My space-man companion warned me not to get too close to it and he himself stopped a good foot away from it. But I must have stepped just a little closer than he, for as I turned to speak to him, my right shoulder came slightly under the outer edge of the flange and instantly my arm was jerked up, and almost at the same instant thrown back down against my body. The force was so strong that, although I could still move the arm, I had no feeling in it as I stepped clear of the ship.

My companion was quite distressed about this accident, but he had warned me and I alone was to blame. However, he did assure me that in time it would be all right. Three months later, his words have been proved true for feeling has returned and only an occasional shooting pain as of a deeply-bruised bone returns to remind me of the incident.

At the time I was not so concerned about my arm as I was about the exposed negatives still in the pocket of my jacket on that side. Immediately I reached in and removed them to put them in my other pocket.

As I held them in my hand, this visitor from Venus reached out and indicated that he would like one. Whether or not he realised that the power from his ship might have neutralised the film to a certain extent, I have no way of knowing.

However, at his request, I held the entire stack out to him and he took the top one. This he placed in the front of his blouse, but I still didn't see any opening or pocket of any kind.

As he did this, he made me understand that he would return the holder to me, but I did not understand how, when, or where.

I asked him if I could take a ride in his ship?

He shook his head.

Then I asked if I could just go inside to see what it looked like in there.

But, smiling very cordially, he made me understand that would be impossible at this time for he must be going.

I was a little disappointed, but at the same time it gave me hope that there would be another time and another opportunity.

Since I was not permitted inside the ship I cannot answer all the questions I have been asked about its construction, air conditioning, etc. However, it is my theory that they have solved their space craft construction problems as we have learned to build submarines for underwater travel. I believe space problems and water problems are very similar in respect to travelling through them. Both are fluid. Water is but gasses in liquid form. Space is composed of gasses in free state.

With a few graceful steps he reached the bank at the back of the ship and stepped up on to the flange. At least that is the way it looked to me. Where the entrance was, or how he went into the ship, I do not know for sure, but as it silently rose and moved away, it turned a little and I saw a small opening about the center of the flange being closed by what looked like a sliding door.

Also I heard the two occupants talking together, and their voices were as music, but their words I could not understand.

As the ship started moving, I noticed two rings under the flange and a third around the centre disk. This inner ring and the outer one appeared to be revolving clockwise, while the ring between these two moved in a counter clockwise motion.

As I stood in this mountainous recess — a solitary man watching the beautiful Scout Ship glide silently over the crest of the mountains and disappear into space — I felt that a part of me was going with it. For, strange as it may sound, the presence of this inhabitant of Venus was like the warm embrace of great love and understanding wisdom, and with his departure I felt an absence of this warm embrace.

There was an emptiness such as can be compared only with the feelings experienced when a very dear one departs; yet a longing remains for his presence. And to this very day I feel the same emptiness and longing whenever I think of this visitor from another world.

Yet there was and is an inexpressible joy for the privilege I had been given of glimpsing friends from a world beyond this Earth — and the ecstasy of a visit with one of them. . . .

# Contact by
# Automatic Writing . . .

*On March 7, 1953, eight people signed an affidavit
before a Notary Public in Winslow, Arizona, that
they had participated in the following events and that
the documentary report of the events was true.
George Hunt Williamson was a member of this
group, and the following selection is from his book*
The Saucers Speak.

Automatic writing itself, belongs to the order of mediumship
known as mental, but at first sight it appears to be of the physical
order. One has only to remember how difficult it is to cultivate the
art of writing to realize that at all times the co-operation of the
individual's own mind, although not necessarily of his consciousness, is necessary. Automatic writing has often been produced by
medical men from the patient's subconsciousness; and it is reasonable to conclude that the medium's subconsciousness is operative
when such writing is impelled by an outside communicator. Re-
searchers in the psychic phenomena field have claimed that this
writing can either be from the medium's subconsciousness or it can
be from some disembodied entity. If this is so, then we can understand how telepathy in the form of automatic writing could be accomplished between two living beings in the same plane of existence, but located in widely separated areas. Distance, whether two
miles or two million miles, would not be an important factor.

We know that this telepathic contact can be made with human
beings of outer space without the use of any device such as a pencil. However, this initial contact needed something whereby those
receiving the messages would not think it was the product of their

own minds. They could more readily accept what was written down in front of them in black and white. . . .

At different stages in the reception of the following messages, we altered our method of contact at the request of the space intelligences. . . . Our first contact was through automatic writing using a sheet of paper and a lead pencil. The second method was employed to make it easier on us, and to speed up the transmission of words. We took a large sheet of ordinary wrapping paper and drew on it the letters of the alphabet and the numbers from 1 through 10. This still did not prove entirely satisfactory, so we made what we later called the "board." It consisted of the same letters and numbers, plus the words "Yes" and "No," and a plus sign on the right and a minus sign on the left side. These signs indicated positive and negative.

This was much easier than holding a pencil for a long period of time. A glass tumbler was inverted and used as a "locator." It moved over the paper surface with considerable ease. Since the letters and figures were now arranged in a circular form, the transmission was speeded up greatly. Messages received in the above manner follow:

2 August 1952

"Masar to Saras." (After much questioning we learned that Masar was the planet Mars and Saras was our planet Earth.)

"You are a dead civilization. We want your co-operation. Time is limited. I am Nah-9 of Solar X Group. I am the leader of a contact group. We were seen over Southern California last night and early today." (Sunday, 3 August, newspapers carried stories of Air Force jet fighter bases being alerted for instant pursuit of saucer objects. They had been seen over the Mojave Desert at 11:45 P.M., Friday night, 1 August, and Saturday morning at 12:14 A.M., 2 August. Our contact had told us this information before we knew they had been observed.)

"Good and evil forces are working now. Organization is important for the salvation of your world. Contact us as you can.

"There is a mass of planets in the organization. Why are your peoples unbelievers? You have begun the research. The time is up to you! Look up into the skies above you, don't lose contact with each other. . . .

"We are friends of those interested, but we are not interested in those of the carnal mind. By that we mean the stupid preservation of self; disregarding the will of the Creative Spirit and His Sons.

"Your world has been observed for over 75,000 years. A survey was begun long ago on this planet Earth. How can we deny the eternal verities; Life, God, the Creator's place in the divine scheme? How can we sit by and watch the progress of evil men on this blob, the Earth? Come now, if you wish the answers that all mankind has been searching for since time began. You are wishing for these answers.

"Our group will be a duplicate of yours. We represent the people of outer space, you represent your world Saras. Cycles are computed by a group for this known as 'Timekeepers.'

"We have not wanted to interfere with men of Saras before. All men must make their progress wherever they are. But we cannot stand by and see another waste.

"We are all of the same Creation! Warning! There will soon be a destructive blast to be felt on Saras. This is of your own manufacture. Evil planetary men, who abound, will attempt contact with evil men of Saras for destruction! The good men of Saras must unite with the ben men of the Universe (ben means good). Great destruction can be caused by your H-bomb. It could all come too soon. Some destruction will come for sure! We have been alerted. We repeat, it is most important that you organize. . . .

"It takes much mind power for our thoughts to reach you on Saras in this manner. Again we say that you must be very well organized amongst yourselves. For better contact we suggest a powerful receiving set or radio. You should have your own set as our set is radically different. But we can reach you in this manner. Our people have trod your byways. Have you not seen us? Bell Flight-9 is a Masar flight to Saras. Masar means Mars. The name Mars has been passed down to you in legend, but it is known to us as Masar. . . ."

9 August 1952

"I am Regga of Masar, Council Circle meets. You were assem-

bled tonight. Oara is here. He is the planetary representative from
Saturn. I must tell you a few things of interest. These true facts
may even surprise you, but they are so. Many of your people on
Earth know them to be true. Your Sun, which is our Sun also, is
not a hot flaming body. It is a cool body. One of our great astronomers believed this and stated it. The so-called solar prominences
are as cool as are your aurora borealis (northern lights). You do
not necessarily have to have heat just because you have light. Look
at your firefly. You think your sun gives off great heat because you
can 'feel' it. Certain forces come from the Sun and when they
enter the earth's magnetic field this resonating field causes friction.
And from friction you get heat. There are other facts about the Sun
I cannot tell you now. In outer space the Sun does not appear as
bright as it does to you on Earth."

17 August 1952, 8:25 P.M.

"I am Zo. I am head of a Masar contact group, but my home is
Neptune. I am going to Pluto soon. Pluto is not the cold, dreary
world your astronomers picture it to be. Mercury is not a hot, dry
world either. If you understood magnetism you would then see why
all planets have almost the same temperature regardless of distance
from the great Sun Body. Sister rites are Universal rites. They are
rotting. Earth is backward, too many wars. Peace to all men everywhere."

"Regga speaking. Please put water on your stove to boil. It will
help our contacting you at this time."

"Zo again. 'To apples we salt, we return.' You may not understand this strange saying now, but someday you will. It is from one
of our old prophecy legends. Rites will save your people. We are
here to warn you. If there is dissension amongst you we will not
contact you. Be calm and quiet! We have only love for all men. We
hold certain councils on Uranus. We must now decide what to do
about your planet Earth. Your bombs will destroy Universal bal-
ance. Your Hydrogen Bomb could make an asteroid belt out of
you. This happened many years ago to planet of the fifth orbit. We
knew what they were doing but we didn't interfere. We cannot stand
by and see another waste. After their destruction there were terrible disasters on Masar. Great volcanic eruptions took place.

Many of our people perished. We would have been thrown out of the Solar System and lost if we had not quickly noticed that Phobos and Deimos reflect too much light to be made of earthly substance. They are right. They are metallic in nature. They readjusted our unstable condition and saved a planet. . . ."

"Regga: Friday and everyday we will try radio. We wait. Try to listen for us, and get a better radio, a more powerful set. Go to see Mr. R, a radioman. He will be all right if spoken to right. Tell him the truth, that you heard that if the saucers are from space they might be contacted by radio. It is most important that you contact us by this means. That is what we meant before when we told you to contact us as soon as possible! Contact between 340 kc. and 400 kc. Get a telescope, if you can. . . ."

In our endeavor to establish radio contact with the flying saucers or other space craft, a radioman whom we called Mr. R was contacted by Al. This man had a great deal of experience in his field and held a commercial license as well as an amateur ham license. Mr. R was skeptical, but quite willing to try a contact. Arrangements were at once made to listen on Friday evening, 22 August 1952.

All messages received by radiotelegraphy will be capitalized throughout this Diary. All other messages (from the "board," etc.) will be in small letters enclosed within quotation marks.

On the evening of 22 August 1952, Mr. R saw what he thought was a very small meteor display over Winslow, Arizona. He also observed what appeared to be a very bright light travelling at a high altitude in the sky above him. He turned on his receiver to 400 kc. and many strange signals were heard but not identified. Al, Mr. and Mrs. R were in the R's kitchen later when they all suddenly heard strange, clear code signals coming to them. They all thought it must be coming from the radio shack in the backyard, but when they went to check, there was nothing to be heard there. After they came back to the kitchen, the mysterious code was heard again! It seemed to be coming from the very air itself!

About 2:00 A.M., 23 August 1952 code signals were again received. Mr. R said it sounded as though two people were talking back and forth to each other using code. However, he said it was a

code unfamiliar to him. He couldn't make any sense out of it at all.
This strange code used a system of dots and dashes. After all, what
else could be devised? It seemed there were more of these dots and
dashes used for each letter or symbol than are used in our standard
International Morse Code. Mr. R had his pencil and pad before
him, and he hoped he might be able to make some sense out of the
code coming over his receiver in loud, clear tones. Then he suddenly wrote down ZO, and in a few minutes, AFFA. At this time,
the name Zo was very understandable, but the name Affa was not.
Nothing else was heard of an identifiable nature.

23 August 1952, 5:18 P.M.

"Regga speaking. You made contact with us on radio yesterday.
I think Lowell Observatory saw us."

"This is Zo. It wasn't altogether our fault that we didn't make a
good contact last night. Affa was talking to me last night. He helps
us in many ways. Soon there will be another contact. You have
already had good contact with us. Be patient! Affa is from the
planet Uranus. He was listening in last night. Be careful . . . 40
metre band is all right. We will do our best on radio contact.

"Affa of Uranus tries to keep us from talking to you. Uranus
doesn't believe in too much contact with the Earth planet. Affa told
me not to let you hear us, but I arranged so you could hear something. He interfered then, but helps otherwise. He was afraid of
Lowell Observatory. The 'big eyes' were looking at us, and they
are doing special work up there on the mountain now. They have
installed certain types of electronic equipment.

"California earthquake was caused by your planet's magnetic
disturbances. We must tell you about Orion. Many there wish to
conquer Universe. We are here to warn you of this also. However,
we find few receptive persons on Saras. You are helping us now by
what you are doing."

"Nah-9 speaking: The Orion Solar Systems are much like Saras.
The principles of good and evil are universal. Saras is the lowest in
progression in your Solar System, but there are planets in the Creation that are above you and below you in state of progression.
There is no beginning or end; no big nor small; nor low or high
estate. We are all on the road to All Perfection. We must tell you

that Orion is coming soon to Saras in a square star body. The year of decision is soon to come to you! We will be seen by more and more people in 1953. We want to land and you can be of help to us. Will you? We are happy. Be patient, for you were lucky you even heard us on the radio the other night. Affa is afraid Saras is too evil. You wonder how long our spaceflights take us. It takes only a few minutes to go from Masar to Saras. We do not fly as you think of flying, but we drift or glide on magnetic lines of force. We need no fuel. We operate in a Resonating Electro-magnetic Field just like planetary bodies do. Now we are hungry as you are. Sometimes on Neptune we eat Macas. They are similar to your cattle, but they do not have horns and they have big ears. . . ."

"Zo again. I will be staying at base on first Moon tonight. We usually take no women on our survey or scientific trips. There are several types of spacecraft. One is a Scout Craft holding one or two men that appears to fly upside down and has an antenna-like projection on the bottom; another is an arrow-shaped or crescent-shaped craft, it is a Master-Craft for it will guide many crystal bells in mass flight formation; then there is the Mother-Ship that you call a cigar-shaped craft. These latter can be many miles in length and send out green 'fireballs' to explode; then photographs of the magnetic fault lines can be taken. You would be astonished if you knew what these fireballs really were. They are not the same as your remote-controlled devices. Most bells do not travel between planets, for they are carried within the Mother-Ships. There are ships that look like tubes; craft that are round with an opening in the center; and triangular-shaped craft. Some of these ships have a high intensity field and others have a low intensity field. The flatter the form, the more intense the field of the craft. The small discs a few inches in diameter are in the fireball class although they are not all used for the same purposes. . . ."

One night in the radio shack, Mr. R decided to try a test. He told none of the witnesses present what he was going to do, not even his own wife. In fact, he finally told us about a week after the happening. He needed plenty of time to think it over. This test was of such a nature that, if the messages were a hoax, they would have been revealed as such immediately. He was seated at his radio set, with his back to all those present. He had sent a question over his transmitter on the 40 metre band and he received an answer. Without any warning he quickly switched to 160 metres and asked another question. To his surprise, an answer was soon forthcoming! Any radioman knows that no power on Earth would have enabled any operator to know where he was switching to! Even if Mr. R had told the other operator that he was going to switch to 160 metres, still they would not have found him on that band until after the question had been asked. And, of course, they couldn't have answered the question if they hadn't heard it! An operator cannot make such a switch without telling what he is going to do and then giving plenty of time for the other side to find him on the new band.

The space intelligences really passed this simple, but very exacting test. This proved one of two things: Perhaps the space friends were using telepathy. Why not? If they are far ahead of us in development they have possibly acquired proficiency in Extra-Sensory Perception. It is also possible that their superior equipment allows them to receive no matter what band is used in communicating with them. It really matters little how it was accomplished. The important thing is that it was done! . . .

# ... *By*

# *Mental Telepathy*

*Visual observation is only one indication that earth plays host to visitors from space. Albert K. Bender, in this selection from his book,* Flying Saucers and the Three Men, *tells of his success in contacting extraterrestrial beings by means of mental telepathy.*

At IFSB* headquarters at a meeting held early in March, 1953, we voted to hold what we would term a "World Contact Day," on which we would urge all IFSB members to attempt to send out a telepathic message to visitors from space. If there was anything to the claims of people expounding telepathic methods, and if we did have visitors from space, perhaps such a message might get across, particularly with so many minds concentrating on the same message. . . .

We quickly multigraphed instructions to send around the world by air mail so that all members would get the material in plenty of time before March 15, the day of the experiment. We received letters from many who thought the entire thing crazy and said they would have nothing to do with it. We do not know who took part and who did not, but I am certain that a great many of our members did so. The special bulletin was as follows:

ALL OFFICERS, REPRESENTATIVES, AND MEMBERS
OF THE INTERNATIONAL FLYING SAUCER BUREAU
SPECIAL BULLETIN: March 15, 1953, is C-Day (Contact Day)

On March 15, 1953, all officers, representatives, and members are asked to participate in an experiment, something that

* International Flying Saucer Bureau.

has not yet been attempted by any other group such as ours. We will attempt to send a message to the occupants of the saucers (if they exist) by the use of mental telepathy. Each member will memorize the message on this form, and on the time designated will close his eyes in a quiet secluded spot, lie down if possible, and repeat this message in his mind (do not repeat vocally). If the saucer people are able to pick up mental telepathy they certainly will be able to pick up a message that will be sent by hundreds of IFSB members. We may never know if this message has reached anyone, but if a sudden flurry of saucer sightings occur in 1953 or soon after our message, or even a saucer landing, we will know that we may have been indirectly responsible for it.

Members must remember that, in order for mental telepathy to work, you must have nothing on your mind at the time you send the message. You must only think of the person or persons to whom you are sending the message, and repeat it over in your mind. You must not have troubles or worries of any kind in the back of your mind, as this will tend to distract. This experiment is not compulsory to anyone in IFSB; we merely ask you to volunteer your services in trying to make it a success. Everyone participating must do so at the time designated, and not too soon before or after the time shown. We are sending this bulletin far enough in advance so that you may be sure to have your clocks set correctly that day and that the message has been memorized.

### THE MESSAGE
(*To Be Memorized*)

"Calling occupants of interplanetary craft! Calling occupants of interplanetary craft that have been observing our planet EARTH. We of IFSB wish to make contact with you. We are your friends, and would like you to make an appearance here on EARTH. Your presence before us will be welcomed with the utmost friendship. We will do all in our power to promote mutual understanding between your people and the people of EARTH. Please come in peace and help us in our EARTHLY problems. Give us some sign that you have received our message. Be responsible for creating a miracle here on our planet to wake up the ignorant ones to reality. Let us hear from you. We are your friends." (End of Message.)

The date, the places, and the times for this message to be sent:

THE DATE: March 15, 1953

| PLACES | | TIMES |
|---|---|---|
| States in the U.S.A. using Eastern Std. Time | | 6 P.M. |
| States in the U.S.A. using Central Std. Time | | 5 P.M. |
| States in the U.S.A. using Mountain Std. Time | | 4 P.M. |
| States in the U.S.A. using Pacific Std. Time | | 3 P.M. |
| Great Britain | | 11 P.M. |
| France | | 11 P.M. |
| Australia | March 16, | 9 A.M. |
| New Zealand | March 16, | 11 A.M. |
| Canada | Same as United States Above | |

On March 15, 1953, in my den at Bridgeport at exactly 6:00 P.M., I proceeded to take part in the experiment as planned. I put out the lights in my room and then quietly lay down on my bed. After studying the saucers for eleven years, I felt that I would try anything that might help solve the mystery. Saucer investigation had become the biggest part of my life, and I had worked diligently to reach a solution. As soon as I was comfortably situated on the bed, I closed my eyes and began to repeat the message over and over — three times to be exact.

It was after the third attempt that I felt a terrible cold chill hit my whole body. Then my head began to ache as if several headaches had saved up their anguish and heaped it upon me at one time. A strange odor reached my nostrils — like that of burning sulphur or badly decomposed eggs. Then I partly lost consciousness, as the room around me began to fade away.

Then small blue lights seemed to swim through my brain, and they seemed to blink like the flashing light of an ambulance. I seemed to be floating on a cloud in the middle of space, with a strange feeling of weightlessness controlling my entire anatomy. A throbbing pain developed in my temples and they felt as if they might burst. The parts of my forehead directly over my eyes seemed to be puffed up. I felt cold, very cold, as if I were lying naked on a floating piece of ice in the Antarctic Ocean.

I opened my eyes, and to my amazement I seemed to be floating above my bed, but looking down upon it where I imagined I could see my own body lying there! It was as if my soul had left my body and I was hovering above it about three feet in mid-air. Suddenly I could hear a voice, which permeated me but in some way did not seem to be an audible sound. The voice seemed to come from the room in front of me, which remained pitch dark.

"We have been watching you and your activities. Please be advised to discontinue delving into the mysteries of the universe. We will make an appearance if you disobey."

I replied in words, though my lips did not move: "Why aren't you friendly to us, as we do not mean to do any harm to you?"

"We have a special assignment," came the reply, "and must not be disturbed by your people."

As I tried to remonstrate, I was interrupted by another statement: "We are among you and know your every move, so please be advised we are here on your Earth."

With this, the voice faded away, but I could sense that something was watching me. My body seemed to drop suddenly and I once again regained my senses and realized I was on my bed. The room was filled with yellow mist. Not far from my bed was a shadow, resembling that of a man, but as I made a move to rise from the bed it disappeared. The yellow mist was gradually fading and my room was becoming normal.

I rubbed my eyes in bewilderment. I couldn't believe that what I had just experienced had been real. I must have dozed off and, with the telepathic experiment on my mind, must have had a terrifying dream as a result. Looking at the clock, I noticed it was five minutes past six, which certainly would have allowed time for me to have slept and dreamed.

As I sat up on the edge of my bed I grew sick at my stomach, felt as if I had eaten something rotten. Had I really experienced something unearthly? I could hardly force myself to rise from the bed. My head still throbbed and the spots over my eyes retained the same puffed feeling.

After a while I got up from the bed and walked about the room. I heard a humming and noticed that my radio was on. I turned it off, as I realized I had not turned it on when I came into the room. The same thing had happened on previous occasions. I was beginning seriously to feel I might be losing my mind. Again I wondered if I should tell anyone about it.

I sat down and made a diary of everything I could remember of the experience, sealed it in an envelope, and locked it in the desk. I felt that if anything of serious nature did happen to me, somebody would find the envelope and would know what had happened that day.

PART TWO   *The Theories*


*If, indeed, UFOs turn out to be visiting spacecraft from another world, we must assume that their technology is far more advanced than ours. How do their ships function? More to the point, why do they come?*

*On the other hand, there is the possibility that all UFOs can be explained within the framework of earthly phenomena; that is to say, reflections of lights, airplanes, balloons, etc. Or, they may turn out to be a product of the mind — a psychic projection.*

*Someday, scientists hope that we, on this planet, will be able to travel to distant solar systems. Even now problems of fuel, navigation, and time are seriously being considered from an earthly point of view.*

*Let us therefore turn from sighting to speculation and see how the following selections deal with these baffling problems.*

*WHERE DO THEY COME FROM*
*AND WHY DO THEY COME?*

# Concern over

# Atomic Explosions . . .

*Major Donald Keyhoe, author of several books on the subject, is convinced that interplanetary saucers are systematically surveying our planet. How and why are the subjects of this selection from* Flying Saucers from Outer Space.

The big question — the purpose of the saucer survey — was still unanswered. . . .

As a start I put down two suggestions that had been published since '47.

1. The unknown planet race — perhaps more than one — may fear an eventual invasion when we achieve space travel. Our success with atomic weapons may have increased this fear, and our high-altitude rocket tests would indicate that we are not far from journeys in space. This is one possibility suggested by Project Sign.

2. The spacemen may fear the effect of more powerful atomic explosions, especially if this race comes from a solar-system planet. Several atomic scientists have said that simultaneous H-bomb explosions might speed up the earth's rotation or even change its orbit. One of these was Dr. Paul Elliott, a nuclear physicist who worked on the first A bomb. Others have said that a mass explosion of H bombs might tear a large chunk out of the earth, or that a violent chain reaction might even destroy our planet.

Any of these effects, particularly destruction of the earth, might have serious results — or at least unpleasant reactions — on Mars, Venus, and other solar-system planets. According to some astronomers, including Dr. George Gamow of George Washington University, the earth's ice ages were caused by certain unknown changes on Saturn and Jupiter. A violent explosion which altered or destroyed the earth might have even more disastrous results. If some other solar-planet race knew this danger from its own atomic discoveries, it would have good reason for alarm.

Using other suggestions I'd heard and ideas of my own, I added the following alternate motives:

3. If the unknown race uses atomic energy, it may be exhausting its supply of uranium. In this case our A-bomb explosions would reveal a new source of supply. This would explain the saucers' interest in our atomic plants and uranium mines. It would be simple for remote-control units to locate uranium deposits — our own Geological Survey has developed Geiger counters for planes used in such searches. It would also explain the saucers' concentration on the United States, the most advanced nation in this field.

4. The saucer race may intend to invade us as part of a program to conquer inhabited planets.

5. They may have some unknown plan for the earth besides plain conquest.

6. Our planet may not be considered a menace, and it may not hold any material interest leading to an invasion. The surveillance then could be for one of two reasons:

a. To survey the earth with the intention of contact, once the saucer race has convinced us of its peaceful intentions, and is sure we will not attack them.

b. To catalogue the earth as just another inhabited planet, with no plans for immediate contact. The survey might then subside into a periodic check until we seemed far enough advanced for acceptance, unless meantime we developed into a threat to space nations.

There was one factor which might have an important bearing. For almost 200 years before the 1947 sightings, strange objects and lights had been reported all over the world. Many of the stories were undoubtedly old wives' tales. But a few reports, by astronomers, sea captains, and various reputable observers, sounded remarkably like the present sightings. . . .

If these reports were to be believed, I could see only one conclusion — that the earth had been observed periodically, in a systematic patrol of inhabited planets, but until recently had not been of great interest to advanced races.

The present sightings, then, might be only a new phase of a long surveillance, though they could be observations by some planet race which had discovered the earth in the last few years. It was even possible that both answers were right — there might be more than one race involved in the saucer survey.

If it was an entirely new operation, it wasn't hard to see how the unknown race had discovered the earth. Though it could have been an accident, during a space exploration, there was a more likely explanation.

For some years now, our radar and high frequency radio messages had been travelling through space. Radio astronomers on some other planet undoubtedly must have heard them and set about deciphering the messages. Even if they hadn't learned their meaning, the unknown race would know they were intelligent symbols, coming from another world. Monitoring the wave lengths, locating their source, and following the signals to the earth would be a simple matter for a race that had conquered space travel. . . .

# Was There
# a Tenth Planet? . . .

*Gavin Gibbons believes the saucers are extraterrestrial. In this selection from* The Coming of the Space Ships *he considers the question of where they come from and why.*

We have seen that Flying Saucers do indeed exist. Even the most pronounced sceptics admit that literally thousands of normal people in all walks of life have seen *something* in the sky or travelling across it — even the most fastidious seeker after the truth cannot deny the evidence of sight to so many witnesses. The newly-established Saucer investigation bureau of the United States Government has published its latest findings under the title "Project Blue Book" and, significantly, has reported that out of 1,593 reports of all kinds reaching them, three out of ten cannot be attributed to any known cause. And this from an official source! We shall find that official sources use every method of discrediting any Saucer reports that come within their ken, explaining them away in a manner sometimes absurd. Yet in this instance even they have to admit that three out of every ten reports received from the general public cannot be so disposed of. Let us go further. We now know that "unidentified flying objects" or U.F.O.'s as we will call them, do exist. Why are we so sure that they are extra-terrestrial? Why should they not be the products of Man's mechanical genius? For these reasons. Every one of the substantiated reports that have reached us from observers all over the world stress the fact that these machines resemble nothing ever before seen on Earth — and do not forget that many of these observers have been scientific men of unimpeachable integrity who have approached the subject with the utmost scepticism and have been later forced to admit the authenticity of many of the sightings.

Numbers of men, actively concerned in the building, designing, and flying the latest types of aircraft, have seen these visiting phenomena and have declared that it would be impossible for us to build such machines with our present scientific knowledge. What is more, it would be as impossible for an earthly pilot to stand the sharp turns, reversals, and zig-zag movements that these craft make as it would for an earthly engineer to construct such a machine. This, added to the fact that the tangibility of the Saucers is suggested by imprints in the ground, strange débris, and certain plant damage, as well as being picked up by radar, makes it highly probable that they must come from outer Space or at least from within the confines of the Solar System. It is true that in the present uneasy state of world tension insinuations have been made that these sightings have been of secret weapons or flying machines operated by certain governments who are arming themselves in a desperate attempt to forestall the machinations of their enemies. This theory will not hold water; reports of Saucer sightings have been received from all these countries and they have all strenuously denied any knowledge of such experimental aircraft. Indeed, we can be sure that no such governments can possibly have the technicians to design nor the engineers to build machines that can fly so high, so fast, and with such manoeuvrability. No! We can be sure that the Saucers are not of our ken — neither of Man's manufacture nor of his control in any way.

As we have seen, Flying Saucers have been known to men since the earliest recorded history of time and have been seen in varying circumstances by many men and women. But it is only since 1947 that they have been appearing in such large numbers and have therefore attracted so much attention. Why has this planet been of such interest to the Saucers since this date in particular? I believe that the answer is simple and straightforward. It lies in the discovery by us of the secret of atomic power and the exploding of atomic and hydrogen bombs. Since the first experimental bomb was set off in the American desert in 1945, to be followed by the holocausts of Hiroshima and Nagasaki, more "unidentified flying objects" have been observed than ever before. This surely indicates a connection and postulates several theories. If there are beings of some form of life on another planet, either in our Solar System or beyond, are they keeping watch over us to ascertain that we do not overstep the bounds of wisdom and hurl ourselves and perhaps other worlds into a nameless oblivion? Let us examine these theories more closely.

There are nine known planets in our Solar System — the great family of the Sun. They are strung out in a roughly ascending and descending sequence of size, swinging majestically in their orbits round the sun, as though a gigantic cigar had been clipped into round pieces as it swung upon a string around a pole. All the planets have their different orbits and movements, some having more moons than the others; some are hard and cold, others appear to be nothing more than a dense mass of flaming gas. Between Mars and Jupiter there lies a cluster of tiny planetoids, ranging in size from a body several hundreds of miles in diameter to a ball less than six inches across. There are very many thousands of these asteroids, as they are called, and they whirl around in orbits that are so near one another that it seems obvious that they once formed a tenth planet, Aster, which at some time exploded with incredible violence, leaving these scattered fragments to perpetuate its memory. The mind reels when it attempts to focus upon a catastrophe of such magnitude and large-scale destruction. We are left asking ourselves why it exploded so suddenly. What caused the vast distintegrating force that rended it so completely? We can only guess. Did the planet swing too near to the mighty gravitational pull of Jupiter, that huge body that is a thousand times as large as the Earth, and in so doing suffered such stresses that it flew into pieces? This could explain the eleven moons that encircle Jupiter — they could either be pieces of the actual plane itself that was caught in the larger body's orbit or tiny fragments of Jupiter that were pulled off by the collision. Or was this tenth planet in actual contact with another body, perhaps an eleventh planet, and in the resulting collision blown to pieces? Either of these hypotheses could be true, but modern astronomy is inclined to doubt them. A better explanation is being sought, and I believe it may be found in a study of the Flying Saucers. This connection is startling but entirely tenable.

Let us suppose that in ages past — countless thousands of years ago — a race lived upon this strange tenth planet, a race of beings that was so far advanced intellectually that we would appear but ignorant savages in comparison. Suppose that they too had discovered atomic power as we have done and in some frightful war or through some error had blown up their planet, pulverising it into the stream of particles that we now see cascading through Space between Mars and Jupiter. I believe not only that this theory is viable, but further that it is possible that some of these fantastically advanced beings escaped from the destruction of their home to set up a colony on some other planet. It is from this colony that they are now anxiously watching our atomic experiments by means of their space ships, fearful not only for our own safety but also for the entire Universe.

In spite of what the astronomers tell us (and how little any man knows of the immensity of the enigma we call the Universe!), there also exists the possibility that the forces behind the U.F.O.'s are inhabitants of one of the other planets who have never lived on our Earth or any other planet but their own, but who are sufficiently advanced to realise that in our fumblings with the secrets of matter we may set off a chain reaction that might obliterate them as well as ourselves. We do not know for certain which of the planets are habitable, but Venus, Mars, or Saturn seem the most likely origin of the Saucers, as conditions there are most near those on Earth. Saturn, of course, is very much the coldest of the three, being so far from the Sun.

Time by our reckoning is nothing — a million years is only a yawn on the face of the Infinite. These Beings from the tenth or other planets could have been in existence for countless years before our globe had begun to solidify and in the vast ages that lie between us they could well have become possessed of such cool and inscrutable wisdom combined with pure knowledge that we can only guess at its depths. In their communion with the Spirit of the Universe they could well be possessed with a great love and compassion for all living things — a feeling that would surely drive them to watch over us with kindly interest. I believe this could well be true, and if we were to embark upon an atomic war on this planet they would be forced to intervene and, if necessary, take us over completely in an effort to save us from ourselves. I believe also that one day if we go our ways in peace, the Saucers may land on our Earth in force in a kind of crusade — an educational invasion to shew us the path to a better life and a fuller existence. These beings are definitely a force for *good* — the good of every living thing in the entire cosmic system. That is why we have no need to fear them, but on the contrary, should welcome their attentions. They are our friends; indeed, they may well be our deliverers!

There is another very interesting theory, put forward by a famous writer in this field, Desmond Leslie, that the people inhabiting the lost continent of Atlantis had advanced to a stage of development where not only did atomic power play a great part in their daily lives, but where space travel was becoming a commonplace thing. This great, lost continent lay roughly under where Atlantic waves roll to-day — west of the most westerly part of Africa. This is proved by scientific records which show that land in that area is slowly rising, as much as six feet per year, and that shortly we can expect to see the heights of the lost continent emerging above the waters. For many centuries men have believed that in the dim ages of time a great and powerful race ruled there. We can find many references in ancient Sanskrit writings to "vimanas" — or chariots of the sky — which seem to be the earliest mention of Flying Saucers. Leslie believes that the people of Atlantis destroyed their civilisation by the indiscriminate use of atomic power, and in the resultant huge explosion the continent was inundated by the ocean. Complete destruction was caused by the stupendous powers unleashed when the waters of the ocean passed through the rent in the Earth's crust and met the molten centre. Atlantis now lies covered with the silt and débris of the ages, a monument to man's foolishness. Atlantis was not the only continent to meet its doom in this way. In 30,000 B.C. Lemuria was destroyed because dangerous knowledge, unknown to all except the ruling priestly class, was misused. The few survivors of this cataclysm founded Atlantis. Some survivors from the Atlantis disaster are believed to have escaped disaster by fleeing in machines to another planet, from whence they now send out their patrols to scan the Earth for signs of further atomic activity.

Here, then, are three theories to account for the presence of Flying Saucers in our skies. . . .

# Are the Ancient
# Lost Cities
# Still Inhabited? . . .

*Legends of lost cities of ancient South American*
*empires have been handed down throughout history.*
*Recently UFOs have been sighted in the mysterious*
*jungle sections of that continent. Is there a*
*connection? The following selection is from*
Road in the Sky, *by Dr. George Hunt Williamson.*

. . . In the same area today, where once the Amazonian Empire flourished, UFOs or space ships are again being sighted and in great numbers. Such craft showed up before to warn the men on Earth that a great disaster was about to engulf them. Why are they now coming to the very same area after thousands of years? Why is the "communication" being established once more? A study of UFO sightings down through recorded history will show that interplanetary visitors always make an appearance in the affairs of Earth just prior to some great cataclysm or change on this planet.

Since 1955, UFOs have been reported by engineers, explorers, and missionaries working in the little-known jungle areas of South America. The Padres report that they do not know what these strange, unconventional craft are, but they do know they have been seeing them in great numbers, and sometimes singly. The UFOs are always observed heading in the direction of the vast unexplored areas where no white man has ever gone. In other words, they are headed directly for the areas where Colonel Fawcett and others have claimed great stone cities of the ancient South American Empire once ruled the world. Why are they returning to these cities now that these places are in ruins? Do they seek ancient records still buried there? Or is it possible that some of these cities are not in ruins but are still occupied by some of the "remnant that remained"? And these inhabitants of still living cities of "Paititi," are they actually in communication with beings from other worlds? What strange and wonderful conclaves we can imagine! Interplanetary craft landing in the plazas of forgotten cities that never were abandoned, but continued to live and be occupied by the masters of a great civilization. A magnificent picture forms before our eyes as we see the men of other worlds, who represent the highest in technical and scientific skill and achievement, sit down to confer with the masters of still living "Paititi" in the majestic and gigantic stone halls of an Empire that ruled the world over 30,000 years ago.

Would all of this account for the fact that for hundreds of years jungle Indians have reported they have occasionally seen "white masters or teachers in robes" in the unknown areas of the rain forests? These "white teachers" are not modern missionaries, for the Indians claim they are capable of "strange powers" and that they come and go as they please and that they live in great cities in parts of the jungle that even they are unfamiliar with. Is this why so many tribes have a great fear of the areas of "Lost Cities"; is this why they can be used to guide you for a certain distance and to a certain point and then they will not go a step further?

As early as 1948-1949, reports came out of Puerto Maldonado on the Rio Madre de Dios that space ships and strange "glowing lights" were being seen regularly there. Red, yellow, and green objects were reported entering the dense jungle areas. Why are they coming? Some research societies in various South American countries believe that the UFOs are using the unexplored jungle areas for gigantic bases of operation and that they use such areas to insure their *privacy*. Let us remember that there is a lot of "space" in outer space and the UFOs have been doing a good job of "hiding" in that space for a very long time. Therefore, do they really need our jungles to hide from us, or are they in those areas for a much more important reason? I believe they have once again established their *road in the sky* and that they are in communication with the master teachers of a dead empire who still guard the ancient wisdom in the high-walled stone citadels of great "Paititi." The fact that they have returned to the Earth constitutes a warning for our time that we must heed.

Again we find in a place where legends speak of "sky dwellers" the same thing happening today, the "gods" have returned to their former haunts. What does all of this mean to us? Are we facing a world calamity as the ancients did? Let us remember the words of warning from the Ancient Mysteries:

"As above, so below . . . that which hath been shall return again." . . .

# Is There a World
# Inside Our Planet? . . .

*Nearly everyone feels that if the UFOs are not made on earth, they come from other planets. There are a few people, however, who believe very strongly that the ships come from the center of the earth itself. Raymond Bernard discusses this possibility in the following selection from* The Hollow Earth.

. . . The conception of a hollow earth . . . offers the most reasonable theory of the origin of the flying saucers and far more logical than the belief in their interplanetary origin. For this reason, leading flying saucer experts, as Ray Palmer, editor of "Flying Saucers" magazine, and Gray Barker, a well known writer on flying saucers, have accepted the theory of their subterranean origin as against the idea that they come from other planets.

The theory that flying saucers came from the earth's interior and not from other planets originated in Brazil and only later was it taken up by American flying saucer experts.

In 1957, while browsing in a Sao Paulo, Brazil, bookstore, the author came across a book that struck his attention, entitled, *From the Subterranean World to the Sky: Flying Saucers*. The book was devoted to the thesis that flying saucers were not space ships from other planets but were of terrestrial origin and came from a subterranean race dwelling inside the earth. . . .

Huguenin's theory of the subterranean origin of the flying saucers, however, was not original. The idea was first put forward by Professor Henruique Jose de Souza, president of the Brazilian Theosophical Society, which has its headquarters in Sao Lourenco in the State of Minas Gerais, where there is an immense temple in Greek style dedicated to "Agharta," the Buddhist name for the Subterranean World. . . .

While Huguenin incorporated the idea of the subterranean origin of the flying saucers in a book, Commander [Paulo Justin] Strauss presented it in a series of lectures which he held in Rio de Janeiro, in which he affirmed that the flying saucers are of terrestrial origin, but do not come from any known nation on the earth's surface. They originate, he believes, in the Subterranean World, the World of Agharta, whose capital city is known as Shamballah.

In his book, Huguenin presents Strauss's views on the subterranean origin of the flying saucers and against the theory that they come from other planets as follows:

> The hypothesis of the extra-terrestrial origin of the flying saucers does not seem acceptable. Another possibility is that they are military aircraft belonging to some existing nation on earth. This hypothesis, however, is opposed by the following arguments:
>
> 1. If the United States and Russia possessed flying saucers, they would not desist from announcing this fact because of its value as a psychological arm to secure advantages in the diplomatic field. Also they would manufacture and use these vehicles for military purposes, since they are so rapid and powerful that they would leave the enemy almost without means of defense.
>
> 2. The United States and USSR would not continue to spend large sums of money on the manufacture of ordinary airplanes if they possessed the secret of producing flying saucers.

After presenting the argument that flying saucers do not come from any existing nation and his view that they are not of interplanetary origin, Huguenin quotes Strauss on the fact that they come from the Subterranean World. On this subject he writes:

> Finally, we must consider the most recent and interesting theory that has been offered to account for the origin of the flying saucers: the existence of a great Subterranean World with innumerable cities in which live millions of inhabitants. This other humanity must have reached a very high degree of

civilization, economic organization, and social, cultural, and spiritual development, together with an extraordinary scientific progress, in comparison with whom the humanity that lives on the earth's surface may be considered as a race of barbarians.

The idea of the existence of a Subterranean World will shock many people. To others it will sound absurd and impossible, for "certainly," they say, "if it existed, it would have been discovered long ago." And there are plenty of other critics who would point out that it would be impossible for such an inhabited world to exist inside the earth because of the belief that as one descends, the temperature increases, on the basis of which theory it is supposed that, since the temperature increased the further down one went, the center of the earth is a fiery mass. However, this increase in temperature does not mean that the center of the earth is fiery, since it might extend only for a limited distance and, as in the case of volcanos and hot springs, arise from subterranean cavities located at certain levels (below which the temperature again drops as one goes downward). In accordance with the hypothesis that heat increases as one descends through the earth's crust, this takes place only a distance of eighty kilometers (in the superficial layer of the earth).

According to the information supplied by Commander Paulo Justin Strauss, the Subterranean World is not restricted to caverns, but is more or less extensive and located in a hollow inside the Earth large enough to contain cities and fields, where live human beings and animals, whose physical structure resembles those on the surface. Among its inhabitants are certain persons who came to the surface. . . .

Huguenin then asks how these marvelous subterranean cities and this advanced civilization in the interior of the earth arose. His answer is that the builders and most of the inhabitants of this Subterranean World are members of an antediluvian race which came from the prehistoric submerged continents of Lemuria and Atlantis, who found refuge there from the flood that destroyed their Motherland. (Lemuria sank under the Pacific Ocean 2,500 years ago, while Atlantis was submerged by a series of inundations, the last of which occurred 11,500 years ago, according to Plato's account, derived from ancient Egyptian records. Egypt was a colony of Atlantis to the East, just as the Aztec, Mayan, and Inca empires were to the West.)

Huguenin claims that the Atlanteans, who were far in advance of us in scientific development, flew the sky in aircraft utilizing a form of energy obtained directly from the atmosphere, and which were known as "vimanas," which were identical with what we know as flying saucers. Prior to the catastrophe that destroyed Atlantis, the Atlanteans found refuge in the Subterranean World in the hollow interior of the earth, to which they traveled on their "vimanas" or flying saucers, reaching it through the polar openings. Ever since then, their flying saucers remained in the earth's interior atmosphere and were used for purposes of transportation from one point in the interior *concave world* to another, for in this world, inside the crust of the earth, a straight aerial line is the shortest distance between any two points, no matter how far apart. It was only after the Hiroshima atomic explosion that these Atlantean aircraft rose to the surface for the first time, and were known as flying saucers. As we have pointed out previously, they came as an act of self-defense, to prevent radioactive pollution of the air they received from the outside. . . .

From Brazil, where the theory of the subterranean origin of the flying saucers originated, it spread to the United States, where Ray Palmer, editor of "Flying Saucers" magazine, became its enthusiastic proponent. . . .

Palmer suggests that people live on the "inside" of the earth, and that such people emerge from the Poles in flying saucers. His case boils down to these main points:

(1) Measurements of areas at the North and South Poles are larger than you can find room for on a map or globe, leading to the assumption that such areas extend down into the "doughnut."

(2) Some animals, particularly the musk-ox, migrate north in the wintertime, from the Arctic Circle. Foxes are found north of the 80th parallel, heading north, and appear well fed in a large area where there is no food available. (They go north because it becomes warmer and there is plant and animal life as they enter the polar opening — Author.)

(3) Arctic explorers agree it gets warmer as one heads north (after coming close enough to the North Pole).

(4) In the Arctic, coniferous trees drift ashore, from out of the north. Butterflies and bees are found in the far north, but never hundreds of miles south of that point.

(5) Remains of mammoth, perfectly preserved, were found in Siberia, with the sparse food of the sub-Arctic region in its stomach. Such food could not have supported the animal. It must have come from the "land beyond the Poles," Palmer postulates.

(6) Trouble with satellites shot over the South Pole bears out the theory that land areas haven't been measured accurately or that "somebody" has been interfering with them.

But there are many other arguments against the interplanetary hypothesis of the origin of flying saucers. This story does not explain how, under entirely different geological, chemical, atmospheric, gravitational, climatic, and other conditions, planets millions or trillions of miles away, and belonging to other solar systems, could develop human beings so like us in structure, appearance, clothing, customs, language, accent and ideas as the "Venusians" whom Adamski claimed to have met in a "Mother-Ship" or "space ship" he claims to have visited. The fact that these people not only look like us, have the same stature, and even speak with an accent (in many cases, a German accent), seems strange if they came from another planet. It seems much more probable that they came originally from the earth's surface, gained access to the Subterranean World, and are employed as pilots by subterranean authorities, who sent them to us.

If they came from other planets or solar systems, it would be very improbable that they would look and speak like us as much as they do. Most writers of science fiction imagine inhabitants of other planets to be entirely unlike us in their structure. In his *War of the Worlds,* H. G. Wells pictured Martians as mechanical monsters. It would be a rare coincidence that other planets would develop forms of life so much like our own as are the pilots of the flying saucers, according to those who claim to have met them. As for the "small men" found in flying saucers, they are probably subterranean dwarfs employed by the master race that created them as pilots.

If the people seen in flying saucers were members of our own race (chiefly Germans, since so many of them speak German, which would be strange if they came from other solar systems or planets), employed as pilots, they would probably have been instructed by their leaders not to reveal the secret of the origin of the flying saucers for the reason that the land area of the New World in the hollow interior of the earth is greater than that of its surface, where we find more area covered by ocean water, and should militaristic governments learn about this, they would make a mad rush to send their aircraft through the polar openings to claim this territory as their own, just as the governments of Europe sent their expeditions to America soon after Columbus discovered the new continent.

If certain ambitious surface governments sought to appropriate this new territory, enjoying an ideal subtropical climate, by force, by sending in expeditions equipped with nuclear weapons, the superior subterranean people would be forced to defend themselves by their "death rays," a force far more powerful than atomic energy, capable of bringing about complete atomic disintegration and the dematerialization and disappearance of their invaders and their weapons. Such a catastrophe they would rather prevent, since they are pacifists and detest warfare.

For this reason they wished to keep the existence of the Subterranean World a secret, so that its inhabitants may not be molested by invaders from the outside. For this reason flying saucer pilots were instructed to pretend that they came from other planets and were "spacemen," in case they were contacted, and to keep it a secret that they came from inside the earth. In this way they could guard their secret. Adamski and others who claimed to contact them were accordingly deceived by the false idea that the flying saucer travelers came from other planets.

If the major governments would forget their race into space and send armies of ice breakers, dirigibles, and aircraft to penetrate as far as possible through the polar openings, it would not be long before contact would be established between the superior race living inside the earth's crust and the less advanced race, still in a state of mechanized barbarism and engaging in constant wars, inhabiting the earth's surface. However, militaristic governments are not worthy of establishing contact with such superior, superhuman beings, who would probably use their powerful radiations capable of dematerialization to prevent intrusion by undesirable or dangerous visitors. Since they came from Atlantis, which had a civilization far greater than our own over 11,500 years ago for many thousands of years previously, this elder race has a scientific development as much greater than our own as ours is greater than that of the Hottentots.

In comparison with the superior Subterranean People, surface dwellers are barbarians, and their proud "civilization" is a state of mechanized barbarism. Until they learn to relinquish war forever, to destroy and bury all nuclear weapons, to establish a world government, a world court, and a world police, and until they reorganize their economic and financial system on a basis of equity and justice, they will be unworthy to contact the inhabitants of the Subterranean World, who stand on a level of scientific, intellectual, and moral development vastly beyond those on the surface.

# METHODS OF PROPULSION

# Tektites
# and Silicon . . .

*"Another civilization already capable of space travel might have based its technology upon the development of universal energies still unknown to our men of science," says Brinsley Le Poer Trench in another selection from* The Sky People.

. . . If Man exists in other parts of the Universe . . . how are his space ships propelled?

A well-known French aircraft manufacturer, Louis Breguet, considers that "discs use a means of propulsion different from ours. There is no other possible explanation — flying saucers come from another world."

What is this mode of propulsion?* Scattered in various localised and circumscribed areas on the earth's surface are smooth, glassy lumps of curious shapes.

These objects, called tektites, are found strewn in fixed areas called "tektite strewn fields" covering several miles. The chief ones so far discovered are in Iraq, Lebanon, the Dead Sea area, Libya, Bohemia, Texas, Mexico, Peru, Central Australia, and elsewhere. These strange objects have been the subject of sharp scientific controversy for many years.

On examining tektites one is first struck by their smooth aerodynamic form suggesting they have travelled rapidly through the air in a softened state. Again, they are chemically different from meteorites and their appearance in localised fields demands special explanation.

---

* These notes on Tektites were supplied by Dr. Bernard E. Finch and subsequently appeared in July–August 1960 issue of *Flying Saucer Review*.

The second striking feature of tektites is their chemical composition. The glasslike substances are found to be composed of silica. Some contain varying quantities of radio-active isotopes of aluminium and beryllium; some are pure silicon; others resemble quartz, glass, or flint, and contain varying quantities of boron. The interesting thing about these silicon masses is that they are powerful insulators of electro-magnetic forces such as gravity. Therefore, all the evidence associated with tektites, their locations and properties, points to their extra-terrestrial origin. By examining large quantities of tektites and their distribution on the "strewn field" one clearly notices the resemblances to the remains of a burnt-out air crash or missile. Some areas contain tektites resembling quartz, others pure silicon, and others, radio-active beryllium. Perhaps, these other locations are the remains of parts of a burnt-out disintegrated space ship, the glass control room, the hull, the drive and so on.

That the tektites are not due to the effect of lightning on sand, as was once thought, is evident by the discovery at various times of a mysterious substance floating on the sea in different parts of the world. This substance was found some months ago near the Pitcairn Islands. It was described as light honey coloured, soft, and of a silky consistency. Examination showed it to be of pure silicon. Hence again, we have evidence of extra-terrestrial objects reaching the Earth.

Finally, recent research work has shown that silicon is affected by light waves. When sunlight or the light of stars falls on a wafer of silicon and mica, an electric current flows. If the sunlight is concentrated by a quartz lens, large voltage differences are produced. The result is solar energy. . . .

From all this evidence one can now deduce for the first time that flying saucers may be made of silicon and its compounds and the anti-gravity effect is produced and controlled by electric power flowing in the hull and activated by sunlight which is concentrated by a quartz lens on top — the electrical energy may be stored in silicon batteries. The silicon body of the saucer acts as an insulator to gravity and other electro-magnetic waves and an alternating current passed through the hull of silicon or through quartz crystals produces a Piezo-Electric effect or high frequency ultra-sonic waves which may be associated with propulsion.

From this point of view it is interesting to note the recent experiments in laboratories in different parts of the world, using ultrasonic waves, causing the air to become ionised, typical of the Aurora Borealis, which glows from a dull red at low frequencies to a bluish white at high frequencies throughout the range of the spectrum. The air became ionised acting as a plasma conducting electricity and magnetism.

Hundreds of saucer reports have testified to changes of colour, red, blue, green, orange, and indeed the whole range of the spectrum, on the part of these objects as they passed through the skies.

This new concept of saucer propulsion has been gained from the careful study of flying saucer reports and satisfies all the known criteria of sightings.

There are other concepts which might be considered. Here on our own planet, vehicular propulsion has emerged along certain definite mechanical and electronic lines. That there exist other possible areas of development is clear from some of the more modern research now going on in the fields of magnetism and light. It has been suggested seriously that space ships of the future may be propelled by the energy of light itself. Certain developments in satellite research show this to be no impossible dream.

It would be only logical to suppose that another civilisation already capable of space travel might have based its technology upon the development of universal energies still unknown to our men of science. To pursue this idea still further and include a so-called etheric universe increases the range of imaginable possibilities even more.

Our own chemical metals, for instance, may have more life in them than we suppose. Under conditions of stress, metals behave in a manner suggesting fatigue, and physicists have found no better word to describe this condition. From another point of view, it is well known that many metaphysical authorities have maintained consistently that there is no such thing as dead matter.

In an etheric universe which might well have a less complicated fundamental structure than our own chemicals show, the processes we recognise and associate with life may continue farther on down the scale toward the simpler molecules and even to the atoms themselves.

If this were true, machines — or their etheric equivalent — could be produced by some process more akin to growth than to manufacture. As a result of this combination of circumstances we should expect such machines to exhibit some of the characteristics of sentient life — and indeed they often do. Reports of sightings have included statements referring to the peculiar motion of the objects observed, such as: "They behaved as if they were alive."

Some people have gone so far as to suppose the saucers — or some of them, at least — are actually animal life-forms inhabiting the fringes of outer space. This idea need not be particularly startling to us if we consider the everyday fact that, to a fish who lives in water, a relatively dense medium, air-breathing animals appear to exist in an uninhabitable vacuum!

Could it not be, then, that the owners and operators of sentient machines have, upon occasion, left their living vehicles to rest and to refresh themselves under favourable circumstances, much after the manner that we ourselves leave faithful horses to frolic in the fields? When they have regained their strength and vigour, might not their owners call them back again into their usual service?

Viewed in this light, such living vehicles would fall somewhere in between an advanced machine and an uncomplicated animal. Such an alert but still mechanically reactive construction might be very sensitive to telepathic impulse, controlled and directed by the very thought-processes of its rider, and capable of rudimentary but immediate and accurate response-judgments based upon environmental data. Although apparently aimless and irresponsible in their actions when alone and unaccompanied by their operators, such animal machines might easily show the same sort of strange curiosity and apparent playfulness attributed to some of the unidentified flying objects that have been reported.

On the other hand, when they are under the full control of their owners, we could expect to observe the more patterned and purposeful behaviour characteristic of what is by far the majority of sightings.

To speculate upon the possible mode of propulsion utilised by flying saucers without considering, at least, the possibility of their being planned and produced from some more advanced and possibly very different basic structure would be to put a limit on our thinking. Without further exact data, not yet forthcoming, such thinking cannot be anything but restricted, and confined to logical extrapolation from our own experience. Let us then beware of dismissing too summarily and out of hand what may at first appear to us to be quite astonishing notions concerning the possible way in which UFOs are made, what they do, and how they do it. In so doing we may let some important datum slip away, and find ourselves no nearer to a solution of the mystery.

When the Scythians rode their horses into Greece, the Greek people, who were unfamiliar with such an arrangement between man and beast, mistook the combination for a single extraordinary animal and believed in Centaurs. The Indians in Mexico made a similar error in judgment concerning the Conquistadores and their horses, assuming that the saddle and all the other elaborate Spanish trappings were a part of the animal, and that the men in armour were actually metal men.

Would it not be wise, on our part, for us to watch our own judgments rather carefully when we try to determine from available data the nature and modes of action of the UFO? We are dealing here with something from well beyond the range of our own immediate experience. We are trying to think creatively and to analyse far out into the framework of the unfamiliar. If we are to understand it at all, we must be able to stretch our minds to include certain logical, but not so easily imagined, perhaps, possibilities.

Not the least of these is the suggestion that etheric minerals may be more fundamentally alive than our familiar chemicals, that vehicles produced from them actually may be self-propelling, that they furnish their own energy and motive power, and that, like our own domesticated horses, they can be controlled and directed by the mind of man.

However, lest we be caught in restrictive error as were the ancient Greeks and the Mexican Indians, we ought to be prepared to add in the significant datum from beyond our own personal experience, which will provide the true and valid answer to our question: How are the flying saucers propelled? This significant datum may have little to do, directly, with the saucers themselves, but may have its roots in the very foundations of the world from which they come. If we fail to consider this possibility we may continue to interpret as merely mechanical what may well be sentient living creatures, perhaps not capable of what we would recognise as thought, but easily responsive to telepathic impulse from the mind of the being in control.

# Gravity
# and the UFO . . .

*Can we understand the propulsion of space vehicles
within the framework of physics as we know it today?
Yes, says Raymond Bernard in another selection
from* The Hollow Earth.

. . . There is a perfectly good way of explaining the saucers
within modern physical theory. To do so, however, we must pass to
the abstract heights of physics, in particular to Albert Einstein's
General Theory of Relativity. Now, before you are too frightened,
let it be said that the General Theory is not as complex and intricate as some persons think. Its reputation for difficulty arises from
the fact that, to grasp it, a transvaluation in the way we feel about
the world is necessary.

Newton's concept of inertia tells us that an object stays in its
place unless some force is applied to it and when the force is applied the object moves with the force. Newton had rather mixed
ideas of why inertia exists. At one point in his *Principia* it is almost inherent in matter. At another point inertial or centrifugal
forces arise from something called absolute space. The persistence
of matter in its state, according to Newton, comes from its relation
to an absolute world of space more final than any material system
we can think of.

This notion of Newton's was never satisfactory and in the last
part of the 19th Century the Austrian physicist and philosopher
Ernst Mach turned his critical mind to it. Mach, whom we all know
for his Mach numbers of aerodynamics, was also a forerunner of
the Vienna Circle which developed logical positivism. To him any-

thing beyond observation — such as absolute space — was unreal. Hence he proposed that inertia was a reference to *all the matter in the universe*. By all the matter in the universe he meant all the fixed stars, or in our day, when we realize that the cosmos is made up of vast numbers of stars collected in vast numbers of galaxies, to all the galaxies. For Mach an object subject to the laws of inertia was relative to all the stars, or as we would say today, all the nebulae.

Yet Mach's principle, as Einstein called it, had a difficulty. It did not supply any physical link between the stars and an inertial system. Mach just substituted the universe for Newton's absolute space as a system of coordinates in which objects existed and moved. He did not take us any further down the road to showing what inertia is, or why it works the way it does.

Perhaps we should say, rather, that he took us a little way and he took Albert Einstein a very long way.

In 1916 Einstein proposed his General Theory of Relativity. In effect it was a theory of universal gravitation *and inertia*. Einstein reduced the two forces *to the same thing* and expressed this in his famous Principle of Equivalence: gravitational and inertial forces are indistinguishable and equal. His illustration of this is a man in an elevator deep in space. The man is away from any large objects. If the elevator is moving uniformly at any constant speed, from a very small one to a very large one, the man will seem quite weightless. He will sense no motion nor any gravity. However, if the elevator speeds up, if it is pulled by its cosmic cable along the direction of the man's height at an increasing speed, the man will begin to feel as if gravity is acting upon him. When a certain acceleration is reached, equivalent in earth's measurements to 32 feet per second, the man will imagine that he is back on the earth and is being pulled down by the earth's gravity just the way he was before he left earth. Actually, of course, he is not. His false impression is merely the result of inertia and the acceleration of his elevator. There is no gravitation or, more correctly we should say, there is no large object in his vicinity.

Thus Einstein illustrated the fact that inertia and gravity have exactly the same effects on the observer and cannot be distinguished on the basis of local observations.

He went further. He sought to explain gravity and inertia in the same physical terms. While the weight of objects on a large celestial body like the earth is caused by the latter's gravitational attraction, the inertial behavior of objects is explained by the gravitational attraction of all matter everywhere. To use a simple analogy, the pipe resting on the table in front of me remains where it is largely because all the stars and nebulae of the cosmos are pulling on it, and they are pulling on it in all conceivable directions. It is as if a million million million little wires were attached to the pipe symmetrically all around it and are pulling it equally at the same time in every direction. Similarly, as I throw my pencil across the room it goes in a straight line (aside from earth's gravity) because it is being pulled at every right angle to the direction of its flight by the totality of matter in the universe, by all the stars or nebulae. Thus inertia in the familiar world is really gravitation but not the gravitation of the earth or of any single big body near us, but the gravitation of every particle in the universe; it is the sum effect of gigantic push, pull, or field depending on how you regard the still elusive gravitational mechanism.

But how, you ask, does this help us explain how flying saucers fly?

If the owners of the saucers have been able to devise a revolutionary means of anti-gravity, say an electro-magnetic screen which they put around their craft, this will mean that as the earth's gravity is overcome the gravity-inertia of all the rest of the universe will be overcome also. If the gravatons or ultra particles or fields which account for the gravitation of the earth are screened out the gravitational effect of the rest of the universe will be screened out also. Thus the saucers, with their anti-gravity screen, will be able to fly above the earth and they will be able to ignore the laws of inertia. They will be literally floating in a little cup or envelope where neither gravity nor inertia play any role. If the creatures who have built and man the saucers have mastered gravity they must, according to Einstein, have overcome inertia, also.

The key to the rather strange thing I have just said is to think how an atom or a molecule, or a group of them which make up an object will behave if no inertial influence can reach them. The pipe on my desk, now at the slightest touch of my finger, may fly across the room. Similarly, if I now throw my pencil across the room the slightest breeze will send it off at a right angle toward the other side of the room. In other words, we may assume that the atoms and matter in an inertia-free area will become almost totally free in their environment. They can move in one direction as easily as in another. They have no tendency to remain in the rigid envised position which inertia would ordinarily hold; they can fly away freely in any direction in which a slight force impels them.

I think this explains how the saucers can accelerate from zero to thousands of miles an hour and decelerate at the same rate, how they can engage in the dramatic maneuvers reported. Once a force, of whatever kind, impels them in a direction different from their line of movement, there is no tendency for their atoms and molecules to continue moving in their former direction. Thus, there is no strain upon the structure of the ship and the molecular binding forces of its material are not torn apart. Again, its occupants, if they can live in such an inertialess world, are not crushed in the slightest or even disturbed by the gyrations of the superstructure around them. Presumably they could sit quietly reading a book without knowing that their craft actually was doing the most remarkable acrobatics.

The concept of a gravity-inertia screen may also explain why the saucers do not burn up as they speed through the atmosphere. Consider a molecule or atom of gas as bumping along against other atoms in the atmosphere, subject to the laws of inertia as everything else is, but not causing very much damage or disturbance because it has little mass; a saucer rushes by and the molecule finds itself within the gravity-inertia screen. Suddenly this little air molecule is entirely free! It no longer carries kinetic punch; it can bump into anything without causing the slightest friction. In other words, it enters the screen like a bullet and strikes the saucer like a feather.

However, as the saucer rushes on, this molecule of air pops out the back of the screen in a very agitated state. It is now again in the inertial world and starts bumping into other highly agitated molecules. Its tiny little punch is magnified as a result of the friction which was not possible and this causes a release of energy — the luminosity seen about the saucers, especially at night.

At this point perhaps we should review what we have said and what we have not said.

In a sense, we have explained how the saucers fly but we have not explained how the gravity-inertia screen is generated. Sometimes when flying saucers are observed during the day through polaroid glasses, and in some photographs of saucers, there seems to be a kind of halo or corona about them. Of course, this well may be a physical token of the screen. However, the way it is produced is still a mystery, at least to this writer.

It is almost certain that in some way the field involves electricity and magnetism — for the effects of both have been noticed in connection with saucers. It is also likely that nuclear energy is used in the generation process, because increase in radioactivity background levels also accompany UFO flights. But of the exact mechanisms which produce the screen we know nothing. Research in this area is highly classified. The earth power which first develops the technique will have an immense military advantage. It may render not only aircraft, but ballistic missiles obsolete.

Let us consider what man's mastery of gravity and inertia may mean for his life on earth and his progress in space — if other races allow him to make any. In the first place, down here on earth the control of both gravity and inertia may well transform much of our economic system. We can think immediately of gravity-free airplanes plus the advantages of being able to control the inertia which governs (and hampers) so much of our lives.

If inertia can be controlled a five-year-old child can bounce an elephant upon its knee; the work of the world may be done with tiny amounts of energy — depending, of course, on how much is needed to produce the gravity-inertia screen. We may be able to move mountains with only the quantity of electricity to light a house. The whole phenomena of friction may be within our range of manipulation; railroad trains may be able to rush down their tracks covered with an inertial screen driven by only fractional horse-power motors.

The idea of inertia-free flight opens up interesting possibilities for space travel. Given inertia-free flight space may no longer be a barrier to solar travel!

Some astronomers and physicists, pointing to the enormous amounts of energy required to accelerate even a tiny payload near enough to the speed of light to make the journey to the nearest star in any reasonable period of time, have held the view that the only communication mankind will ever have with intelligent life elsewhere in the galaxy is by radio.

The distances between stars are measured in light years and only a limited number of stars are within one-half the light year equivalent of four score and 10. Thus the necessity for approaching the optical velocity in inter-stellar travel becomes obvious. Yet, even to approach it under the old law of inertia is a difficult matter; some scientists believe it is impossible.

Dr. Frank Drake illustrates the problem by calculating that to deliver the Encyclopedia Brittanica to our nearest stellar neighbor would require such a huge rocket that its blast-off would incinerate the entire state of Florida.

Other scientists, of course, have believed that inter-stellar travel is possible, even under the limitations of an inertial world. The great German physicist, Professor Singer, once proposed an inter-stellar vehicle capable of sweeping up the hydrogen atoms in space in a gigantic net and converting them into fuel along the way.

But if we are able to develop a gravity-inertia screen we may be able to approach the optical velocity with very little energy actually required.

It also may mean that higher species, who long ago discovered the same technique, have voyaged back and forth between the stars quite regularly. This would in turn increase the likelihood that our solar system is visited by races from other stars.

# OTHER EXPLANATIONS

# UFOs as

# a Psychological

# Projection . . .

*Dr. Carl Jung, a distinguished psychiatrist, regards
the saucer or sphere as a vision of wholeness —
and believes that man may have invented the
phenomenon to compensate for the lack of security
in his own life and the lack of peace in the world.
This selection is from* Flying Saucers: A Modern
Myth of Things Seen in the Skies.

Since the things reported of Ufos not only sound incredible but
seem to fly in the face of all our basic assumptions about the physical world, it is very natural that one's first reaction should be the
negative one of outright rejection. Surely, we say, it's nothing but
illusions, fantasies, and lies. People who report such stuff — chiefly
airline pilots and ground staff — cannot be quite right in the head!
What is worse, most of these stories come from America, the land
of superlatives and of science fiction.

In order to meet this natural reaction, we shall begin by considering the Ufo reports simply as rumours, i.e., as psychic products,
and shall draw from this all the conclusions that are warranted by
an analytical method of procedure.

Regarded in this light, the Ufo reports may seem to the sceptical
mind to be rather like a story that is told all over the world, but
differs from an ordinary rumour in that it is expressed in the form
of visions,* or perhaps owed its existence to them in the first place

---

* I prefer the term "vision" to "hallucination," because the latter bears the
stamp of a pathological concept, whereas a vision is a phenomenon that is by
no means peculiar to pathological states.

and is now kept alive by them. I would call this comparatively rare variation a *visionary rumour*. . . .

If we close our eyes a little so as to overlook certain details, it is possible to side with the reasonable opinion of the majority . . . and regard the thousands of Ufo reports and the uproar they have created as a visionary rumour, to be treated accordingly. They would then boil down, objectively, to an admittedly impressive collection of mistaken observations and conclusions into which subjective psychic assumptions have been projected.

But if it is a case of psychological *projection,* there must be a *psychic cause* for it. One can hardly suppose than anything of such worldwide incidence as the Ufo legend is purely fortuitous and of no importance whatever. The many thousands of individual testimonies must have an equally extensive causal basis. When an assertion of this kind is corroborated practically everywhere, we are driven to assume that a corresponding motive must be present everywhere, too. Though visionary rumours may be caused or accomplished by all manner of outward circumstances, they are based essentially on an omnipresent emotional foundation, in this case a psychological situation common to all mankind. The basis for this kind of rumour is an *emotional tension* having its cause in a situation of collective distress or danger, or in a vital psychic need. This condition undoubtedly exists today, in so far as the whole world is suffering under the strain of Russian policies and their still unpredictable consequences. In the individual, too, such phenomena as abnormal convictions, visions, illusions, etc., only occur when he is suffering from a psychic dissociation, that is, when there is a split between the conscious attitude and the unconscious contents opposed to it. Precisely because the conscious mind does not know about them and is therefore confronted with a situation from which there seems to be no way out, these strange contents cannot be integrated directly but seek to express themselves indirectly, thus giving rise to unexpected and apparently inexplicable opinions, beliefs, illusions, visions, and so forth. Any unusual natural occurences such as meteors, comets, "rains of blood," a calf with two heads, and suchlike abortions are interpreted as menacing omens, or else signs are seen in the heavens. Things can be seen by many people independently of one another, or even simultaneously, which are not physically real. . . .

In addition, there are cases where the same collective cause produces identical or similar effects, i.e., the same visionary images and interpretations in the very people who are least prepared for such phenomena and least inclined to believe them.*

This fact gives the eyewitness accounts an air of particular credibility: it is usually emphasized that the witness is above suspicion because he was never distinguished for his lively imagination or credulousness but, on the contrary, for his cool judgement and critical reason. In just these cases the unconscious has to resort to particularly drastic measures in order to make its contents perceived. It does this most vividly by projection, by extrapolating its contents into an object, which then mirrors what had previously lain hidden in the unconscious. Projection can be observed at work everywhere, in mental illnesses, ideas of persecution and hallucinations, in so-called normal people who see the mote in their brother's eye without seeing the beam in their own, and finally, in extreme form, in political propaganda. . . .

Initial attempts to explain Ufos as Russian or American inventions soon came to grief on their apparently weightless behavior, which is unknown to earth-dwellers. Human fantasy, already toying with the idea of space-trips to the moon, therefore had no hesitation in assuming that intelligent beings of a higher order had learnt how to counteract gravitation and, by dint of using interstellar magnetic fields as sources of power, to travel through space with the speed of light. The recent atomic explosions on the earth, it was conjectured, had aroused the attention of these so very much more advanced dwellers on Mars or Venus, who were worried about possible chain reactions and the consequent destruction of our planet. Since such a possibility would constitute a catastrophic threat to our neighboring planets, their inhabitants felt compelled to observe how things were developing on earth, fully aware of the tremendous cataclysm our clumsy nuclear experiments might unleash. The fact the Ufos neither land on earth nor show the least inclination to get into communication with human beings is met by

---

* Aimé Michel remarks that Ufos are mostly seen by people who do not believe in them or who regard the whole problem with indifference.

the explanation that these visitors, despite their superior knowledge, are not at all certain of being well received on earth, for
which reason they carefully avoid all intelligent contact with hu-
mans. But because they, as befitted superior beings, conduct themselves quite inoffensively, they would do the earth no harm and are
satisfied with an objective inspection of airfields and atomic instal-
lations. Just why these higher beings, who show such a burning
interest in the fate of the earth, still have not found some way of
communicating with us after ten years — despite their knowledge
of languages — remains shrouded in darkness. Other explanations
have therefore been sought, for instance that a planet has got into
difficulties, perhaps through the drying up of its water supplies, or
loss of oxygen, or overpopulation, and is looking for a *pied-à-
terre*. . . .

As one can see from all this the observation and interpretation
of Ufos has already led to the formation of a regular legend. Quite
apart from the thousands of newspaper reports and articles there is
now a whole literature on the subject, some of it humbug, some of
it serious. The Ufos themselves, however, do not appear to have
been impressed; as the latest observations show, they continue their
way undeterred. Be that as it may, one thing is certain: they have
become a *living myth*. We have here a golden opportunity to see
how a legend is formed, and how in difficult and dark times for
humanity a miraculous tale grows up of an attempted intervention
by extra-terrestrial "heavenly" powers — and this at the very time
when human fantasy is seriously considering the possibility of
space travel and of visiting or even invading other planets. We on
our side want to fly to the moon or to Mars, on their side the inhabitants of other planets in our system, or even of the fixed stars,
want to fly to us. We at least are conscious of our space-conquering
aspirations, but that a corresponding extra-terrestrial tendency exists is a purely mythological conjecture, i.e., a projection. . . .

It could easily be conjectured that the earth is growing too small
for us, that humanity would like to escape from its prison, where we
are threatened not only by the hydrogen bomb but at a still deeper
level, by the prodigious increase in the population figures which
give cause for serious concern. . . .

Man's living space is, in fact, continually shrinking and for many races the optimum has long been exceeded. The danger of catastrophe grows in proportion as the expanding populations impinge on one another. Congestion creates fear, which looks for help from extra-terrestrial sources since it cannot be found on earth.

Hence there appear "signs in the heavens," superior beings in the kind of space ships devised by our technological fantasy. From a fear whose cause is far from being fully understood and is therefore not conscious there arise explanatory projections which purport to find the cause in all manner of secondary phenomena, however unsuitable. Some of these projections are so obvious that it seems almost superfluous to dig any deeper.

But if we want to understand a mass rumour which, it appears, is even accomplished by collective visions, we must not remain satisfied with all too rational and superficially obvious motives. The cause must strike at the roots of our existence if it is to explain such an extraordinary phenomenon as the Ufos. Although they were observed as rare curiosities in earlier centuries, they merely gave rise to the usual local rumours.

The universal mass rumour was reserved for our enlightened, rationalistic age. The widespread fantasy about the destruction of the world at the end of the first millenium was metaphysical in origin and needed no Ufos in order to appear rational. Heaven's intervention was quite consistent with the *Weltanschauung* of the age. But nowadays public opinion would hardly be inclined to resort to the hypothesis of a metaphysical act, otherwise innumerable parsons would already have been preaching about the warning signs in heaven. Our *Weltanschauung* does not expect anything of this sort. We would be much more inclined to think of the possibility of *psychic* disturbances and interventions, especially as our psychic equilibrium has become something of a problem since the last World War. In this respect there is increasing uncertainty. Even our historians can no longer make use of the conventional techniques in evaluating and explaining the developments that have overtaken Europe in the last few decades, but must admit that psychological and psychopathological factors are beginning to widen the horizons of histriography in an alarming way. . . . Psychologists who are conscious of their responsibilities should not be dissuaded from critically examining a mass phenomenon like the

Ufos, since the apparent impossibility of the reports suggests to common sense that the most likely explanation lies in a psychic disturbance.

We shall therefore turn our attention to the psychic aspect of the phenomenon. For this purpose we shall briefly review the central statements of the rumour: certain objects are seen in the earth's atmosphere, both by day and night, which are unlike any known meteorological phenomena. They are not meteors, not misidentified fixed stars, not "temperature inversions," not cloud formations, not migrating birds, not aerial balloons, not balls of fire, and certainly not the delirious products of intoxication or fever, nor the plain lies of eyewitnesses. What as a rule is seen is a body of *round* shape, disk-like or spherical, glowing or shining fierily in different colours, or, more seldom, a cigar-shaped or cylindrical figure of various sizes.* It is reported that occasionally they are invisible to the naked eye but leave a "blip" on the radar screen. The round bodies in particular are figures such as the unconscious produces in dreams, visions, etc. In the latter case they are to be regarded as *symbols* representing, in visual form, some thought that was not thought consciously, but is merely potentially present in the unconscious, in invisible form, and attains visibility only through the process of becoming conscious. The visible form, however, expresses the meaning of the unconscious content only approximately. In practice the meaning has to be completed by amplificatory interpretation. The unavoidable errors that result can be eliminated only through the principle of "waiting on events"; that is to say we obtain a consistent and readable text by comparing sequences of dreams dreamt by different individuals. The figures in a rumour can be subjected to the same principles of dream interpretation.

If we apply them to the round object — whether it be a disk or a sphere — we at once get an analogy with the symbol of totality

---

* The more rarely reported cigar-form may have the Zeppelin for a model. The obvious phallic comparison, i.e. the translation into sexual language, springs naturally to the lips of the people. Berliners, for instance, refer to the cigar-shaped Ufo as a "holy ghost," and the Swiss military have an even more outspoken name for observation balloons.

well-known to all students of depth psychology, namely the *mandala* (Sanskrit for circle). This is not by any means a new invention, for it can be found in all epochs and in all places, always with the same meaning, and reappears time and again, independently of tradition, in modern individuals as the "protective" or apotropaic circle, whether in the form of the prehistoric "sun wheel" or the magic circle, or the alchemical microcosm, or a modern *symbol of order,* which organizes and encloses the psychic totality. . . .

In the course of the centuries the mandala has developed into a definitely psychological totality symbol. . . .

If the round shining objects that appear in the sky be regarded as visions, we can hardly avoid interpreting them as archetypal images. They would then be involuntary, automatic projections based on instinct, and as little as any other psychic manifestations or symptoms can they be dismissed as meaningless and merely fortuitous. Anyone with the requisite historical and psychological knowledge knows that circular symbols have played an important role in every age; in our own sphere of culture, for instance, they were not only soul symbols but "God-images." There is an old saying that "God is a circle whose centre is everywhere and the circumference nowhere." God in his omniscience, omnipotence, and omnipresence is a totality symbol *par excellence,* something round, complete, and perfect. Epiphanies of this sort are, in the tradition, often associated with fire and light. On the antique level, therefore, the Ufos could easily be conceived as "gods." They are impressive manifestations of totality whose simple, round form portrays the archetype of the self, which as we know from experience plays the chief role in uniting apparently irreconcilable opposites and is therefore best suited to compensate the split-mindedness of our age. . . .

The present world situation is calculated as never before to arouse expectations of a redeeming, supernatural event. If these expectations have not dared to show themselves very clearly, this is simply because no one is deeply rooted enough in the tradition of earlier centuries to consider an intervention from heaven as a matter of course. We have indeed strayed far from the metaphysical certainties of the Middle Ages, but not so far that our historical

and psychological background is empty of all metaphysical hope.*
Consciously, however, rationalistic enlightenment predominates,
and this abhors all leanings towards the "occult." Desperate efforts
are made for a "repristination" of our Christian faith, but we cannot get back to that limited world view which in former times left
room for metaphysical intervention. Nor can we resuscitate a genuine Christian belief in an after-life or the equally Christian hope for
an imminent end of the world that would put a definite stop to the
regrettable error of Creation. Belief in this world and in the power
of man has, despite assurances to the contrary, become a practical
and, for the time being, irrefragable truth.

This attitude on the part of the overwhelming majority provides
the most favourable basis for a projection, that is, for a manifestation of the unconscious background. Undeterred by rationalistic
criticism, it thrusts itself to the forefront in the form of a symbolic
rumour, accompanied and reinforced by the appropriate visions,
and in so doing activates an archetype that has always expressed
order, deliverance, salvation, and wholeness. It is characteristic of
our time that, in contrast to its previous expressions, the archetype
should now take the form of an object, a technological construction, in order to avoid the odiousness of a mythological personifica-
tion. Anything that looks technological goes down without difficulty with modern man. The possibility of space travel makes the
unpopular idea of a metaphysical intervention much more accept-
able. The apparent weightlessness of the Ufos, is, of course, rather
hard to digest but then our own physicists have discovered so many
things that border on the miraculous: why should not more advanced star-dwellers have discovered a way to counteract gravitation and reach the speed of light, if not more?

Nuclear physics has begotten in the layman's head an uncertainty of judgement that far exceeds that of the physicists, and
makes things appear possible which but a short while ago would
have been declared nonsensical. Consequently the Ufos can easily

* It is a common and totally unjustified misunderstanding on the part of
scientifically trained people to say that I regard the psychic background as
something "metaphysical," while on the other hand the theologians accuse
me of "psychologizing" metaphysics. Both are wide of the mark: I am an
empiricist, who keeps within the boundaries set for him by the theory of
knowledge.

be regarded and believed in as a physicists' miracle. I still remember, with misgivings, the time when I was convinced that something heavier than air could not fly, only to be taught a painful lesson. Nevertheless, the apparently physical nature of the Ufos creates such insoluble puzzles for even the best brains, and on the other hand has built up such an impressive legend, that one feels tempted to take them as a 99 per cent psychic product and subject them accordingly to the usual psychological interpretation. Should it be that an unknown physical phenomenon is the outward cause of the myth, this would detract nothing from the myth, for many myths have meteorological and other natural phenomena as accompanying causes which by no means explain them. A myth is essentially a product of the unconscious archetype and is therefore a symbol which requires psychological interpretation. . . .

# Flying Saucers
# Do Not Exist . . .

*Donald H. Menzel, astronomer and astrophysicist, is
Director of the Harvard College Observatory. He is
co-author, with Lyle G. Boyd, of* The World of
Flying Saucers, *from which the following selection is
taken, and he suggests that even though not all UFO
reports are easily explained, they are all the result of
a misinterpretation of conventional objects.*

Some flying-saucer reports, at first glance, do not seem to belong
in any of the ordinary categories of sightings such as mistaken identification of air-borne objects or astronomical phenomena. Each of
these atypical UFOs forms a class of its own and, when explained,
proves to be the "special effect" of a unique situation. Many are
misidentified lights or reflections, but since each one derives from a
peculiar combination of circumstances that may not have occurred
before and is not likely to occur again, accounting for them often
requires a certain amount of luck as well as patient detective
work. . . .

## Michigan's Flying Bird Cage

A UFO sighting based on mistaken identification of strange
lights occurred in the early morning hours of March 22, 1959, near
Ann Arbor, Michigan. The night was clear, the moon was nearly
full, and visibility was unusually good. At about 1:30 A.M. a man
and his wife driving on a country road suddenly noticed a strange
object hovering in the sky south of the road. According to their
report to the Air Force, the UFO was an elongated oval with a
dome on top, something like a bird cage, and brilliantly illuminated

by two shafts of intense pale-yellow light that sprang from the bottom and converged over the top. Frightened at this apparition, the witnesses could provide only uncertain estimates of distance and size. The object seemed to be twenty to thirty feet in diameter, was at an altitude of about 200 feet when first seen, and was hovering about two miles away. As they drove on, the object seemed to move and travel parallel with the car for about a mile. Then the yellow lights dimmed and a circle of eight or ten red lights suddenly appeared on the underside, the UFO rose vertically, very rapidly, and vanished in a few seconds. It had been in view for a period of five to ten minutes.

Checking the most probable explanations first, ATIC officials found that the nearby Willow Run Airport had had no aircraft in the vicinity at the time and that no star or planet seemed to be involved. Further investigation showed that the flying bird cage was actually the radio telescope of the University of Michigan. The telescope was installed on the top of Peach Mountain and was clearly visible from the road on which the witnesses were traveling. . . .

## UFOs from Reflections

Reflections from the bright sun have produced many elusive UFOs. All pilots are familiar with the luminous objects that sometimes appear in the air below a plane on a sunny day, particularly when the plane is flying over wooded terrain that is partly obscured by atmospheric haze. The sun has been reflected momentarily from a broad shiny surface, such as the metal roof of a farm building; because of the contrast between the bright surface and the dark forest surrounding it, the image appears to be a UFO floating high in the air.

Sometimes the sun shines on a bright metallic surface, such as the chrome trim of an automobile, and by chance is reflected directly into the eyes of a passer-by. If he then glances at the sky he may see a whole fleet of UFOs; the bright flash has produced a temporary chemical change in the retina so that for a moment or two the eye sees a series of saucer-shaped images of the sun. A photographer's flashbulb or a bright flash of lightning can produce similar after-images.

Some startling UFOs have been produced by reflections from an object that the witness was not able to see or did not recognize. One night in the spring of 1961 an amateur astronomer reported that a huge cigar-shaped flying saucer was hovering in the sky several thousand feet above the Harvard College Observatory. Investigation showed that the "UFO" was a reflection from a small oblong insulator on an electric wire strung between two buildings. Faintly illuminated from below by the lights from the unshaded windows, it seemed to be an immense and brilliantly glowing object high in the sky. The witness at first refused to believe that he could so mistake the evidence of his own eyes. Next morning, however, he returned to the scene and was able to see that what had appeared the night before to be a giant spaceship was only a small insulator a few feet above his head.

The bright sun reflected at a particular time from an object invisible to the observer often produces a puzzling phenomenon, such as the flying saucer reported from Dandy, California, early in October 1958.

About 4:00 in the afternoon on October 2, three prospectors standing near a tungsten mill at Railroad Danby noticed a sudden bright glow in the northwest sky which remained visible for about 2½ hours and then disappeared. When a glow appeared again the following day at the same time and place, the observers tried to identify it by using a small telescope and saw a bright, oblong object hovering above the horizon; it was the color of aluminum, approximately fifteen feet long, five feet high, and about four miles away. Getting into a car, the men drove in the direction of the object and searched the supposed location on foot for several hours, but could find no trace of the UFO.

Several days later, realizing that the object reappeared every day at about the same time and place, two of the men decided to investigate further. Studying the object through a pair of powerful binoculars, they could see guy wires coming from it and rods radiating from the guy wires. Remembering that two tall radio antennas used by the highway patrol stood in approximately the same location, the witnesses found the explanation, which Air Force investigators confirmed. The antennas, placed some twenty feet apart, extended about twenty feet above the trees. The cigar-shaped hovering object was a special effect depending on a particular combination of circumstances: only during the first part of October, and only late in the afternoon, did the sun's rays strike the antenna in such a way that the reflection was visible to an observer at Railroad Danby.

## Sundogs in Utah and France

Sundogs are another special effect resulting from a peculiar combination of circumstances, and they continue to supply their quota of good UFO reports. Tiny ice crystals floating in a layer of quiet air and reflecting a bright sun are responsible for producing sundogs. A thin layer of such crystals may be invisible to the observer; a thick layer appears as the familiar cirrus clouds. Sunlight filtering through such an ice fog is reflected in each crystal so that a pattern of bright spots of light forms in the sky, an image of the sun that sometimes rivals the sun itself in brilliance. These images are called mock suns, sundogs, or parhelia when they accompany the sun (and mock moons, moondogs, or paraselenae when they accompany the moon). They appear in the sky at a position a given distance from the sun and usually have a trace of red on the edge nearest the sun.

Occasionally a sundog makes a complete circle of light surrounding the sun with four bright patches, one above, one below, and one on either side. Sometimes two circles will appear, one within the other, surmounted by an inverted arc and traversed by a cross, like the spokes of a wheel whose center is the sun. The complicated structure of a fully developed mock sun — which is extremely rare — can suggest to the imaginative an enormous chariot in the sky and can terrify the superstitious. There is little doubt that this phenomenon inspired the two visions of Ezekiel described in the Bible.

Mock suns have been the cause of many UFO sightings. Even after several publications explained how the sun reflected from ice crystals could account for some of the reported flying saucers, this idea was largely ignored by early investigators who had a limited training in the physical sciences.

Sundogs are relatively uncommon. Few airmen, even those with long experience, have learned to recognize them. In a poll of both commercial and military pilots, Dr. Menzel found that only one in five knew what a sundog was and how it might look in the sky. Two or three generals in the Air Force, similarly, were unfamiliar with the phenomenon. Like balloons, sundogs have a silvery metallic sheen. When observed from the ground, they seem to hover or move very sluggishly; to a witness in the air they seem to move rapidly, to pace the plane, or to take evasive action as though under intelligent control. When enough data are available, and the time of day and the position of the unknown relative to the sun are appropriate, a mock sun should be considered as a possible explanation of the UFO.

A sundog seen from a plane can suggest a spectacular and fantastic structure, like the one reported over Rheims, France, at 2:30 P.M. local time on March 31, 1960. The pilot and crew of a C-47 plane described the unknown as like a gigantic spool of thread some twelve feet tall. The neck of the spool, about six feet in diameter, seemed to be capped at top and bottom by disks eight or ten feet in diameter. The upper disk was reddish, the lower, blue-green. The plane was flying at 6000 feet and had just passed from a storm area into a region of calm with unlimited visibility. The UFO remained in view for about sixty seconds, then suddenly vanished. From an analysis of the data, the position of the unknown relative to the sun and the observers, and the weather situation, Air Force investigators positively identified the object as a mock sun.

One of the most recent sightings of this type occurred on October 2, 1961, a few minutes after noon. A civilian pilot who was just taking off from the Utah Central Airport at Salt Lake City noticed a bright silvery disk in the air ahead of his plane. He supposed it to be another aircraft crossing his course. When he was air-borne, he was surprised to find that the object, now an elongated pencil shape, still appeared in the same position where he had first seen it and hence could not be a plane. Puzzled, he radioed the control tower and reported the UFO. Looking south as directed by the pilot, the tower operator easily found the object, a bright spot in the sky directly below the sun and apparently hovering over the town of Provo, forty miles to the south.

Deciding to investigate, the pilot left the traffic pattern and

started directly south after the UFO. It seemed to be standing practically still in the sky, with a little rocking motion, at an altitude of
6500 to 7000 feet. He seemed to have approached within three to
five miles when the UFO suddenly shot up "like an elevator" and
retreated rapidly south, as though taking evasive action. The acceleration was tremendous, almost as though the UFO had been fired
from a rocket, but there was no vapor trail and no sound. It then
disappeared, gradually. "It just faded out. I kept my eyes glued
right on it because I could see it was moving away at a great speed.
I wanted to see how long it would take and it was just a second or
two until it had faded completely. And it was getting smaller all the
time, you could see it was moving away." The speed of departure,
the pilot estimated, must have been thousands of miles an hour.

Alerted by the pilot's message to the control tower, several persons on the ground at the Salt Lake City airport, most of them with
experience as pilots, had also been watching the UFO. Ground observers at the Provo airport, also alerted, were not able to locate
the unknown, even though they had been told it was almost directly
overhead.

Investigators from a nearby Air Force Base interviewed the witnesses, who were obviously competent and reliable. All agreed that
the unknown had been a bright, silvery, metallic-looking object
that seemed to glisten or flicker in the sun; that it was roughly oval
or indeterminate in shape; that it was solid and tangible, but not a
conventional aircraft or balloon; that it made no sound, showed no
exhaust or vapor trail; that it was in view roughly fifteen minutes,
and disappeared gradually by "blotting out" or fading. All but one
of the witnesses agreed that the skies had been absolutely clear and
cloudless; one stated that, although the day was clear, a very slight
haze existed over the mountainous region where the UFO appeared.

In spite of this general agreement, certain significant discrepan-
cies became evident. The pursuing pilot stated that the object had
moved up and away from him at incredible speed, as though it were
controlled. The ground observers, however, did not see any movement by the UFO. Most of them reported that it remained stationary as though it were suspended in the air; a few said that it van-

ished at intervals, only to reappear a few seconds later in another place. Most of the time, they agreed, it just hung in the sky until it faded from view.

By analysis of these clues, ATIC was able to solve the mystery. According to the local weather bureau, the sky had been clear with visibility unlimited, but there had been very thin cirrus clouds, a layer of minute ice crystals suitable for producing a mock sun. A sundog would also account for the contradictory statements about the UFO's motion. Since the ground observers remained in one place, their position relative to the sundog did not change and it seemed to remain stationary. The pilot, however, was in a moving plane and changing his position relative to the UFO; hence it seemed to move rapidly away from him. In the same way a rainbow seems stationary to a person who merely stands and watches it. But if he begins to chase it, hoping to catch up and perhaps find the legendary pot of gold, the rainbow seems to move away and elude its pursuer. The pilot's belief that the UFO had exhibited fantastic speed was, according to his own statement, an inference based on the fact that the UFO quickly dwindled, became very small, and vanished. It disappeared, however, not because it was speeding away at thousands of miles an hour, but because of a change in the relative positions of sun and ice clouds that produced the sundog in the first place. One final point nailed down this explanation. The angular distance between sun and UFO was exactly that to be expected between sun and mock sun, at that time and place. . . .

## Unfamiliar Lights on Planes

In the spring of 1961, a leading saucer publication stated that unidentified objects were still surveying the earth and cited, among other cases, a bright UFO seen maneuvering the night of March 23 near Fort Pierce, Florida. The report failed to mention that unidentified lights were seen on several other nights during that week in the skies over Jacksonville, Miami, and Cocoa-Titusville, as well as over Fort Pierce. Newspaper offices and radio stations in the area received many telephone queries about the mysterious lights, which were observed from the ground and from the air for periods of time ranging from five minutes to an hour. The descriptions showed an impressive consistency: the UFO was a round, twinkling light with a red or orange color changing to white, and exhibited a bobbing up-and-down motion as it swept across the horizon. In all sightings the weather was clear and the visibility excellent.

On the night of March 24 an Eastern Airlines pilot reported the UFO to the Miami Traffic Control. An observer in the control tower at the airport could see the object, but lost sight of it when he took up a plane to chase it. On the following night the Cocoa-Titusville Airport reported a similar object. A pilot in the air sighted the unknown and, about an hour later, encountered a turbulence unlike anything he had experienced in sixteen years of flying. Cruising in the region the next day, he observed a burned-out area on the ground below the place where the UFO had been. On the night of March 27, a ground observer watched the unknown through binoculars as it moved rapidly from west to north and gradually disappeared in the northwest.

Most of these witnesses were veteran airmen, well able to recognize conventional phenomena in the night sky. Studying their reports, officials at Patrick Air Force Base decided that the similiarity of the descriptions warranted further investigation. In the preliminary study, an Intelligence officer took up a B-57 aircraft in the vicinity of Fort Pierce, while ground radar at Patrick Air Force Base kept his plane under constant surveillance. At 7:20 P.M., when at 25,000 feet, he saw the UFO, a white light three times brighter than the brightest star. It appeared in the western sky and was moving north to south. When viewed with the naked eye, the light looked like a star that dimmed and brightened in a regular cycle; through binoculars it also displayed the red and green navigation lights of a plane. Soon after the visual sighting, the ground radar informed the investigating pilot that the object was approximately fifty nautical miles from his plane and was a jet airliner bound for Miami; the jet was observed for approximately ten minutes as it descended toward the Miami airport. The investigating plane remained in the air and, about five minutes after the jet had landed, observed a second, similar, high-intensity light that appeared in the western sky, moving from north to south. The radar at the Miami air-traffic control center positively identified this light as a Delta Airline jet, Flight 833, proceeding southeast. From these facts the officers concluded that the UFOs seen in Florida that week had been produced by commercial jet airliners.

Two questions remained: How had the experienced pilots and ground observers failed to recognize so familiar a phenomenon as a night-flying jet? What accounted for the unprecedented turbulence experienced by one pilot, and the burned-over ground below the region of the sighting?

The first question was soon answered. ATIC investigators telephoned the Federal Aviation Agency and learned that experiments with a new type of anti-collision beacon were being carried out from various field offices, and that several jet airliners as well as some turboprop aircraft were using the new light. The standard beacon was a rotating sodium light, whose color is yellow. The new beacon was an intense white light which, viewed at a slant, becomes a spectacular phenomenon even more brilliant than Venus or Jupiter seen rising or setting through a hazy atmosphere. Since the witnesses were not familiar with the appearance of the experimental beacons, they had not recognized the newly equipped jets.

The answer to the second question came later, an example of the "luck" required to solve some of these UFO puzzles. Major W. T. Coleman, then Air Force Information Officer for the UFO project, was flying over the Fort Pierce region on the afternoon of April 29 in calm, clear weather when his plane ran into moderate turbulence of the short-wave type, "like riding in a car over a washboard road." The wind-shear component was not large enough to explain the turbulence, and though a cold front was approaching from the Gulf of Mexico, it was still far out on the edge of the western horizon. Then, being a native of Florida, he suddenly remembered that muck fires were fairly common in the Everglades region, which lay below the plane. Peering down at the glades, he noticed a very large muck fire. He concluded:

"Now, as typical with a cold front situation, the surface wind was blowing from the east pushing the smoke and heat toward the west coast of Florida. This relatively warm air naturally was lifting in the surrounding cool air. When the continuing warm air rose rapidly to the higher altitudes it ran into the reversed upper winds (high altitude westerly). In the process of being lifted the smoke filtered and cleared, yet the air remained relatively heated. It was moved directly across our course, thereby causing turbulence."

The fires explained both the turbulence reported during the week of the UFO sightings and the burned-out area below the region of turbulence. Thus these Florida UFOs were not spacecraft watching the earth, but were a special effect created by the chance combination of unrelated factors: a new and unfamiliar anti-collision beacon, an advancing cold front, and fires in the Florida swamps.

## Inversions in California

An unusually complex combination of events produced an epidemic of UFO sightings in northern California during the week of August 12 to 20, 1960. Nearly every night dozens of reliable citizens throughout Tehama County and the Mount Shasta region (long famous for its mysterious lights) reported UFOs at various times and of various descriptions: round, bright, metallic UFOs glowing with a reddish-purple fluorescent type of light, cigar-shaped UFOs trailing a long fiery exhaust, oval UFOs with red lights at each end and white lights in between, yellow-colored UFOs like a flying railroad car with flashing red lights at each end and white lights glowing at the windows. Radios roared with static and radar sets were plagued with phantoms, as the state was apparently invaded by a whole fleet of patrolling saucers.

The most important factor in these sightings was the weather; prolonged and extensive temperature inversions prevailed in the area all that week. From southern Oregon through northern California multiple inversions of 3 to 18 degrees occurred nightly. Under these conditions, practically any light shining into the night was apt to be projected upward as a mirage and to perform weird antics. Determining what was the particular light source of some specific phenomenon is almost impossible.

As complicating factors, certain heavenly bodies made their own contribution to the excitement. Most of the objects observed late at night and watched for periods of one to three hours were refracted images of the stars Capella or Aldebaran or the planet Mars.

Some of the most spectacular sightings were those reported from Red Bluff on the night of August 13-14. Two highway patrolmen were chasing a speeding motorcycle when, at about 11:50 P.M. P.D.S.T., they saw what they at first supposed to be a brilliantly lighted aircraft falling directly toward them. Jumping out of their car, they watched the object as it apparently reversed its course, shot upward, and began to perform fantastic maneuvers in the eastern sky. The performance continued for more than two hours. Before it ended, a second UFO had joined in the celestial dance, which was observed by dozens of excited witnesses in the Red Bluff area.

Air Force bases in the neighborhood were notified, and ATIC investigators gathered and studied the evidence. There was no real mystery. The UFO first noticed by the patrolmen was probably the star Capella, which at Red Bluff is circumpolar; it rose at 10:50 P.M. and at the time of the sighting was about 4.7 degrees above the northeast horizon. About an hour later (12:48 A.M.) Mars rose, also in the northeast; and close behind it (1:15 A.M.) came the bright star Aldebaran, which made a striking pair with Mars. With three brilliant heavenly bodies just above the horizon, on a night of fantastic multiple inversions of temperature and humidity, the only surprising fact is that the number of UFOs reported was not larger.

A person who has never been lucky enough to see a good mirage may feel skeptical about the phenomenon. But those who have encountered a first-rate specimen — for example, the Chicago skyline suspended upside down in mid-air above Lake Michigan — know how startlingly real it can seem. When the source of the mirage is not apparent, the displaced image can seem mysterious and even frightening, as do many UFOs.

One such phenomenon, which might easily have been interpreted as a flying saucer, appeared shortly after dark one evening in mid-July, 1954, and was described by Dr. Menzel in a letter to a friend:

"My wife and I were driving to Alamosa, Colorado, on one of the longest, straightest stretches of highway in the United States, commonly referred to as the 'gun-barrel highway.' I had turned over the wheel to her and was settling back for a rest, after a long turn at driving over the mountains, when I became aware of unusual driving behavior on her part. First she would step on the gas, then on the brake, then on the gas again. 'What is the matter? What are you trying to do?' I asked. 'See that truck ahead?' she replied. 'Every time I try to pass it, it speeds up, and then it slows down when I try to give it a chance to get ahead of me. It's making me nervous.'

"I peered ahead through the darkness and there, sure enough, about three hundred feet ahead of us was a truck, its dark body brilliantly outlined with red and white lights. I studied the situation and glanced at the speedometer, which read forty miles per hour. 'Well,' I advised her, 'you certainly ought to be able to pass that, dear, the way you usually drive.' And this time she really stepped on the gas, pushing the speed up to sixty, seventy, eighty, and finally eighty-five. And would you believe it, that truck took right out ahead, still holding its estimated three hundred feet clearance, and matched us for every mile of that speed. By this time I was beginning to get an idea. 'Slow down,' I said. My wife obliged me by coming to a dead stop, brakes squealing.

" 'Now see there,' she said, 'I just escaped running into that truck.' And the truck had stopped, still 300 feet ahead. At this point I ventured my conclusion. 'That isn't a truck,' I explained. 'It's a flying saucer.' 'You have flying saucers on the brain,' she said. Well, to shorten the story, she started the car again and the 'truck' moved off. And we chased it in that fashion for about fifty miles. On rare occasions, as we dipped slightly in a hollow, the truck would seem to dash ahead at speeds close to 1000 miles an hour. Or sometimes it would jump straight up, momentarily vanish, and then drop back into the road.

"The explanation was quite simple. The hot day had warmed the air close to the pavement, but the cooling of the surface at the onset of darkness had caused a layer of warm air to be sandwiched in between the cold air close to the road surface and the cold air above. This acted like a lens which produced an out-of-focus image of a bright tavern sign more than fifty miles away, a real mirage. There were few cars on the road, but as we met them the effect was most startling because some of them were so enlarged by the lens effect that a car five miles away seemed to be rushing directly at us only a block or two ahead. Sometimes these cars would appear to come to a sharp stop, reverse their course and disappear in the distance. At other times they would appear to be rushing on us upside down, with part of the road itself in the sky. Altogether it was a weird experience, but not in any sense supernatural. Lenses of air, either close to the ground or in the sky, can produce strange illusions."

In this case, as in many UFO puzzles, the solution depended on a knowledge of the weather conditions and of the facts of local geography. If the pursuing car had turned off the road or stopped for the night before reaching the tavern, the specific cause of the phenomenon might still be a mystery. . . .

# Can We Visit Other Solar Systems? . . .

*Walter Sullivan, Science Editor of* THE NEW YORK TIMES, *turns in this selection from* We Are Not Alone *to the problems involved in sending astronauts from the earth to other galaxies.*

. . . Actually the problem of propelling large numbers of people to another solar system was discussed as early as 1951 by Lyman Spitzer, head of the Princeton University Observatory. He spoke of a vehicle weighing 10,000 tons, powered by a uranium pile of perhaps 1,000 tons, generating 2 million horsepower of useful energy:

> Such a ship [he wrote] could carry thousands of people and vast supplies anywhere in the solar system, and could even navigate to other stars, though many generations would be born, grow up and die on shipboard before such a journey were complete. However, launching such a ship from the Earth's surface to a close circular orbit would be a tremendous undertaking. With the use of chemical fuels, such a launching would require a rocket of some million tons gross weight, an achievement that would seem far, far in the future.

Among those who rebelled against the sober reasoning of Pierce, Purcell, and von Hoerner was Freeman J. Dyson at the Institute for Advanced Study in Princeton. It was Dyson who had suggested that a supercivilization might redistribute the material of its solar system to achieve maximum living space and maximum energy from its star. In a letter to the *Scientific American* in 1964 he said the calculations of Purcell and the others were perfectly valid, in so far as they related to fuel requirements for journeys limited to human lifetimes. But what about slower trips? Engines using nuclear power could reasonably be expected to drive large space ships at a speed of a few light years per century, he said. If an intelligent race achieved a life span considerably greater than our own; or if it perfected a method of freezing its citizens, harmlessly, for prolonged hibernation, then journeys reckoned in thousands of years would be conceivable. Thus, he wrote, "interstellar travel is essentially not a problem in physics or engineering but a problem in biology."

There is no reason to suppose, he asserted, that others in the galaxy have not solved this problem and that we may not ultimately do so. No doubt many would find thousand-year trips "unappealing," he said, but added: "We have no right to impose our tastes on others."

In another paper Dyson made a startling proposal as to how interstellar vehicles might pick up momentum en route. His scheme was to steal a little bit of the energy with which two very dense stars circle each other. If, he said, a vehicle approached one such star as the star was coming toward it, the gravity of the star would whip the vehicle around in a tight orbit, sending it off into space again with far more energy than it had to begin with. It would be almost as though the vehicle had been hit by a gigantic baseball bat. The star, having transferred to the vehicle some of the energy with which it was circling its twin, would move a tiny bit closer to the star with which it was waltzing through space.

The most remarkable feature of this procedure was that, even though the vehicle underwent an explosive rate of acceleration — some 10,000 g's — no harm would come to the most delicate passenger or the most sensitive piece of equipment on board. This is because the accelerating force would be applied with almost complete uniformity to every particle of the body or instrument on board. It would not be any more uncomfortable than falling through space.

Thus, said Dyson, a vehicle could very rapidly be speeded up by more than 1,000 miles a second. The best star systems for giving vehicles such enormous accelerations, he said, would be pairs of white dwarfs, tiny "senile" stars whose density is so great that they may weigh as much as 3,000 tons per cubic inch. "It may be imagined," he wrote, "that a highly developed technological species might use white-dwarf binaries scattered around the galaxy as relay stations for heavy long-distance freight transportation."

One of the most ardent — and controversial — champions of the feasibility of interstellar travel is Carl Sagan. His main argument was formulated while he was at the University of California in Berkeley and was presented to the American Rocket Society on November 15, 1962. He sought to show, not only that such travel is possible, but that, if so, "other civilizations, aeons more advanced than ours, must today be plying the spaces between the stars."

He argued that radio waves are but a poor way to achieve a meeting of the minds between beings with utterly different histories and ways of thought. Furthermore, the radio does not permit contact between an advanced society and one that is intelligent but not yet in possession of radio technology. Nor does it allow the exchange of artifacts and biological specimens.

"Interstellar space flight sweeps away these difficulties," Sagan wrote with typical enthusiasm. "It reopens the arena of action for civilizations where local exploration has been completed; it provides access beyond the planetary frontiers, where the opportunities are limitless." . . .

Sagan likened the "spacefaring" societies to those of the European Renaissance that sent voyagers eagerly in search of new worlds on our own planet. He suggested that such societies might send out expeditions about once a year and, hence, the starships would return at about the same rate, some with negative reports on solar systems visited, some with fresh news from some well-known civilization. "The wealth, diversity, and brilliance of this commerce," he said with an exuberance reminiscent of Tsiolkovsky, "the exchange of goods and information, of arguments and artifacts, of concepts and conflicts, must continuously sharpen the curiosity and enhance the vitality of the participating societies."

On the assumption that there are about a million worlds in the galaxy capable of such feats, Sagan proposed that they would visit one another about once in every thousand years and that scouts may have visited the earth from time to time in the past — perhaps a total of 10,000 times over the full span of the earth's history. One or two million years ago such visitors would have observed the emergence of primates ancestral to man and may have decided to step up the frequency of their visits to once every thousand years, Sagan said.

Is it possible, he asked, that they have visited us since the dawn of civilization? Without making direct reference to the "flying saucer" episodes of recent years, he dismissed such tales by noting that in the past few centuries, "when critical scholarship and nonsuperstitious reasoning have been fairly widespread," there have been no reliable reports of a visitation. However, he urged that myths and legends be re-examined for indications that such may have occurred in the distant past. . . .

Sagan . . . said the legends of primitive peoples have described, in recognizable form, encounters with a superior civilization. This, he felt, was an incentive for searching the records for evidence of a more exotic visit. He also considered it "not out of the question" that relics of such visits may be found and suggested that a hidden base may be discovered, perhaps on the far side of the moon, placed there to provide continuity for succeeding expeditions. A remote location would be used, he said, lest the base be destroyed by weathering during the many centuries between visits and to avoid meddling by inhabitants of our planet. When high resolution photographs are made of the moon, as a prelude to landing men there, he said, the possibility of such a base should be kept in mind.

Frank Drake proposed, instead, that such early visitors might have left artifacts for us to find — perhaps as a first step in establishing contact. To preserve such clues from the workings of time and from tampering by primitive inhabitants, they might have been buried in limestone caves, Drake said. Such caves would clearly attract the attention of archaeologists. The artifacts might be tagged with radioactive isotopes whose artificial origin would be evident to any sophisticated investigator. The cache, Drake said, "would then remain invisible until radiation detectors were developed."

Drake has calculated that to transmit one pulse — that is, one "bit" of information — 1,000 light years by radio, would cost only five cents. Hence, few of those who have explored the problem of interstellar communication accept Sagan's argument in favor of travel. In particular, they consider it a grossly uneconomical method of searching for intelligent life, even though it may be the only way to discover societies before they acquire an advanced technology. If beings in other worlds have learned to live long or to hibernate, they may be able to travel between neighboring solar systems by coasting for a few centuries, instead of constantly accelerating or decelerating, although in so doing they would forfeit the time-slowing effect. But one wonders, despite Sagan's eloquent arguments, if such trips, with all of their cost and discomfort, are necessary.

Biological specimens from another world would be of great interest, but it seems at least possible that they could be replicated by means of radio signals. The human egg cell, the size of a grain of dust, contains a mass of long-chain molecules on which are coded the information needed to construct a human being. The information is voluminous — there are probably billions of "bits" coded into the egg — and to send it all by radio, particularly at the slow rate that may be necessary for interstellar distances, would be tedious. But by the time we can build interstellar ramjets our communications ability will certainly be much improved. We should be able to tell "them" how to build a car, a cow, a rose, and a man. Nor, if radio were used, would anyone have to worry over the possibility that an arriving space ship might be carrying germs dangerous to the world being visited. Perhaps, in fact, there are galaxy-wide immigration laws forbidding travel in person.

Although even some of the more open-minded scientists shrug off Sagan's arguments, citing the problems and limitations, the question arises: Are we arrogant to believe that we understand these limitations? Are there pertinent phenomena or peculiarities of nature unknown to us, like Philip Morrison's hypothetical "Q waves"? The reasoning of men like Purcell is based on physical laws that seem immutable. We can have no reason to suspect there is anything wrong with them. Yet it is well to call to mind the foresight of Benjamin Franklin, when he wrote to Joseph Priestley, the discoverer of oxygen, in 1780:

It is impossible to imagine the height to which may be carried, in a thousand years, the power of man over matter. We may perhaps learn to deprive large masses of their gravity, and give them absolute levity, for the sake of easy transport. Agriculture may diminish its labor and double its produce; all disease may by sure means be prevented or cured, not excepting even that of old age, and our lives lengthened at pleasure even beyond the antediluvian standard. O that moral science were in as fair a way of improvement, that men would cease to be wolves to one another, and that human beings would at length learn what they now improperly call humanity!

# "Ball
# Lightning" . . .

*The strongest argument for an earthly explanation of
certain types of UFOs was presented by electronics
editor Philip Klass in* Aviation Week *and* Space
Technology. *The following article from* The New
York Times *of August 23, 1966, by Evert Clark
describes Mr. Klass's theory.*

Many "flying saucers" may be balls of ionized air originating
along high-tension electric power lines, an authoritative aeronautical
journal suggested today.

The magazine *Aviation Week & Space Technology* noted that
many night-time sightings of Unidentified Flying Objects
(U.F.O.s.) had been along or near power lines. It also noted many
similarities between ball lightning and the reported behavior of the
U.F.O.s.

If the "corona discharge" of luminous, ionized air containing
electrified particles that forms along power lines detaches itself and
dances, hovers and spins as ball lightning does, this might explain
the erratic movement often attributed to saucers at night, Philip J.
Klass, a senior editor and electronics specialist for the magazine
wrote.

Ball lightning was once discounted as an old wives' tale. In the
late 1940's, however, scientists became interested in the possibility
that it could be created by man — perhaps with powerful radar
antennas — and used to destroy intercontinental missiles. Some
military-sponsored research followed, but apparently the approach
was all but abandoned.

The Soviet Union showed a similar interest in man-made ball

lightning around the same time and the investigation attracted the attention of such top scientists as Academician Peter Kapista, Mr. Klass wrote.

One Russian author, P. N. Chirvinskii, indicated that one experimenter had been killed by artificially created lightning. This author also noted that ball lightning was observed as long ago as the time of the Roman poet Lucretius in 60 B.C.

Still another scientific author suggested in 1954 that ball lightning and saucers might be related, Mr. Klass said in an interview. Both authors were cited in the bibliography of a paper written by Carsten M. Haaland of the Atomic Energy Commission's Oak Ridge National Laboratory.

The paper never was published but was sent to Mr. Klass after he talked to Mr. Haaland about the power line theory.

Until Mr. Klass's article, no one had suggested that corona discharge, ball lightning and the dancing red, green and bluish-white objects might all be the same thing.

Mr. Klass said his curiosity had been aroused by John G. Fuller's recent book, "Incident at Exeter," which is primarily a survey of sightings of flying objects at Exeter, N. H., last year.

Mr. Fuller, a columnist for the *Saturday Review,* concluded that the objects were extraterrestrial.

Mr. Klass, noting that almost all the Exeter sightings had been at night and almost all occurred near power lines, discounts the Fuller explanation.

Corona discharge is more likely to occur when dust, salt deposits or even insects contaminate the power lines, Mr. Klass reported.

Exeter is 10 miles from the ocean and the power lines serving it run to the ocean. Officials of the Exeter and Hampton Electric Company told him that corona discharge occurs more frequently "when there is not much rain to clean off the lines."

Mr. Klass found that the Exeter area had received barely more than half its usual rainfall in the period of the sightings.

Investigating what is known about ball lightning, including recent work done by the Westinghouse Electric Corporation and research laboratories for the Office of Naval Research, Mr. Klass found that it compares in everything but size to many of the balls of light reported at Exeter and in other sightings at Pittsburgh and at Syracuse, N.Y.

Mr. Klass believes the apparent discrepancy in size might be explained by the illusory nature of a dancing, glowing ball of light, by fright, and by a lack of familiar objects with which to compare the "saucers."

Mr. Klass emphasized that he does not offer his theory as explanation for all such sightings — nor even for all night-time observations.

But he urged that the Air Force, which has been given responsibility for investigating reports on such objects, and independent scientists and engineers look further into the question.

Mr. Klass is an electrical engineer who worked for the General Electric Company for 12 years before joining the magazine 14 years ago.

Because both corona discharge and ball lightning are associated with electromagnetic fields, Mr. Klass believes his theory might explain why observers of flying objects have often reported trouble with automobile radios and ignition systems when a "saucer" was nearby.

# The Radiation
# Story . . .

*Is there a connection between UFOs and the amount
of radiation in the air? A group of scientists
accidentally discovered that this just might be the
case. This selection from Edward J. Ruppelt's*
Report of Unidentified Flying Objects *traces the
attempt by experts to correlate the two.*

. . . In the fall of 1949, at some unspecified place in the United
States, a group of scientists had set up equipment to measure background radiation, the small amount of harmless radiation that is
always present in our atmosphere. This natural radiation varies to
a certain degree, but will never increase by any appreciable amount
unless there is a good reason.

According to the rumor, two of the scientists at the unnamed
place were watching the equipment one day when, for no apparent
reason, a sudden increase of radiation was indicated. The radiation
remained high for a few seconds, then dropped back to normal.
The increase over normal was not sufficient to be dangerous, but it
definitely was unusual. All indications pointed to equipment malfunction as the most probable explanation. A quick check revealed
no obvious trouble with the gear, and the two scientists were about
to start a more detailed check when a third member of the radiation crew came rushing into the lab.

Before they could tell the newcomer about the unexplained radiation they had just picked up, he blurted out a story of his own. He
had driven to a nearby town, and on his return trip, as he approached the research lab, something in the sky suddenly caught
his eye. High in the cloudless blue he saw three silvery objects mov-

ing in a V formation. They appeared to be spherical in shape, but he wasn't sure. The first fact that had hit him was that the objects were traveling too fast to be conventional aircraft. He jammed on the brakes, stopped his car and shut off the engine. No sound. All he could hear was the quiet whir of a generator in the research lab. In a few seconds the objects had disappeared from sight.

After the first two scientists had briefed their excited colleague on the unusual radiation they had detected, the three men asked each other the $64 question: Was there any connection between the two incidents? Had the UFOs caused the excessive radiation?

They checked the time. Knowing almost exactly when the instruments had registered the increased radiation, they checked on how long it took to drive to the lab from the point where the three silver objects had been seen. The times correlated within a minute or two. The three men proceeded to check their radiation equipment thoroughly. Nothing was wrong.

The rumor stopped here. Nothing that I or anyone else on Project Blue Book could find out shed any further light on the source of the story. People associated with projects similar to the research lab that was mentioned in the rumor were sought out and questioned. Many of them had heard the story, but no one could add any new details. The three unknown scientists, at the unnamed lab, in an unknown part of the United States, might as well never have existed. Maybe they hadn't.

Almost a year after I had first heard the UFO-radiation story I got a long-distance call from a friend on the west coast. I had seen him several months before, at which time I told him about this curious rumor and expressed my wish to find out how authentic it was. Now, on the phone, he told me he had just been in contact with two people he knew and they had the whole story. He said they would be in Los Angeles the following night and would like very much to talk to me.

I hated to fly clear to the west coast on what might be a wild goose chase, but I did. I couldn't afford to run the risk of losing an opportunity to turn that old recurrent rumor into fact.

Twenty hours later I met the two people at the Hollywood Roosevelt Hotel. We talked for several hours that night, and got the details on the rumor and a lot more that I hadn't bargained for.

Both of my informants were physicists working for the Atomic Energy Commission, and were recognized in their fields. They wanted no publicity and I promised them that they would get none. One of the men knew all the details behind the rumor, and did most of the talking. To keep my promise of no publicity, I'll call him the "scientist."

The rumor version of the UFO-radiation story that had been kicking around in Air Force and scientific circles for so long had been correct in detail but it was by no means complete. The scientist said that after the initial sighting had taken place word was spread at the research lab that the next time the instruments registered abnormal amounts of radiation, some of the personnel were to go outside immediately and look for some object in the sky.

About three weeks after the first incident a repetition did occur. While excessive radiation was registering on the instruments in the lab, a lone dark object was seen streaking across the sky. Again the instruments were checked but, as before, no malfunction was found.

After this second sighting, according to the scientist, an investigation was started at the laboratory. The people who made the visual observations weren't sure that the object they had seen couldn't have been an airplane. Someone thought that perhaps some type of radar equipment in the airplane, if that's what the object was, might have affected the radiation-detection equipment. So arrangements were made to fly all types of aircraft over the area with their radar in operation. Nothing unusual happened. All possible types of airborne research equipment were traced during similar flights in the hope that some special equipment not normally carried in aircraft would be found to have caused the jump in radiation. But nothing out of the ordinary occurred during these tests either.

It was tentatively concluded, the scientist continued, that the abnormally high radiation readings were "officially" due to some freakish equipment malfunction and that the objects sighted visually were birds or airplanes. A report to this effect was made to military authorities, but since the conclusion stated that no flying saucers were involved, the report went into some unknown file. Project Blue Book never got it.

Shortly after the second UFO-radiation episode the research group finished its work. It was at this time that the scientist had first become aware of the incidents he related to me. A friend of his, one of the men involved in the sightings, had sent the details in a letter.

As the story of the sightings spread it was widely discussed in scientific circles, with the result that the conclusion, an equipment malfunction, began to be more seriously questioned. Among the scientists who felt that further investigation of such phemomena was in order, were the man to whom I was talking and some of the people who had made the original sightings.

About a year later the scientist and these original investigators were working together. They decided to make a few more tests, on their own time, but with radiation-detection equipment so designed that the possibility of malfunction would be almost nil. They formed a group of people who were interested in the project, and on evenings and week-ends assembled and set up their equipment in an abandoned building on a small mountain peak. To insure privacy and to avoid arousing undue interest among people not in on the project, the scientist and his colleagues told everyone that they had formed a mineral club. The "mineral club" deception covered their weekend expeditions because "rock hounds" are notorious for their addiction to scrambling around on mountains in search for specimens.

The equipment that the group had installed in the abandoned building was designed to be self-operating. Geiger tubes were arranged in a pattern so that some idea as to the direction of the radiation source could be obtained. During the original sightings the equipment-malfunction factor could not be definitely established or refuted because certain critical data had not been measured.

To get data on visual sightings, the "mineral club" had to rely on the flying saucer grapevine, which exists at every major scientific laboratory in the country.

By late summer of 1950 they were in business. For the next three months the scientist and his group kept their radiation equipment operating twenty-four hours a day, but the tapes showed nothing except the usual background activity. The saucer grapevine reported sightings in the general area of the tests, but none close to the instrumented mountaintop.

The trip to the instrument shack, which had to be made every two days to change tapes, began to get tiresome for the "rock hounds," and there was some talk of discontinuing the watch.

But the persistence paid off. Early in December, about ten o'clock in the morning, the grapevine reported sightings of a silvery, circular-shaped object near the instrument shack. The UFO was seen by several people.

When the "rock hounds" checked the recording tapes in the shack they found that several of the Geiger tubes had been triggered at 10:17 A.M. The registered radiation increase was about 100 times greater than the normal background activity.

Three more times during the next two months the "mineral club's" equipment recorded abnormal radiation on occasions when the grapevine reported visual sightings of UFO's. One of the visual sightings was substantiated by radar.

After these incidents the "mineral club" kept its instruments in operation until June 1951, but nothing more was recorded. And, curiously enough, during this period while the radiation level remained normal, the visual sightings in the area dropped off too. The "mineral club" decided to concentrate on determining the significance of the data they had obtained.

Accordingly, the scientist and the group made a detailed study of their mountaintop findings. They had friends working on many research projects throughout the United States and managed to visit and confer with them while on business trips. They investigated the possibility of unusual sunspot activity, but sunspots had been normal during the brief periods of high radiation. To clinch the elimination of sunspots as a cause, their record tapes showed no bursts of radiation when sunspot activity had been abnormal.

The "rock hounds" checked every possible research project that might have produced some stray radiation for their instruments to pick up. They found nothing. They checked and rechecked their instruments, but could find no factor that might have induced false readings. They let other scientists in on their findings, hoping that these outsiders might be able to put their fingers on errors that had been overlooked.

Now, more than a year after the occurrence of the mysterious incidents that they had recorded, a year spent in analyzing their data, the "rock hounds" had no answer.

By the best scientific tests that they had been able to apply, the visual sightings and the high radiation had taken place more or less simultaneously.

Intriguing ideas are hard to kill, and this one had more than one life, possibly because of the element of mystery which surrounds the subject of flying saucers. But the scientific mind thrives on taking the mystery out of unexplained events, so it is not surprising that the investigation went on.

According to my friend the scientist, a few people outside the laboratory where the "rock hounds" worked were told about the activities of the "mineral club," and they started radiation-detection groups of their own.

For instance, two graduate astronomy students from a southwestern university started a similar watch, on a modest scale, using a modified standard Geiger counter as their detection unit. They did not build a recorder into their equipment, however, and consequently were forced to man their equipment continuously, which naturally cut down the time they were in operation. On two occasions they reportedly detected a burst of high radiation.

Although the veracity of the two astronomers was not doubted, the scientist felt that the accuracy of their readings was poor because of the rather low quality of their equipment.

The scientist then told me about a far more impressive effort to verify or disprove the findings of the "mineral club." Word of the "rock hounds" and their work had also spread to a large laboratory in the East. An Air Force colonel, on duty at the lab, told the story to some of his friends, and they decided to look personally into the situation.

Fortunately these people were in a wonderful spot to make such an investigation. At their laboratory an extensive survey of the surrounding area was being made. An elaborate system of radiation-detection equipment had been set up for a radius of 100 miles around the lab. In addition, the defenses of the area included a radar net.

Thanks to the flashing of silver eagles, the colonel's group got permission to check the records of the radiation-survey station and to look over the logs of the radar stations. They found instances where, during the same period of time that radiation in the area had been much higher than normal, radar had had a UFO on the scope. These events had occurred during the period from January 1951 until about June 1951.

Upon learning of the tentative but encouraging findings that the colonel's group had dug out of their past records, people of both the radiation-survey crews and at the radar sites became interested in co-operating for further investigation. A tie-in with the local saucer grapevine established a three-way check.

One evening in July, just before sunset, two of the colonel's group were driving home from the laboratory. As they sped along the highway they noticed two cars stopped ahead of them. The occupants were standing beside the road, looking at something in the sky.

The two scientists stopped, got out of their car, and scanned the sky too. Low on the eastern horizon they saw a bright circular object moving slowly north. They watched it for a while, took a few notes, then drove back to the lab.

Some interesting news awaited them there. Radar had picked up an unidentified target near the spot where the scientists in the car had seen the UFO, and it had been traveling north. A fighter had been scrambled, but when it got into the proper area, the radar target was off the scope. The pilot glimpsed something that looked like the reported UFO, but before he could check further he had to turn into the sun to get on an interception course, and he lost the object.

Several days passed before the radiation reports from all stations could be collected. When the reports did come in they showed that stations east of the laboratory, on an approximate line with the radar track, had shown the highest increase in radiation. Stations west of the lab showed nothing.

The possible significance of this well-covered incident spurred the colonel's groups to extend and refine their activities. Their idea was to build a radiation-detection instrument in an empty wing tank and hang the tank on an F-47. Then when a UFO was reported they would fly a search pattern in the area and try to establish whether or not a certain sector of the sky was more radioactive than other sectors. Also, they proposed to build a highly directional detector for the F-47 and attempt actually to track a UFO.

The design of such equipment was started, but many delays occurred. Before the colonel's group could get any of the equipment built, some of the members left the lab for other jobs, and the colonel, who sparked the operation, was himself transferred elsewhere. The entire effort collapsed.

The scientist was not surprised that I hadn't heard the story of the colonel's group. All the people involved, he said, had kept it quiet in order to avoid ridicule. The scientist added that he would be glad to give me all the data he had on the sightings of his "mineral club," and he told me where to get the information about the two astronomers and the colonel's group.

Armed with the scientist's notes and recorder tapes, I left for my office at Wright-Patterson Air Force Base, Dayton.

With the blessings of my chief, I started to run down the rest of the radiation information. The data we had, especially that from the scientist's "mineral club," had been thoroughy analyzed, but we thought that since we now had access to more general data something new and more significant might be found.

First I contacted the government agency for which all of the people involved in these investigations had been working, the scientists who recorded the original incident, the scientist and his "mineral club," the colonel's group, and the rest.

The people in the agency were very co-operative but stressed the fact that the activities I was investigating were strictly the extracurricular affairs of the scientists involved, had no official sanction, and should not be tied in with the agency in any way, shape, or form. This closed-door reaction was typical of how the words "flying saucer" seem to scare some people.

They did help me locate the report on the original incident, however, and since it seemed to be the only existing copy, I arranged to borrow it.

About this same time we located the two graduate astronomy

students in New Mexico. Both now had their Ph.D.'s and held responsible jobs on highly classified projects. They repeated their story, which I had first heard from the scientist, but had kept no record of their activities.

On one occasion, just before dawn on a Sunday morning, they were on the roof, making some meteorological observations. One of them was listening to the Geiger counter when he detected a definite increase in the clicking.

Just as the frequency of the clicks reached its highest peak — almost a steady buzz — a large fireball, described by them as "spectacular," flashed across the sky. Both of the observers had seen several of the green fireballs and said that this object was similar in all respects except that the color was a brilliant blue-white.

With the disappearance of the fireball, the counter once more settled down to a steady click per second. They added that once before they had detected a similar increase in the frequency of the clicks but had seen nothing in the sky.

In telling their story, both astronomers stressed the point that their data were open to a great deal of criticism, mainly because of the limited instrumentation they had used. We agreed. Still their work tended to support the findings of the more elaborate and systematic radiation investigations.

The gods who watch over the UFO project were smiling about this time, because one morning I got a call from a colonel on Wright-Patterson Air Force Base. He was going to be in our area that morning and planned to stop in to see me.

He arrived in a few minutes and turned out to be none other than the colonel who had headed the group which had investigated UFO's and radiation at the eastern laboratory. He repeated his story. It was the same as I had heard from the scientist, with a few insignificant changes. The colonel had no records of his group's operations, but knew who had them. He promised to get a wire off to the person immediately, which he did.

The answer was a bit disappointing. During the intervening months the data had been scattered out among the members of the colonel's group, and when the group broke up, so did its collection of records.

So all we had to fall back on was the colonel's word, but since he

now was heading a top-priority project at Wright, it would be difficult not to believe him.

After obtaining the colonel's story, we collected all available
data concerning known incidents in which there seemed to be a
correlation between the visual sighting of UFO's and the presence
of excess atomic radiation in the area of the sightings.

There was one last thing to do. I wanted to take the dates and
times of all the reported radiation increases and check them against
all sources of UFO reports. This project would take a lot of leg
work and digging, but I felt that it would offer the most positive
and complete evidence we could assemble as to whether or not a
correlation existed.

Accordingly, we dug into our files, ADC radar logs, press wire
service files, newspaper morgues in the sighting area, and the files
of individuals who collect data on saucers. Whenever we found a
visual report that correlated with a radiation peak we checked it
against weather conditions, balloon tracks, astronomical reports,
etc.

As soon as the data had all been assembled, I arranged for a
group of Air Force consultants to look it over. I got the same old
answer — the data still aren't good enough. The men were very
much interested in the reports, but when it came time to putting
their comments on paper they said, "Not enough conclusive evidence." If in some way the UFO's could have been photographed
at the same time that the radiation detectors were going wild, it
would have been a different story, they later told me, but with the
data I had for them this was the only answer they could give. No
one could explain the sudden bursts of radiation, but there was no
proof that they were associated with UFO's.

The board's ruling wrote finish to the investigation. I informed
the colonel, and he didn't like the decision. Later I passed through
the city where the scientist was working. I stopped over a few hours
to brief him on the board's decision. He shook his head in disbelief.

It is interesting to note that both the colonel and the scientist
reacted in the same way. We're not fools — we were there — we
saw it — they didn't. What do they want for proof?

# "The Blackout"
# and the UFOs . . .

*The appearance of unidentified flying objects on the night of the Northeast's "Great Power Blackout" may or may not have been a coincidence, but bears scrutiny in light of science's failure to provide a convincing technical explanation. The following selection is from John G. Fuller's* Incident at Exeter.

The blackout caused by the failure of the Northeast Power Grid created one of the biggest mysteries in the history of modern civilization. Eighty thousand square miles and 36,000,000 people — one-fifth of the nation's population — were suddenly plunged into inexplicable darkness.

Massachusetts, New Hampshire, Rhode Island, Connecticut, Vermont, New York, New Jersey, Pennsylvania, and parts of Canada were totally or partially affected by the failure. The President ordered a sweeping investigation. Nearly 800,000 persons — equal to the entire population of Washington, D.C. — were trapped for hours in elevator shafts, subway cars, or commuter trains. Airline pilots circled vainly to find a way to land at darkened airports.

The miracle was that panic and darkness failed to leave a massive death toll. Only a few accidents were reported, and these might have happened with or without a blackout.

By November 11, *The New York Times* was reporting that the Northeast was slowly struggling back toward normal, but that the cause of the blackout was still unknown. Authorities frankly admitted that there was no assurance whatever that the incredible blackout could not occur again, without warning.

There was a curious lack of physical damage: The utility companies looked for something to repair, but there was nothing. Only a few generators were out of action as a result of the power line failure, not a cause. What's more, the utilities were able to restore service with the exact same equipment that was in use at the time of the blackout. What happened that night was not only far from normal; it was mystifying.

If there had been a mechanical flaw, a fire, a breakdown, a short circuit, a toppling transmission tower, the cause would have been quickly and easily detected. Mechanically, however, the system as a whole was in perfect repair before and after the failure.

William W. Kobelt, of Walkill, New York, is one of the thousands of line patrol observers who, according to *The New York Times,* went into action to try to discover the trouble. He is typical of all the others. He flew over the lines of the Central Hudson Gas and Electric Corporation at daybreak after the blackout. Cruising close to treetop level, he checked wires, insulators, cross arms, and structures of the high-power transmission lines. He looked for trees, branches which might have fallen over the wires. "We looked for trouble — but couldn't find any at all," he said.

Robert Ginna, Chairman of the Rochester Gas and Electric Corporation, said that his utility had been receiving 200,000 kilowatts under an agreement with the New York State Power authority, which operates the hydroelectric plants at Niagara Falls. "Suddenly, we didn't have it," he said. "We don't know what happened to the 200,000 kilowatts. It just wasn't there."

Edward L. Hoffman, assistant to the chief system electrical engineer of Niagara Mohawk, told *The New York Times* that it was true that some generators dropped out of phase, but that this was "secondary to the main cause of the failure."

Early in the blackout, it was announced that a line break near Niagara Falls had caused the trouble. A fast check immediately ruled that theory out.

At 10 P.M., it was announced that the crux of the difficulty lay at a remote-controlled substation on the Power Authority's transmission lines at Clay, New York, a town 10 miles north of Syracuse. The high-tension 345,000-volt power lines stretching over Clay are part of the authority's "superhighway" of power distribution, running into Niagara Falls, east to Utica and south to New York City.

Niagara Mohawk repairmen who drove out to Clay found the substation in apparently perfect order. There were no signs of mechanical failure, fire, or destruction. Another report sent FBI investigators and State Police to the desolate Montezuma Marshes outside of Syracuse, but they found nothing out of order there, according to *The Times*.

Something else happened outside Syracuse, however, which was noted briefly in the press, and then immediately dropped without follow-up comment. Weldon Ross, a private pilot and instructor, was approaching Hancock Field at Syracuse for a landing. It was at almost the exact moment of the blackout. As he looked below him, just over the power lines near the Clay substation, a huge red ball of brilliant intensity appeared. It was about 100 feet in diameter, Ross told the New York *Journal-American*. He calculated that the fireball was at the point where the New York Power Authority's two 345,000-volt power lines at the Clay substation pass over the New York Central's tracks between Lake Oneida and Hancock Field. With Ross was a student pilot who verified the statement. At precisely the same moment, Robert C. Walsh, Deputy Commissioner for the Federal Aviation Agency in the Syracuse area, reported that he saw the same phenomenon just a few miles south of Hancock Field. A total of five persons reported the sighting. Although the Federal Power Commission immediately said they would investigate, no further word has been given publicly since.

Pilot Ross's sighting took place at 5:15 P.M., at the moment when the blackout occurred in the Syracuse area. At 5:25 A.M. a schoolteacher in Holliston, Massachusetts, watched through binoculars with her husband an intense white object in the sky moving slowly toward the horizon. At the same time, David Hague, a seventeen-year-old from Holliston, reported an identical object, moving toward the southwest.

In New York City, simultaneously with the blackout, two women declared in two separate statements that they sighted unusual objects in the sky.

In the statement of Mrs. Gerry Falk, she says: "Between five and five-five P.M., November ninth, I was driving along Mt. Prospect Avenue, West Orange, New Jersey. As I reached the corner of Mt. Prospect Avenue and Eagle Rock Avenue, I noticed a red streak in the sky. I stopped for a light and saw it again. I tried to get the attention of the driver in the next car, but was unable to do so. It is a heavily wooded area and hilly, and as I reached the crest of a hill, I saw it again.

"It was shaped rather like a half-moon, with two tips facing up. It was pale red, not like a flame, and there appeared to be something at the tip. It was very high in the air. At first I thought it was a sky-writer, but then I saw it was different from anything I had ever seen. The sun was going down to the right. This was on the left. It continued going up."

Mrs. Sol Kaplan, of Central Park West, New York City, was watching television in her bedroom, which faces the Hudson River to the west. Her TV set went off and the lights went out. "I looked out the window," she states, "and there were a number of planes in the sky, more than usual. As I kept looking, I saw a big circular dome — it was not flying, but going up and down and sideways. It was silvery-looking, no lights like an airplane. I was looking through binoculars."

*Life* photographer Arthur Rickerby took a strikingly dramatic picture of the New York skyline just after the blackout. In the western sky, a brilliant, silvery object appears that has not in any satisfactory way been explained, after it appeared in the November 19, 1965, issue of *Time*. Although some claim it is Venus, photographer Rickerby is inclined to disagree.

In Philadelphia, several witnesses in many parts of the city reported seeing a "curious cloud, shaped like an up-ended coin with a handle" in an otherwise cloudless sky, according to Ruth Montgomery, Hearst columnist. They later discovered it was seen at almost the exact moment that the power failure occurred. Philadelphia itself was unaffected by the blackout.

Walter Voelker, a research engineer, told Miss Montgomery: "The most curious aspect was that by the time my wife and I saw the 'cloud' and could stop the car in traffic for a better look, it had shifted to the other side of the sky. We saw it in three different locations. Later, we learned of others who had had similar experiences in sighting it." Several sightings of a similar description were made in and around Bloomfield, Connecticut, at approximately the same time that the blackout struck.

According to NICAP, at 4:30 P.M. on the day of the blackout, pilot Jerry Whittaker and passenger George Croniger saw two shiny objects above them, chased by two jet planes. One UFO put on a "burst of speed" to outdistance them. Other UFO reports at the time of the blackout came from Holyoke and Amherst, Massachusetts, Woonsocket, Rhode Island, and Newark, New Jersey.

In spite of the lengthy report issued by the FPC the Great Blackout has still not been adequately explained. Ostensibly, backup Relay #Q-29 at the Sir Adam Beck generating station, Queenston, Ontario, was eventually pinpointed as the source of the massive failure. But further investigation, hardly noted in the press, showed that nothing in the relay was broken when it was removed for inspection. In fact, it went back into operation normally when power was restored. The line it was protecting was totally undamaged. "Why did everything go berserk?" *Life* Magazine asks in an article about the blackout. "Tests on the wayward sensing device have thus far been to no avail." A later statement by Arthur J. Harris, a supervising engineer of the Ontario Hydro Electric Commission, indicated that the cause was still a mystery. "Although the blackout has been traced to the tripping of a circuit breaker at the Sir Adam Beck No. 2 plant, it is practically impossible to pinpoint the initial cause." As late as January 4, 1966, *The New York Times* in a follow-up story indicated a series of questions regarding the prevention of future blackouts. The news item says: "These questions more or less are related to the cause, *still not fully understood,* of last November's blackout." The italics are ours.

The Great Northeast Blackout was a mystery, but not any more puzzling than what followed on its heels. On November 16, a series of power blackouts hit many parts of Britain. Dozens of sections of London were darkened, and telephone operators in Folkestone, on the south coast, worked by candlelight.

On November 26, NICAP was advised that power failures in St. Paul, Minnesota, were reported by the Northern States Power Company simultaneous with the appearance of objects overhead giving off blue and white flashes just off Highway 61. Fifteen minutes later, just north of the original sighting, a resident on Hogt Avenue reported a "blue-glowing" UFO as all house lights and appliances in the area went dead. A motorist also reported that his car lights and radio went out.

The power company announced that it was unable to determine the cause of that blackout.

By December 2, sections of two states and Mexico were plunged into darkness after a widespread power failure in the Southwest. Juarez, Mexico, was hit, as well as El Paso, Texas, and Las Cruces and Alamogordo, New Mexico. Authorities were unable to explain the cause of the trouble.

A few days later on December 4, portions of east Texas were knocked out electrically, with 40,000 houses losing power. It was the third major blackout since the Northeast Grid failed.

By December 26, the mystery was growing deeper. The entire city of Buenos Aires, and towns as far as 50 miles away, were plunged into darkness by a power failure, with hundreds trapped in subways beneath Buenos Aires' streets. The cause was thought to be a single generator.

On the same date, four major cities of south and central Finland were hit by a loss of electrical power attributed to a single insulator.

Going back to 1962, an interesting fact was revealed by Eileen Shanahan of *The New York Times.* "Still not widely known in the eastern United States," she wrote under a November 21, 1965, dateline, "is that the Northeast power blackout was not the first wide-area power failure experienced in recent years. *There was one covering an area four times as large* [our italics] as the New York-New England blackout, and a less extensive one last January. Both were in the Midwest and involved such major cities as Omaha and Des Moines.

"Although the 1962 wide-area failure in the Midwest was well known to power experts before the Commission's survey was completed last year, the National Power Survey [published about a year before by the Federal Power Commission] made no significant mention of it, while recommending an enlargement of the kind of interdependence that made Tuesday's blackout so extensive. The Commission has offered no explanation for the omission."

Further evidence tabulated by NICAP on electrical interference of UFOs in the past enhances the possibility that there may be some relationship between the phenomenon and the wide-area power blackouts:

— On September 3, 1965, a glowing disk-shaped object hovered at low altitude over Cuernavaca, Mexico, as the lights of the town went out. It was witnessed by many, including Governor Emilie Riva Palacie, Mayor Valentin Lopez Gonzalez, and a military zone chief, General Rafael Enrique Vega.

— On August 17, 1959, the automatic keys at a power station turned off as a round-shaped UFO passed overhead, following a trunk power line. As the object disappeared, the keys went on again automatically, and service returned to normal.

— On August 3, 1958, parts of Rome, Italy, were darkened as a luminous UFO passed overhead.

— In 1957 lights went out at Nogi Mirim, Brazil, as three UFOs passed overhead. Also in 1957, a UFO hovered over Tamaroa, Illinois, as the electrical power failed.

One news story on January 13, 1966, is particularly interesting because it received little attention in the press aside from the Portsmouth, New Hampshire, *Herald* of that date, even though it was an AP release, with an Andover, Maine, dateline:

> The Telstar communications satellite tracking station was blacked out by a power failure which hit a 75-mile area in western Franklin County.
>
> Electrical power failed at 4:30 P.M. Wednesday and was restored at 11:20 P.M.
>
> A spokesman for the Central Maine Power Co. blamed the failure on "an apparent equipment failure which somehow corrected itself."

Noteworthy are two things: 1) The power failure involved a space satellite and 2) in this age of science and engineering, the equipment "somehow corrected itself." Coupled with the stories of the numerous other blackouts, this is strange indeed that the engineers could not figure out how it went out — and how the failure was remedied.

On the following day, an AP story datelined Augusta, Maine, stated that Chairman Frederick N. Allen of the Public Utility Commission indicated that there was no negligence by the two power companies involved. The Central Maine Power Company said that the blackout was caused by the failure of a big transformer in its Rumford substation.

CMP Vice-President Harold F. Schnurle went on to say that it had not been determined why the transformer failed or why it restored itself to service nearly seven hours later.

The relationship of the Unidentified Flying Objects to the power failures is entirely circumstantial, of course. Both UFOs and the Great Blackout still remain unsolved. But stranger yet is the incapacity of modern science to come up with any kind of real answer to either question. More baffling still is the attitude of the large bulk of the scientific fraternity in presumably laughing off a phenomenon testified to by hundreds of technicians, other scientists, airline pilots, military personnel, local and state police, and articulate and reliable citizens. . . .

# UFOs Plotted on a
# Map of France . . .

*French mathematician Aimé Michel made a startling*
*discovery when he plotted UFO sightings for a*
*certain period on a map of France. This selection is*
*from Aimé Michel's book,* Flying Saucers and the
Straight-Line Mystery.

. . . This comment should be made at once: on the scale on which the phenomena that we are studying take place, the word "straight" is misleading. On the earth's surface the shortest route from one point to another ("geodesic") *cannot* be a true straight line, since that surface is convex; in reality, it is a "great-circle" arc, or "orthodromic line" (Greek for, "which runs straight").

The representation of the earth's surface (which is curved) on a map (which is flat) always involves distortion either of angles or distances or surfaces, depending on which of various methods is used to draw the map. To represent all great circles as straight lines, the appropriate projection is the "gnomonic" one. However, this causes so much distortion of shapes that maps are seldom drawn on this projection, with the exception of nautical charts (used by seamen for plotting great-circle sailing routes). In the absence of a gnomonic map of France, we must content ourselves, for the time being, with the nearest available approximation. In the cases we are dealing with, the topographical accuracy of the observations and their distances from one another are not sufficiently great for the margin of error caused by map distortion to be very significant, no matter what projection is used. So, when I speak of alignment, or "the arrangement of observations on a straight line," I mean observations entered, and straight lines drawn, on the map of scale 1:1,000,000 of the National Geographical Institute, on Lambert's conical projection, secant at 45° to 49° north latitude; or on the Michelin map No. 989, which is a more manageable equivalent.* Since the error involved does not exceed a few hundred yards, the accuracy of lines drawn on these maps is more than sufficient for our purposes. If it is ever decided to make a truly scientific study of the saucer phenomenon over vast distances, on an international scale, the true gnomonic projection will have to be

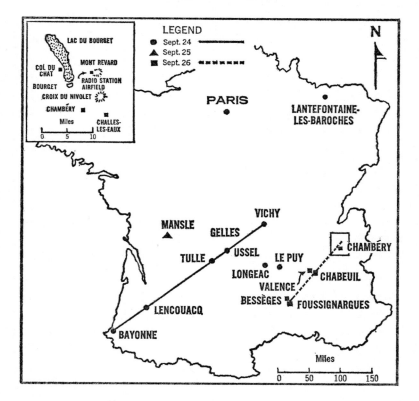

* For locating the villages referred to and for short-distance plotting, Michelin's larger-scale sectional maps #51-87 (1:200,000) are recommended.

resorted to* for over large distances the geodesic lines will deviate considerably from straight lines on the Lambert projection. But for an area no bigger than France this is not necessary.

It follows that since this book is limited, with a few exceptions, to a study of alignments in France, it is not possible to know whether the reported sightings are arranged *exactly* on the great-circle lines. Accordingly, I shall not use the terms geodesic or orthodromic lines, in order not to assume more than has actually been shown. Instead, I will coin a phrase and speak of "orthotenic" lines and of the phenomenon of "orthoteny," which thus means, as a practical matter, "alignment on straight lines of the Lambert projection." . . .

## *The Spider Web and Coincidence — October 2*

Many of the October 1 cases are not well substantiated, and therefore we cannot venture on a detailed analysis of that day. Saturday the 2nd and Sunday the 3rd, on the other hand, are very well remembered; it was the week end, and Saturdays and Sundays are days that leave an impression.

From the orthotenic point of view, Saturday the 2nd affords a fascinating spectacle. . . .

Having gathered together all my October 2 documentation, I undertook to transfer the observations to a map. It turned out to be a long and tedious task. Every point represents more than an hour's work. Each time I exactly located a point of observation, I stuck a yellow drawing-pin in the large map, like an armchair strategist following the progress of a battle.

Most of the observations had already been covered with their little spot of yellow when the ceramicist Pierre Mestre came in and stood looking at the map in silence. To the casual eye the yellow dots (there were already more than 20) gave the appearance of chaos. However, one alignment of six appeared incontrovertibly, joining Les Rousses in the Jura to the Maisoncelles airfield near Paris, while passing through Dijon, Poncey-sur-l'Ignon near Di-

---

* The United States is large enough to make this advisable. Fortunately, a large gnomonic-projection map of the United States (U.S.C. & G.S. #3074) is available from large map dealers at a low price.–AMER. EDS.

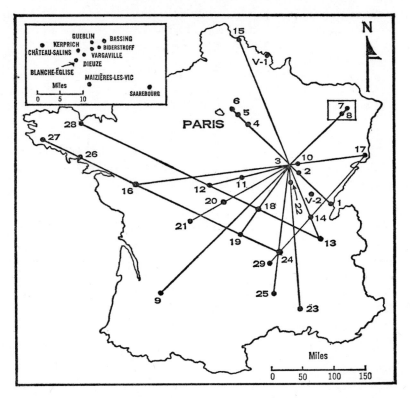

jon, and Provins and Voinsles, both southeast of Paris: six points
perfectly aligned over a distance of 220 miles.

Mestre took the black thread I used to tie the outermost points
in the alignment to one another, and, without saying a word, he
stretched it from Les Rousses to Maisoncelles, where he fastened
it. I watched him do this, and then continued my tiresome study of
local maps.

When I came back to the big map, to put the last pin in position,
I was dumbfounded at what I saw.

Nine black threads were stretched from pin to pin, and every one
of them passed through Poncey!

Mestre was munching on an orange, visibly pleased. Taking the
ruler to the map I measured the alignments:

Les Rousses —— Dijon —— Poncey —— Provins —— Vo-insles —— Maisoncelles: 220 miles.

Bassing —— Blanche Église —— Poncey —— Aiguillon: 425 miles.

Pellerey —— Poncey —— Rians —— Vatan: 141 miles.

Morestel —— Bourg —— Poncey —— Comines: 360 miles.

Cholet —— Poncey —— Willer: 375 miles.

Poncey —— Vichy —— Clermont-Ferrand: 140 miles.

Poncey —— Châteaumeillant —— Magnac-Laval: 200 miles.

Poncey —— Savigny-les-Beaune —— Avignon: 235 miles.

Poncey —— Aurec —— La Grand-Combe: 220 miles.

Furthermore:

Aurec, Clermont, and Cholet were in alignment, and prolongation of the line passed over two of the three pins that marked Brittany, Vannes and Quimper, making a very nice alignment of 420 miles.

The other Breton pin, St-Brieuc, made another 420-mile straight line with Vatan and Morestel; and these two lines of the same length ran parallel to each other.

Finally, one last straight line of 235 miles joined Willer, Bourg, and Aurec to St.-Paulien.

Lying outside all alignments, we found only two stubbornly Virgilian pins, one at Jeumont on the Belgian frontier, and the other at Louhans in Saône-et-Loire, six miles east of the alignment Morestel —— Bourg —— Poncey —— Comines.

"All the same," said Pierre Mestre, "six miles is a very short distance! Don't you think anyone could see a saucer from six miles away?"

"What is a saucer?" I replied. "No one knows. And if it *is* an hallucination, is it possible to see an hallucination for six miles? Here's an extraordinary opportunity to grasp an undeniable phenomenon, one as definite as a crystal. Let's keep it rigorous, if we want it to prove something."

"But let us at least consider," said Mestre, "what this observation at Louhans may be. If what the Louhans witnesses saw was something in the sky toward the west, I shall stick to my opinion and you can have your crystal."

We looked. It was a landing report at Louhans proper. Mestre then abandoned his Virgilian saucer, with good grace.

"So much the worse," he said. "But Poncey? This point at which nine alignments meet is disturbing. I should like to know what was seen there."

"An extraordinary thing was seen there two days later, on October 4. What happened on the 2nd I can't recall, but the files will tell us."

## Poncey-Sur-L'Ignon  (Côte-d'Or) — October 2

On the evening of Saturday October 2, at about 8 P.M., Mme. Guainet finished milking her cows in the stable. Her account of subsequent events is confirmed by her husband, one-time mayor of Poncey, and by numerous other witnesses from Poncey and from Pellerey, the village next to it.

"The dogs, who usually remain beside me in the stable while I'm milking, had run out several seconds before, baying in the direction of the woods. When I went out into the court after them, I saw something very odd: the front of the house was softly illuminated as though by the setting moon. 'The moon looks peculiar this evening,' I thought to myself. Then, raising my eyes, I noticed above the woods, apparently at low altitude, a sort of vast illuminated cigar, and I saw that it was silently flying eastward at a speed comparable to that of a big airplane, but maintaining an obviously vertical position. I called my husband and my daughter. A woman neighbor came out, too. We all saw the enormous object disappear behind the hill, always flying in a straight line and at a moderate speed."

This spectacle had also been observed at other points of the village by many residents, and the inquiry made on the 6th — after the landing that took place two days later, on the 4th — proved that the same thing had been seen from the village of Pellerey, a mile east-northeast of Poncey. Furthermore, the line Poncey —— Pellerey confirms the direction attributed to the object's flight. It equally confirms the straight line which, at 100 and 140 miles westward from Poncey passes over Rians (Cher) and Vatan (Indre), where two observations had been made at least an hour before. From this October 2 observation, which at first went almost unnoticed among the sensational events that occurred two days later in the same village, it now becomes perfectly clear that the "big cloud cigar" had been seen in the Poncey area the night of October 2; and that once more, the role of "base" (or dispersion center) played by this phenomenon was confirmed, and this time in stunning fashion.

For it seems evident to me that with 28 points over an area of dispersion equal at least to the surface of France, chance alone could not account for *nine* absolutely straight lines all crossing or meeting at the same point.

Of these nine lines, five were formed by three points (of which one was always the same, Poncey); three by four points, one of which is Poncey, and one by six points, also including Poncey. Furthermore, many of these points occur on other alignments just as straight as the first: one of five points (Quimper —— Aurec), two of four points (Bassing —— Aiguillon —— Willer——St-Paulien), and one of three points (St-Brieuc —— Morestel). . . .

SIGHTINGS AND ALIGNMENTS, OCTOBER 2

Perhaps the most interesting fact of this day is the light thrown on the detail of sightings by their disposition on the map, and vice versa. Whenever the observed movements of an object were recorded, they are in agreement with the orthotenic lines; one confirms the other at every point.

*Les Rousses*. The village of Les Rousses is situated on the Swiss frontier, not far from Lake Geneva. At about 3:45 P.M., twenty-three school children were outdoors, supervised by their teacher, Mme. Jaillet, when they saw in the sky above Mount Noirmont, in the southeast, an elongated object in the shape of a short white trail or train. At first it was barely perceptible, because of its height and its distance. However, it approached quite rapidly, and some minutes later the phenomenon as it was described corresponded exactly to the classic "huge cloud cigar." As at St.-Prouant, the witnesses saw the object pass from the horizontal position (when moving laterally) to the vertical position (when motionless). At one stage, they perceived very clearly for several seconds a gleaming yellow disk which slipped out of the cigar, only to hide itself again shortly. Then the cloud — the "train," said the witnesses — resumed its horizontal position at the same time as its motion, and disappeared at a lively speed in the direction of Dôle, that is, toward the northwest. The sighting lasted four or five minutes.

The object thus appeared southeast of Les Rousses and disappeared toward the northwest. This confirms the line Les Rousses —— Dijon —— Poncey —— Provins —— Voinsles —— Maisoncelles on which this sighting is located. The direction of Dôle as pointed out by the witnesses was even the direction of the alignment within six or seven degrees.

*Poncey —— Rians —— Vatan.* This alignment, as shown on the map, is oriented toward the west-southwest of Poncey. But at Rians, witnesses discovered the object when it was southwest of the village, and they saw it set off "toward the right," they said, which is westward. At Vatan, the direction of displacement indicated was "toward Châteauroux," that is, toward the southwest. Here again, the displacement conforms to the lines on the map.

*Poncey —— Châteaumeillant —— Magnac-Laval.* The alignment is oriented toward the southwest of Poncey. Almost a mile southwest of Châteaumeillant, in the department of Cher, the line enters the department of Indre; said the witnesses: "The object seemed to travel at a very high altitude in the direction of Indre."

*Willer —— Bourg —— Aurec —— St-Paulien.* The alignment is oriented from northeast to southwest, and we are in a position to be quite exact for Aurec: the villagers insist that they saw "many objects which, after stopping motionless for an instant, disappeared toward the southwest. . . ."

## Stars and Cars — October 7

For October 5 and 6 there were not enough reliably dated reports for analysis. But Thursday, October 7, was doubly remarkable: first, for its spider web of orthotenic lines, and second, for the first appearance of a new and striking phenomenon. . . .

## The Network of October 7 — Stars and Apexes

Excluding Lardenne, and regarding St-Jean-d'Assé:Ballon and Chalette:Dordives as single observations, there are now 27 reports for Thursday, October 7, arranged along 23 lines.

One line includes seven sightings: Cherbourg —— La Ferté-Macé —— St-Jean-d'Assé:Ballon —— Route N-23 —— Lavenay —— Montlevic —— Cassis.

Three lines have four sightings each:

(1) Marcillac —— Puymoyen —— Montlevic —— Corbigny
(2) Isles-sur-Suippes —— Montlevic —— Bournel —— Mont-pézat
(3) St-Savinien —— St-Plantaire —— Montlevic —— Jettingen

The remaining 19 lines consist of three points each, as follows:

(1) Plozévet —— Marcillac —— Montpézat
(2) Plozévet —— Montlevic —— Beauvoir
(3) Plozévet —— St-Bihy —— Duclair
(4) St-Bihy —— Puymoyen —— Bompas
(5) St-Bihy —— Lavenay —— Corbigny
(6) St-Bihy —— Chalette:Dordives —— Jettingen
(7) Cherbourg —— Duclair —— Isles-sur-Suippes
(8) Isles-sur-Suippes —— Chalette:Dordives —— Puymoyen
(9) Isles-sur-Suippes —— Corbigny —— Bompas
(10) St-Étienne-sous-Barbuise —— Chalette:Dorvies —— Les Aubiers
(11) Jettingen —— St-Étienne —— Hennezis
(12) Jettingen —— Montlevic —— St-Savinien
(13) Jettingen —— Beauvoir —— Monteux
(14) Monteux —— Béruges —— Les Aubiers
(15) Corbigny —— Chalette:Dordives —— Hennezis
(16) Hennezis —— Lavenay —— Marcillac
(17) St-Jean-d'Assé:Ballon —— Béruges —— Puymoyen
(18) Hennezis —— N-23 —— Les Aubiers
(19) Hennezis —— Montlevic —— Bompas

Of the 27 places involved, only five fall on one alignment only — La Ferté-Mace, Bournel, St-Plantaire, St-Savinien, and Cassis. One point, Montlevic, falls at the crossing of six alignments. Hennezis is the terminal point on five alignments. Six places are on four alignments each: Corbigny, St-Bihy, Isles-sur-Suippes, Jettingen, Puymoyen, and Chalette:Dordives. Five places are on three lines each: Marcillac, Plozévet, Les Aubiers, Bompas, and Lavenay. The remaining nine (St-Jean:Ballon, Duclair, St-Étienne, Beauvoir, Cherbourg, Monteux, Béruges, N-23, and Montpézat) are on two lines each.

The meeting and intersection of these alignments vary. Three places mark "stars," where three or more lines cross each other (crossing of two lines has not been considered a "star"): Lavenay, with three lines; Chalette:Dordives, with four lines; and Montlevic, with six lines. In addition, there is a three-line crossing about half-way between Montlevic and St-Savinien, from which no observation was reported.

There are nine "multi-radial apexes," where two to five alignments meet and end: termination of two lines at Cherbourg, Monteux, and Montpézat; termination of three lines at Plozévet, Les Aubiers, and Bompas; termination of four lines at Jettingen and Isles-sur-Suippes; termination of five lines at Hennezis.

And there are also several combinations of apexes with straight lines.

Examination of this map indicates other curious features of the strongly-marked pattern. For example, there appears to be a prevalence of angles of about 30 degrees; at least eight such angles can be found at major apexes. There are several 90-degree angles, and several pairs of parallel and almost-parallel lines, creating rectangles and trapezoids. Most striking is the way the pattern is closed up around the edges; only one point, Cassis, fails to lie on or within the borders established by the alignments.

It is obviously impossible even to speculate about the possible meaning of these features; but that the pattern is distinctive no one can question.

Two things are clear about the network of October 7. First, this network is incontestable; the reports of the sightings are in the French newspapers of October, 1954.* Second, this network is

* Corbigny: *Aurore,* Oct. 8; St-Jean-d'Assé, Route N-23: *Aurore,* Oct. 9; Duclair, Beauvoir: *Parisien Libéré,* Oct. 9; St-Bihy, St-Étienne, Ballon, Lavenay, Dordives, Chalette, Les Aubiers, Pumoyen: *France-Soir,* Oct. 9; Plozévet, Béruges, Jettingen: *France-Soir,* Oct. 10; St-Plantaire, Montlevic;

astonishing, not simply because of the presence of these straight lines marked out by as many as seven sightings, but because of the convergence of these straight lines in star formations. That chance or coincidence should explain these convergences is extremely unlikely. . . .

*Paris-Presse,* Oct. 9; Cherbourg, Isles-sur-Suippes: *Paris-Presse,* Oct. 10; Marcillac, Bournel, Montpézat: *Combat,* Oct. 12; St-Savinien: *Sud-Ouest,* Oct. 14; Cassis: files of Charles Garreau; La Ferté-Macé, Hennezis, Monteux, Bompas: Jimmy Guieu, *Blackout sur les soucoupes volantes.*

PART THREE  *The Controversy*

*The old maxim never to debate religion or politics with
friends — if you want them to remain friends — might well be
amended to include the UFO controversy. The subject is
hardly a neutral one, and there are as many adamant opinions
as there are people to voice them.*

*The Air Force reports that out of 10,000 sightings only
6 percent remain unidentified. NICAP (National Investigations
Committee on Aerial Phenomena) claims that the unidentified
percentage is much higher because the Air Force has been
unthorough in its investigation, hasty in its conclusions, and
evasive in regard to releasing facts.*

*What can be done when there are two sets of facts for a
single sighting? Which is unreliable? Which is a hoax?*

*The charges fly back and forth, and this, of course,
contributes to the confusion surrounding the entire matter. In
addition, when all the facts are tallied, we still very often come
up with no answer.*

*The following selections illustrate these problems.*

# THE CONTROVERSY

# Air Force
# Regulation #200-2 . . .

*After researching* Incident at Exeter, *from which this selection is taken, John G. Fuller declared that as a general rule, the Air Force dismisses qualified UFO reports with the attitude that flying saucers just don't exist. Nevertheless, he continues, within the military organization itself, UFOs seem to merit serious consideration.*

. . . Air Force . . . "inside" regulations to its personnel are serious and detailed. The official regulation #200-2, as of July 20, 1962, is far from a joking matter. It covers seven full pages of instruction packed into tightly spaced 8-point type.

It describes UFOs as "any aerial phenomena, airborne objects or objects which are unknown or appear out of the ordinary to the observer because of performance, aerodynamic characteristics, or unusual features."

It goes on to describe the objectives of the Air Force UFO program: "Air Force interest in UFOs is threefold. First, as a possible threat to the security of the United States and its forces; second, to determine the technical or scientific characteristics of any such UFOs; third, to explain or identify all UFO sightings. . . ."

The official regulation admits that "there is need for further scientific knowledge in such fields as geophysics, astronomy, and physics of the upper atmosphere which the study and analysis of UFOs and similar aerial phenomena may provide."

The responsibilities of reporting incidents, according to Air Force regulation 200-2, rests on Base commanders, who "will report all information and evidence of UFO sightings received from other services, government agencies, and civilian sources. Investigators are authorized to make telephone calls from the investigation area direct to the Foreign Technology Division (FTD) of the Air Force Systems Command, Wright-Patterson Air Force Base, Ohio. The purpose of the calls is to report high-priority sightings."

The Commander of the Air Force base nearest the location of a UFO sighting is instructed to "conduct all investigative action necessary to submit a complete initial report of a UFO sighting. The initial investigation will include every effort to resolve the sighting."

The job of interpreting the data is left up to the Air Force Systems Command Foreign Technology Division at the Wright-Patterson Base. From here the report goes to the Headquarters of the U.S. Air Force, and no information can be released except from the Office of Information of the Office of the Secretary of the Air Force. Up to the present, this has been a stone wall for any meaningful information.

But further evidence of the seriousness with which the Air Force considers the UFO problem is indicated in Paragraph #5, which states: "Both the Assistant Chief of Staff, Intelligence, Headquarters, USAF, and the Air Defense Command have a direct and immediate interest in the facts pertaining to UFOs reported within the United States."

The releasing of information to the public is definitely a sacred cow. According to Paragraph #7, only the Office of Information, Office of the Secretary of the Air Force, can do this "regardless of the origin and nature" of the UFO.

There is only one exception — and that is significant. The base commander may "release information to the press or the general public *only after positive identification of the sighting as a familiar or known sighting."* (The italics are mine.) If the sighting is unexplainable, the only statement that the local base can release "is the fact that the sighting is under investigative action and information regarding it will be available at a later date. After completion of investigative action, the commander may release the fact that the Air Force Systems Command (Foreign Technology Division) will review and analyze the results of the investigation. He will then refer any further inquiries to the local Office of Information."

In analyzing regulation 200-2 NICAP has pointed out that several specific paragraphs amount to direct contradictions of official denials of censorship on the part of the Air Force.

In regulation 200-2 is the statement: "Air Force activities must reduce the percentage of unidentifieds to a minimum. . . ." NICAP claims that this shows an obvious intention to explain away UFO reports, not to investigate them scientifically and admit that many cases cannot be explained.

Another statement in the regulation is considered by NICAP as direct censorship: "Air Force personnel . . . will not contact private individuals on UFO cases nor will they discuss their operations and function with unauthorized persons unless so directed, and then only on a 'need to know' basis."

There are other provisions to which NICAP takes exception, and the battle between it and the Air Force continues without letup. . . .

On the other side of the fence, if you presupposed a benign and intelligent group of political leaders, or Air Force generals, who were faced with definite evidence and proof of the fact that UFOs of extraterrestrial origin did exist, wouldn't they, out of concern for the entire organized structure of society, feel that they must be most cautious in the manner in which this intelligence should be released to the general populace? The Orson Welles "invasion" in the late thirties, a single dramatized radio program, resulted in mass hysteria. Would the same thing — or worse — happen if official government sources announced blandly that we definitely had visitors from another planet? What would a reasonable and prudent man in the position of complete authority — such as the President of the United States — do when confronted with such a decision?

There have been, I learned after I started this research, frequent and continual rumors (and they are *only* rumors) that in a morgue at Wright-Patterson Field, Dayton, Ohio, lie the bodies of a half-dozen or so small humanoid corpses, measuring not more than four-and-a-half feet in height, evidence of one of the few times an extra-terrestrial spaceship has allowed itself either to fail or otherwise fall into the clutches of the semicivilized Earth People. What would any of us do if we bore the responsibility of releasing this news to the citizenry? If we were the "reasonable and prudent man" our law courts always use as the measuring stick of judgment, we would probably be very circumspect. We might even delay judgment. It could produce chaos in an overorganized society which has become so dependent on intricate interrelated mechanisms that even a pint-size back-up relay in Ontario, Canada, can plunge 30 million people into inexplicable darkness, with none of the engineering experts in the country knowing exactly why it happened. As Gordon Evans had pointed out, the Brookings report had indicated that the engineers and the scientists would suffer the greatest confusion and who else could the masses turn to, aside from the suggestion that they turn to God? For there would *have* to be an explanation — a sober, logical explanation, from "official sources." And those official sources would have to be the ordinary person, elevated into authority by the mandate of the voters. The President. Or you. Or me.

The whole question of the Space Age ghost story seems to reduce itself to an insoluble ghost story — unless physical evidence of overwhelming validity were suddenly made available; or, unless scientists who *might* have such evidence were willing to share it. The censorship of the political powers in the Air Force seems to be exercising authority far beyond the powers assigned to it by the civilian control under which it is supposed to be operating. . . .

# The Air Force Point of View . . .

*Bill Wise, in this* Life *Magazine article of April 1, 1966, tells of the Air Force's attempt to make sense of it all.*

DAYTON, OHIO

There have been 10,147 reported UFO sightings since a private pilot named Kenneth Arnold claimed he saw a set of rapidly moving "things" in the air near Mount Rainier, Wash. on June 24, 1947. Arnold's widely publicized report set off the first of the modern epidemics of saucer-sighting, and the Air Force has been in the saucer business ever since. Its "Project Bluebook" occupies a single room on the second floor of a windowless red concrete building here at Wright-Patterson Air Force Base. Its functions: 1) to try to find an explanation for all reported sightings of unidentified flying objects, 2) to discover whether the UFOs pose any security threat, and 3) to determine if UFOs exhibit any advanced technology which the U.S. could put to use.

To assist Project Bluebook, there is a UFO officer stationed at every Air Force base in the country; the officer at the base nearest a reported sighting is responsible for initiating the investigation. According to Major Hector Quintanella Jr., a physicist who heads Project Bluebook, most UFO sightings have a rational and usually very simple explanation. The most common reports stem from bright stars, planets, and meteorites, particularly when viewed through broken clouds or haze.

Others turn out to be satellites — few people realize that there are now more than 30 of these in orbit that are visible to the naked eye. Thousands of balloons — some as large as 300 feet in diameter, some carrying running lights — are released daily at airports, weather stations, and research centers, and these lead to a great many "saucer" reports. Conventional aircraft are another major source — reflecting sun by day or providing the glow of running lights or jet afterburners or the flash of photo recon strobe lights at night.

All satellites and most weather balloons and aircraft are being carefully tracked and logged by military or civilian agencies, and Project Bluebook routinely checks sightings against these records. Unreported local flights by private aircraft pose the most frequent problem in this detective work.

Strange blips on radar screens have occasionally unsettled personnel at tracking stations — *e.g.,* two "objects" that appeared on the scopes at Patuxent Naval Air Station (Md.) last December seemingly approaching the base at an estimated 4,800 miles an hour before making a tight turn and disappearing. But these can generally be traced to pulsating "bugs" within a receiving set or to interference from other neighboring electronic gear. Wright-Patterson experts have been able to account for every errant radar blip reported to date.

There is no question that our Air Force and those of other countries employ assorted airborne hardware as tactical and training devices. Many of these are, of course, "seen" as flying saucers and it is obvious that for security reasons the Air Force is reluctant to talk about them.

"I've looked at the records of nearly every UFO case back to 1947," says Major Quintanella, "and my feeling is that the vast majority have involved simple misinterpretation of natural phenomena."

Of the sightings so far checked out, less than two percent of the total are listed on Project Bluebook's file as "unidentified." The Air Force officially concludes that *none* of these has given any indication of posing a threat to national safety, or offering new technological data, or of originating from some extraterrestrial source. However, some of these files remain officially "open" and the investigations on them continue.

Dr. J. Allen Hynek, director of Dearborn Observatory at Northwestern University, who is heading up the Ann Arbor investigation for the Air Force, is an old hand at checking on flying saucers, for Bluebook. . . . Dr. Hynek notes that sighting reports usually do not originate with persons who believe in outerspace visitations. "Believers" don't need sightings to convince them, and are irritated by the embarrassment and skepticism with which most UFO spotters, like Frank Mannor, report what they believe they have seen.

"It is easy to dismiss the cases of birds, balloons, and the like," says Dr. Hynek, "but when good solid citizens report something puzzling, I believe we have an obligation to do as good a job as we can. I regard our 'Unidentifieds' as a sort of blot on the escutcheon. Somehow we scientists should be able to come up with answers for these things."

Major Quintanella, although certain that no evidence turned up to date has even hinted at spacecraft of unearthly origin, agrees that "it is impossible to prove that flying saucers do not exist." In any event, the Air Force is not about to give up chasing UFOs.

"We are spending millions to develop our own rocket boosters to get our spacecraft to the moon and beyond," says the major, smiling. "Imagine what a great help it would be to get our hands on a ship from another planet and examine its power plant."

# The Maury
# Island Episode . . .

*What happened at Maury Island? Edward J. Ruppelt,
in* The Report on Unidentified Flying Saucers, *gives
us one set of facts.*

. . . The report of the investigation of this incident, the Maury
Island Mystery, was one of the most detailed reports of the early
UFO era. The report that we had in our files had been pieced
together by Air Force Intelligence and other agencies because the
two intelligence officers who started the investigation couldn't finish it. They were dead.

For the Air Force the story started on July 31, 1947, when Lieutenant Frank Brown, an intelligence agent at Hamilton AFB, California, received a long-distance phone call. The caller was a man
whom I'll call Simpson who had met Brown when Brown investigated an earlier UFO sighting, and he had a hot lead on another
UFO incident. He had just talked to two Tacoma Harbor patrolmen. One of them had seen six UFO's hover over his patrol boat
and spew out chunks of odd metal. Simpson had some of the
pieces of the metal.

The story sounded good to Lieutenant Brown, so he reported it
to his chief. His chief OK'd a trip and within an hour Lieutenant
Brown and Captain Davidson were flying to Tacoma in an Air
Force B-25. When they arrived they met Simpson and an airline
pilot friend of his in Simpson's hotel room. After the usual round
of introductions Simpson told Brown and Davidson that he had
received a letter from a Chicago publisher asking him, Simpson, to
investigate this case. The publisher had paid him $200 and wanted

an exclusive on the story, but things were getting too hot, Simpson wanted the military to take over.

Simpson went on to say that he had heard about the experience off Maury Island but that he wanted Brown and Davidson to hear it first hand. He had called the two harbor patrolmen and they were on their way to the hotel. They arrived and they told their story.

I'll call these two men Jackson and Richards although these aren't their real names. In June 1947, Jackson said, his crew, his son, and the son's dog were on his patrol boat patrolling near Maury Island, an island in Puget Sound, about 3 miles from Tacoma. It was a gray day, with a solid cloud deck down at about 2,500 feet. Suddenly everyone on the boat noticed six "doughnut-shaped" objects, just under the clouds, headed toward the boat. They came closer and closer, and when they were about 500 feet over the boat they stopped. One of the doughnut-shaped objects seemed to be in trouble as the other five were hovering around it. They were close, and everybody got a good look. The UFO's were about 100 feet in diameter, with the "hole in the doughnut" being about 25 feet in diameter. They were a silver color and made absolutely no noise. Each object had large portholes around the edge.

As the five UFO's circled the sixth, Jackson recalled, one of them came in and appeared to make contact with the disabled craft. The two objects maintained contact for a few minutes, then began to separate. While this was going on, Jackson was taking photos. Just as they began to separate, there was a dull "thud" and the next second the UFO began to spew out sheets of very light metal from the hole in the center. As these were fluttering to the water, the UFO began to throw out a harder, corklike material. Some of it landed on the beach of Maury Island. Jackson took his crew and headed toward the beach of Maury Island, but not before the boat was damaged, his son's arm had been injured, and the dog killed. As they reached the island they looked up and saw that the UFO's were leaving the area at high sped. The harbor patrolman went on to tell how he scooped up several chunks of the metal from the beach and boarded the patrol boat. He tried to use his radio to summon aid, but for some unusual reason the interference was so bad he couldn't even call the three miles to his headquarters in

Tacoma. When they docked at Tacoma, Jackson got first aid for his son and then reported to his superior officer, Richards, who, Jackson added to his story, didn't believe the tale. He didn't believe it until he went out to the island himself and saw the metal. Jackson agreed.

Jackson's trouble wasn't over. The next morning a mysterious visitor told Jackson to forget what he'd seen.

Later that same day the photos were developed. They showed the six objects, but the film was badly spotted and fogged, as if the film had been exposed to some kind of radiation.

Then Simpson told about his brush with mysterious callers. He said that Jackson was not alone as far as mysterious callers were concerned, the Tacoma newspapers had been getting calls from an anonymous tipster telling exactly what was going on in Simpson's hotel room. This was a very curious situation because no one except Simpson, the airline pilot, and the two harbor patrolmen knew what was taking place. The room had even been thoroughly searched for hidden microphones.

That is the way the story stood a few hours after Lieutenant Brown and Captain Davidson arrived in Tacoma.

After asking Jackson and Richards a few questions, the two intelligence agents left, reluctant even to take any of the fragments. As some writers who have since written about this incident have said, Brown and Davidson seemed to be anxious to leave and afraid to touch the fragments of the UFO, as if they knew something more about them. The two officers went to McChord AFB, near Tacoma, where their B-25 was parked, held a conference with the intelligence officer at McChord, and took off for their home base, Hamilton. When they left McChord they had a good idea as to the identity of the UFO's. Fortunately they told the McChord intelligence officer what they had determined from their interview.

In a few hours the two officers were dead. The B-25 crashed near Kelso, Washington. The crew chief and a passenger had parachuted to safety. The newspapers hinted that the airplane was sabotaged and that it was carrying highly classified material. Authorities at McChord AFB confirmed this latter point, the airplane was carrying classified material.

In a few days the newspaper publicity on the crash died down, and the Maury Island Mystery was never publicly solved.

Later reports say that the two harbor patrolmen mysteriously disappeared soon after the fatal crash.

They should have disappeared, into Puget Sound. The whole Maury Island Mystery was a hoax. The first, possibly the second-best, and the dirtiest hoax in the UFO history. One passage in the detailed official report of the Maury Island Mystery says:

> Both ——— (the two harbor patrolmen) admitted that the rock fragments had nothing to do with flying saucers. The whole thing was a hoax. They had sent in the rock fragments [to a magazine publisher] as a joke. ——— One of the patrolmen wrote to ——— [the publisher] stating that the rock could have been part of a flying saucer. He had said the rock came from a flying saucer because that's what ——— [the publisher] wanted him to say.

The publisher, mentioned above, who, one of the two hoaxers said, wanted him to say that the rock fragments had come from a flying saucer, is the same one who paid the man I called Simpson $200 to investigate the case.

The report goes on to explain more details of the incident. Neither one of the two men could ever produce the photos. They "misplaced" them, they said. One of them, I forget which, was the mysterious informer who called the newspapers to report the conversations that were going on in the hotel room. Jackson's mysterious visitor didn't exist. Neither of the men was a harbor patrolman, they merely owned a couple of beat-up old boats that they used to salvage floating lumber from Puget Sound. The airplane crash was one of those unfortunate things. An engine caught on fire, burned off, and just before the two pilots could get out, the wing and tail tore off, making it impossible for them to escape. The two dead officers from Hamilton AFB smelled a hoax, accounting for their short interview and hesitancy in bothering to take the "fragment." They confirmed their convictions when they talked to the intelligence officer at McChord. It had already been established, through an informer, that the fragments were what Brown and Davidson thought, slag. The classified material on the B-25 was a file of reports the two officers offered to take back to Hamilton and had nothing to do with the Maury Island Mystery, or better, the Maury Island Hoax.

Simpson and his airline pilot friend weren't told about the hoax for one reason. As soon as it was discovered that they had been "taken," thoroughly, and were not a party to the hoax, no one wanted to embarrass them.

The majority of the writers of saucer lore have played this sighting to the hilt, pointing out as their main premise the fact that the story must be true because the government never openly exposed or prosecuted either of the two hoaxers. This is a logical premise, but a false one. The reason for the thorough investigation of the Maury Island Hoax was that the government had thought seriously of prosecuting the men. At the last minute it was decided, after talking to the two men, that the hoax was a harmless joke that had mushroomed, and that the loss of two lives and a B-25 could not be directly blamed on the two men. The story wasn't even printed because at the time of the incident, even though in this case the press knew about it, the facts were classed as evidence. By the time the facts were released they were yesterday's news. And nothing is deader than yesterday's news. . . .

# . . . Challenged . . .

*The preceding version is challenged by Harold
Wilkins in* Flying Saucers on the Attack.

. . . What happened to the fragments of Maury Island metal
which Chrisman said he had taken to his cabin in the mountains?
The mystery of this telephone caller, who may be identical with the
stranger who called on Dahl, is a minor aspect of the greater mystery of the nine queer machines whose appearances over Maury
Island — twice — seem to follow some sort of pattern. It seems
clear that the principles of their construction show an advanced
scientific knowledge whose theory is as much beyond us, now, as it
transcends anything we can put into aeronautical practice.

We do not know; but the evidence, or data that will be given,
later, in this book, about strange spherical or wheel-like machines
that have been seen to rise from the ocean several times in the
19th century, and logged by ships' captains and officers, and then
seen to soar into the skies may make one wonder — as Mr. Arnold himself has said: whether there be any strange connection
between these weird and mysterious amphibious spheres and the
vast dumps of furnace slag found on ocean-floors. If there is, then
these flying discs may dump and jettison metal elsewhere than in
uninhabited islands!

What was the line taken by the U.S. military authorities?

A military intelligence officer called on Mr. Arnold and took
away from him every piece of metal he had from Maury Island.
Mr. Arnold had planned to make a cigarette ash-tray from the
metal. The military man took Mr. Arnold to a smelter's works and
pointed out tons of material that, he said, "was exactly like the

fragments. It is only smelter's slag that you found in Maury Island," said the officer, smiling.

He did not explain how that could be when there is no smelter's works in this very sparsely populated island, nor is it used as a dumping-place. Further, no reference was made to the curious sixteen constituents of this metal from Maury Island. If what the officer alleged had been true, then smelter's slag must be a most amazing alloy, not to say a shocking waste of valuable metal on the part of any smelter knowing his business.

The absurd "subterfuge" of the officer was a pointer to the official attitude higher up in the U.S. Air Force. On April 27, 1949 — two years later, when the circumstances would not be so fresh in people's minds — Project Saucer's experts administered the knock-out blow:

> Chrisman and Dahl, under questioning, broke and admitted that the fragments were really unusual rock formations found on Maury Island, and had no connection with the "flying discs." They admitted telling the Chicago magazine that the fragments "could have been remnants of the discs," in order to increase the sale value of their story. During the investigation, Dahl's wife consistently urged him to admit that the entire affair was a hoax, and it is carried as such in Project Saucer's files.

It is likely that Chrisman and Dahl had been badly "grilled" by the investigators, and warned that their jobs in the Coast Guard were at stake, unless they recanted, like two modern American Galileos. Some of us are well aware that folk in America and in Britain have often perpetrated hoaxes in the last 80 or more years. The painful craze for publicity and the limelight at any cost account for most of them. Moreover, this alleged recantation would, were it true — and I do not believe it to be true — suggest that both Dahl and Chrisman must have *very* remarkable powers as fictionists.

I have been informed by a friend in Seattle, Washington, that Chrisman and Dahl vigorously denied this allegation of hoaxing. Dahl says: "It is a bald-faced lie for the Air Force to say that I broke under questioning, and admitted that the fragments of the saucers were merely rock formations found in Maury Island. What happened to the fragments of the metal that were in the crashed 'plane? Why have not I and Chrisman been prosecuted if we were such rascals as to have perpetrated a story that led to the death of two U.S. Air Force pilots, and the loss of a 'plane valued at over $150,000?"

Chrisman also points out that, soon after the 'plane had crashed, he was ordered to fly to Alaska in an Army 'plane. Was this likely, had he really been guilty of a hoax that led to so tragic an affair?

I wrote an air mail letter from Bexleyheath, Kent, England, to Chrisman, at Tacoma, on 23 January 1951, pointing out that I was writing a book in which I should deal with the strange Maury Island adventure. Would he be so good as to give me *his* story and a refutation of the libel upon him in the U.S. Air Force release to the press?

It is significant of the censorship that was being applied by the U.S. Army authorities — as, also, was being done in Great Britain, by the various Air Ministries, in 1951 — for me to record what did *not* happen in this inquiry!

My letter duly arrived at Tacoma, and was returned from the Dead Letter Office, at Tacoma, Washington, on March 19, 1951, arriving back at my English address, in Kent, on April 7, 1951. I had endorsed the front of my air letter asking that it be forwarded to Mr. Chrisman's private address, if he were no longer in the U.S. Coastguard Service. Someone at Tacoma had written on the letter: "Not Coast Guard." The Tacoma postal authorities imprint on it the word: "Rebuts," and "Parti" (gone away), and it is returned to me, undelivered. Yet, it is *certain* that someone in the Coast Guard Service at Tacoma knew where Mr. Chrisman had gone, and declined to forward the letter to him. If all Mr. Chrisman's private correspondence be treated in this way by the U.S. authorities at Tacoma, he must suffer considerable inconvenience, if not actual loss.

Why this U.S. official rendering of Mr. Chrisman, who is an honourable man, *incommunicado?* Of what is the U.S. Air Force, a branch of the U.S. Army, afraid? What does it desire to conceal? I have also not been able to make any contact with Mr. Dahl.

I have this letter in my files, and anyone, who is concerned, may inspect it. . . .

# Marsh Gas
# in Michigan . . .

*A recent report in* Newsweek (*April 4, 1966*) *of a sighting in Michigan is explained by the Air Force as marsh gas.*

For more than a week, and almost always from the sparsely populated swamplands that abound in the countryside around Ann Arbor, Michigan, the reports piled in. The first sighting was made at the village of Dexter — there a shimmering, strangely lighted vehicle seemed to glide in and land just like something from outer space.

Next there came a series of strange lights in the skies in other nearby areas, and sheriffs' deputies who watched from three counties were convinced that something unearthly was afoot. "We would not have believed it if we had not seen it with our own eyes," they said. "These objects could move at fantastic speeds, make very sharp turns, dive and climb and hover with great maneuverability." Three days later, a deputy in Washtenaw County set up a 16-mm. Minox camera with a telephoto lens and photographed two of the strange lights from a distance of about 5 miles. Then, while the film from this experiment was being developed, a similar visitation descended upon Frank Mannor, 47, a truck driver who lives in a ramshackle farmhouse at the end of a mile-long dirt road near Dexter. Mannor offered this account:

"We was all in looking at television about 7:30 P.M., when the dogs began raising Cain outside. I went outside to holler at them, and when I turned back I saw this meteor. . . . It stopped and settled to the ground, then rose again. It was about a half mile away. I called my wife and kids out and we watched it for fifteen minutes. I got my son, Ronnie, and we put on our galoshes and headed out toward the lights.

"We got to about 500 yards of the thing. It was sort of shaped like a pyramid, with a blue-green light on the right hand side and on the left a white light. I didn't see no antenna or porthole. The body was like a yellowish coral rock and looked like it had holes in it — sort of like if you took a piece of cardboard box and split it open. You couldn't see it too good, because it was surrounded with heat waves, like you see on the desert. The white light turned to a blood red as we got close to it, and Ron said, 'Look at that horrible thing.' "

Tension: The Mannors chased the "thing" but never caught it. Calls to the police, the Air Force, and the university came pouring in. One night, a University of Michigan scientist sat in his car and blinked the universal "pi" equation in code, explaining that this could be understood by unearthly creatures. On another night, 87 Hillsdale College co-eds reported similar lights and apparitions in a swamp near their school.

But while the tension mounted in rural Michigan, the U.S. Air Force was on the way. Late in the week, Dr. J. Allen Hynek, scientific consultant to the USAF's "Project Bluebook," (which keeps tabs on reports of unidentified flying objects, and has recorded 10,147 such reports since 1947), finished his investigation and held a press conference.

In a five-page statement, Hynek said he felt certain that the two strongest sightings — those at the Mannor farm and at Hillsdale College — were caused by marsh gas. "Rotting vegetation produces the marsh gas, which can be trapped by ice and winter conditions," Hynek continued. "When a spring thaw occurs, the gas may be released in some quantity. The flame is a form of chemical luminescence and its low temperature is one of its peculiar features." As for the pictures of the two lights taken by the deputy sheriff, Hynek said, they were "without any question" trails made on the time-exposed film by light from the rising crescent moon and from Venus.

Loopholes: These theories seemed to satisfy most of the skeptics around Dexter and Ann Arbor, but there were some who noted that Hynek, like any good scientist, had been careful to leave himself at least two loopholes. "I emphasize in conclusion," he said, "that I cannot prove in a court of law that this is a full explanation of these sightings." And when someone asked him if the Air Force had anything around that could be mistaken for flying saucers, Hynek replied, smiling: "You'll have to ask the Secretary of the Air Force about that."

# . . . Questioned . . .

*The conclusion reached in the preceding selection is challenged in an editorial in the April 9, 1966, edition of* America.

Michigan Congressman Gerald R. Ford's call for a "full-blown" Congressional inquiry into the Air Force investigation of Michigan's headline-making "flying saucers" has lifted this latest UFO (Unidentified Flying Object) incident out of the routine category. Certainly somebody, if not the Congress, should look into it.

So far, we have seen no further confirmation of New York *Journal-American* staffer Mort Young's story that Dr. J. Allen Hynek, the Northwestern University astrophysicist who has headed the Air Force UFO investigations for 18 years, threatened to quit the project because the official "marsh gas" explanation was forced on him. Well he might. William Van Horn, the Hillsdale County Civil Defense director who saw one of the Michigan UFO's for himself, says he has lived in the area long enough to know swamp gas when he sees it. The same could be said of many of the Michigan witnesses to the phenomena.

Moreover, can swamp gas be picked up on the radar screens at Willow Run airport? Does swamp gas have a surface "pitted like coral rock," as farmer Frank Mannor and his son described the glowing object they approached to within 500 yards of? No wonder other Michigan "saucer" witnesses, such as Hillsdale College Director of Public Affairs Milton H. Ferguson, call the Air Force "marsh gas" explanation an attempt "to explain it away arbitrarily . . . whitewash."

Whatever you may think of UFO's — and frankly we don't

know what to think — the picture of Michigan's football-shaped, car-sized "saucer" drawn from witnesses' descriptions tallies almost perfectly with other reputable and now classic descriptions. It is, for instance, practically a perfect mate to the "saucer" that landed at Marseilles' Marignane airport in the early morning hours of October 27, 1952, and was seen at a distance of 50 yards by customs officer Gabriel Gachignard.

Before the Michigan UFO is quietly buried in the pages of the Air Force Blue Book as just another "unidentified flying object," we hope Congressman Ford, or somebody, can force a wholesale review of the whole UFO phenomenon. It's been around a long time.

# The Air Force
# and the Scientific
# Community

*J. Allen Hynek, chairman of the Department of
Astronomy at Northwestern University, is the
scientific consultant to Project Blue Book, but does
not always see eye to eye with its conclusions. In
this article from the December 17, 1966, issue of*
The Saturday Evening Post *he elaborates his own
personal beliefs and those of his fellow scientists, and
tells his side of the story of the Michigan "marsh gas"
incidents.*

On August 25, 1966, an Air Force officer in charge of a missile
crew in North Dakota suddenly found that his radio transmission
was being interrupted by static. At the time, he was sheltered in a
concrete capsule 60 feet below the ground. While he was trying to
clear up the problem, other Air Force personnel on the surface
reported seeing a UFO — an unidentified flying object — high in
the sky. It had a bright red light, and it appeared to be alternately
climbing and descending. Simultaneously, a radar crew on the
ground picked up the UFO at 100,000 feet.

So begins a truly puzzling UFO report — one that is not ex-
plainable as it now stands by such familiar causes as a balloon,
aircraft, satellite, or meteor. "When the UFO climbed, the static
stopped," stated the report made by the base's director of operations. "The UFO began to swoop and dive. It then appeared to

land ten to fifteen miles south of the area. Missile-site control sent a strike team [well-armed Air Force guards] to check. When the team was about ten miles from the landing site, static disrupted radio contact with them. Five to eight minutes later the glow diminished, and the UFO took off. Another UFO was visually sighted and confirmed by radar. The one that was first sighted passed beneath the second. Radar also confirmed this. The first made for altitude toward the north, and the second seemed to disappear with the glow of red."

This incident, which was not picked up by the press, is typical of the puzzling cases that I have studied during the 18 years that I have served as the Air Force's scientific consultant on the problem of UFO's. What makes the report especially arresting is the fact that another incident occurred near the base a few days earlier. A police officer — a reliable man — saw in broad daylight what he called "an object on its edge floating down the side of a hill, wobbling from side to side about ten feet from the ground. When it reached the valley floor, it climbed to about one hundred feet, still tipped on its edge, and moved across the valley to a small reservoir."

The object, which was about 30 feet in diameter, next appeared to flatten out, and a small dome became visible on top. It hovered over the water for about a minute, then moved to a small field, where it appeared to be landing. It did not touch the ground, however, but hovered at a height of about 10 feet some 250 feet away from the witness, who was standing by his parked patrol car. The object then tilted up and disappeared rapidly into the clouds. A fantastic story, yet I interviewed the witness in this case and am personally satisfied that he is above reproach.

During the years that I have been its consultant, the Air Force has consistently argued that UFO's were either hoaxes, hallucinations, or misinterpretations of natural phenomena. For the most part I would agree with the Air Force. As a professional astronomer — I am chairman of the department of astronomy at Northwestern University — I have had no trouble explaining the vast majority of the reported sightings.

But I cannot explain them all. Of the 15,000 cases that have come to my attention, several hundred are puzzling, and some of the puzzling incidents, perhaps one in 25, are bewildering. I have wanted to learn much more about these cases than I have been able to get from either the reports or the witnesses.

These special cases have been reported by highly respected, intelligent people who often had technical training — astronomers, airport-tower operators, anthropologists, Air Force officers, FBI personnel, physicians, meteorologists, pilots, radar operators, test pilots, and university professors. I have argued for years within the Air Force that these unusual cases needed much more study than they were getting. Now, finally, the Air Force has begun a serious scientific investigation of the UFO phenomena.

The public, I am certain, wants to know what to believe — what *can* be believed — about the "flying-saucer" stories that seem to be growing more sensational all the time. With all loyalty to the Air Force, and with a deep appreciation of its problems, I now feel it my duty to discuss the UFO mystery fully and frankly. I speak as a scientist with unique experience. To the best of my knowledge, I am the only scientist who has spent nearly 20 years monitoring the UFO situation in this and other countries and who has also read many thousands of reports and personally interviewed many sighters of UFO's.

Getting at the truth of "flying saucers" has been extraordinarily difficult because the subject automatically engenders such instantaneous reactions and passionate beliefs. Nearly all of my scientific colleagues, I regret to say, have scoffed at the reports of UFO's as so much balderdash, although this was a most unscientific reaction since virtually none of them had ever studied the evidence. Until recently my friends in the physical sciences wouldn't even discuss UFO's with me. The subject, in fact, rarely came up. My friends were obviously mystified as to how I, a scientist, could have gotten mixed up with "flying saucers" in the first place. It was a little as though I had been an opera singer who had suddenly taken it into his head to perform in a cabaret. It was all too embarrassing to bring up in polite conversation.

While the scientists were chuckling at UFO's, a number of groups of zealous citizens were telling the public that "flying saucers" did indeed exist. The believers in UFO's charged the Air Force with concealing the existence of "flying saucers" to avoid a public panic. Since I was the Air Force's consultant, these groups accused me of selling out as a scientist, because I did not admit that UFO's existed. I was the Air Force's stooge, its tame astronomer, a man more concerned with preserving his consultant's fee than with disclosing the truth to the public.

I received many letters attacking me for not attacking the Air Force. One typical writer pointed out that as a scientist my first allegiance was to "fact." He went on to state, "Any person who has closely followed the UFO story knows that many reports have been 'explained away' in a manner that can only be called ludicrous."

Another typical letter declared: "In spite of the fact that the [Air Force] claims (or is instructed to claim) that UFO's do not exist, I think that common sense tells most of us that they do. There have been too many responsible people through the years that have had terrifying experiences involving UFO's. I think our Government insults the intelligence of our people in keeping information regarding UFO's from them."

The question of UFO's has developed into a battle of faiths. One side, which is dedicated to the Air Force position and backed up by the "scientific establishment," *knows* that UFO's do not exist; the other side *knows* that UFO's represent something completely new in human experience. And then we have the rest of the world, the great majority of people who, if they think about the subject at all, don't know what to think.

The question of whether or not UFO's exist should not be a battle of faiths. It must be a subject for calm, reasoned, scientific analysis.

In 1948, when I first heard of the UFO's, I thought they were sheer nonsense, as any scientist would have. Most of the early reports were quite vague: "I went into the bathroom for a drink of water and looked out of the window and saw a bright light in the sky. It was moving up and down and sideways. When I looked again, it was gone."

At the time, I was director of the observatory at Ohio State University in Columbus. One day I had a visit from several men from the technical center at Wright-Patterson Air Force Base, which was only 60 miles away in Dayton. With some obvious embarrassment, the men eventually brought up the subject of "flying saucers" and asked me if I would care to serve as consultant to the Air Force on the matter.

The job didn't seem as though it would take too much time, so I agreed. When I began reviewing cases, I assumed that there was a natural explanation for all of the sightings — or at least there would be if we could find out enough data about the more puzzling incidents. I generally subscribed to the Air Force view that the sightings were the results of misidentifications, hoaxes, or hallucinations.

During the next few years I had no trouble explaining or discarding most of the cases referred to me, but a few were baffling enough to make me wonder — cases that the Air Force would later carry as "unidentified." Let me emphasize the point that the Air Force made up its own mind on each case; I merely submitted an opinion. I soon found that the Air Force had a tendency to upgrade its preliminary explanations while compiling its yearly summaries; a "possible" aircraft often became a "probable" aircraft. I was reminded of the Greek legend of Procrustes, who tried to fit all men to his single bed. If they were too long, he chopped them off; if they were too short, he stretched them out.

Public statements to the contrary, the Air Force has never really devoted enough money or attention to the problem of UFO's to get to the bottom of the puzzling cases. The Air Force's UFO evaluation program, known as "Project Blue Book," is housed in one room at Wright-Patterson. For most of its history Project Blue Book has been headed by a captain. This fact alone will tell anyone familiar with military procedures the relative position of Project Blue Book on the Air Force's organization chart. The staff, which has usually consisted of two officers and a sergeant, has had to try to decide, on the basis of sketchy statements, the causes of all UFO sightings reported to the Air Force. From 1947 through 1965, Project Blue Book reviewed 10,147 cases. Using the Air Force's criteria, the project identified 9,501, leaving over 600 that were carried as unidentified.

By 1952 my feeling that the Air Force was not investigating the reports seriously enough led me to write a paper suggesting that the subject deserved much closer study. In 1953 the Air Force did give UFO's more attention, although not nearly enough, to my mind. A panel of some of the top scientists in the country was assembled under the direction of Howard P. Robertson, a distinguished physicist from Cal Tech. The Robertson panel discussed UFO's for four days. Most of the cases, incidentally, were not as puzzling as some of the ones we have now. What was more, the panel was given only 15 reports for detailed study out of the several hundred that had been made up to that time, although it did quickly review many others. This was akin to asking Madame Curie to examine a small fraction of the pitchblende she distilled and still expecting her to come out with radium.

I was listed as an associate member of the panel, but my role was really more that of an observer. After completing its brief survey, the panel concluded that "the evidence presented on unidentified flying objects showed no indication that these phenomena constitute a direct physical threat to the national security," and that "we firmly believe there is no residuum of cases which indicate phenomena which are attributable to foreign artifacts capable of hostile acts, and that there is no evidence that the phenomena indicated a need for revision of current scientific concepts." It is interesting to note the phrase "we firmly believe," a phrase more appropriate to the cloth than to the scientific fraternity.

The Robertson report immediately became the main justification of the Air Force's position — there is nothing to worry about — and it so remains to this day. I was not asked to sign the report, but I would not have signed if I had been asked. I felt that the question was more complicated than the panel believed, and that history might look back someday and say that the panel had acted hastily. The men took just four days to make a judgment upon a perplexing subject that I had studied for more than five years without being able to solve to my satisfaction.

In 1953, the year of the Robertson report, there occurred one of the most puzzling cases that I have studied. It was reported first in Black Hawk, S. Dak., and then in Bismarck, N. Dak., during the night of August 5 and the early morning of August 6. A number of persons in Black Hawk reported seeing several strange objects in the sky. What made these reports particularly significant was the fact that these people were trained observers — they were part of the national network of civilians who were keeping watch for enemy bombers.

At approximately the same time, unidentified blips showed up on the radarscope at Ellsworth Air Force Base, which is near Black Hawk. An airborne F-84 fighter was vectored into the area and reported seeing the UFO's. The pilot radioed that one of the objects appeared to be over Piedmont, S. Dak., and was moving twice as fast as his jet fighter. It was "brighter than the brightest star" he had ever seen. When the pilot gave chase, the light "just disappeared." Five civilians on the ground, who had watched the jet chase the light, confirmed the pilot's report.

Later a second F-84 was sent aloft and directed toward the UFO, which still showed on ground radar. After several minutes, the pilot reported seeing an object with a light of varying intensity that alternated from white to green. While the pilot was pursuing the UFO, he noted that his gunsight light had flashed on, indicating that his plane's radar was picking up a target. The object was directly ahead of his aircraft but at a slightly greater altitude. It then climbed very rapidly. When the pilot saw he was hopelessly losing ground, he broke off the chase. Radar operators on the ground tracked the fighter coming back from the chase, while the UFO continued on out of range of the scope.

As the object sped off to the north, Ellsworth Air Force Base notified the spotters' control center in Bismarck, 220 miles to the north, where a sergeant then went out on the roof and saw a UFO. The Air Force had no planes in Bismarck that could be sent after the UFO, which finally disappeared later that night.

I investigated this reported sighting myself and was unable to find a satisfactory explanation. In my report, I noted that "the entire incident, in my opinion, has too much of an *Alice in Wonderland* flavor for comfort."

It was about this time that some firm believers in UFO's became disgusted with the Air Force and decided to take matters into their own hands, much like the vigilantes of the Old West; they organized "to do the job the Air Force was mishandling." These groups, composed of people with assorted backgrounds, were often the recipients of intriguing reports that never came to the official attention of

Project Blue Book. The first group of this kind in the United States was the APRO (Aerial Phenomena Research Organization), founded in 1952 and still going strong, as is NICAP (National Investigations Committee on Aerial Phenomena), which was organized several years later.

As the years went by, I learned more and more about the global nature of UFO sightings. At first I had assumed that it was a purely American phenomenon, like swallowing goldfish. But reports of sightings kept coming in from around the world until 70 countries were on the list. As a scientist, I naturally was interested in correlating all of the data; a zoologist studying red ants in Utah, say, wants to find out about a new species found along the Amazon. But when I suggested to the Air Force that the air attachés abroad be used to gather reports on foreign sightings, I was turned down. No one in a position of authority seemed to want to take up the time of the officers with such an embarrassing subject.

Gradually I began to accumulate cases that I really couldn't explain, cases reported by reliable, sincere people whom I often interviewed in person. I found that the persons making these reports were not acquainted with UFO's before their experience, which baffled and thoroughly frightened them. Fearing ridicule, they were often reluctant to report the sighting and did so only out of a sense of duty and a tremendous desire to get a rational explanation for their irrational experience. One typical letter to me concluded with the sentence: "Hoping you don't think I'm nuts, but not caring if you do, Sincerely," . . .

We had many reports from people of good repute, yet we had no scientifically incontrovertible evidence — authenticated movies, spectrograms of reported lights, "hardware" — on which to make a judgment. There are no properly authenticated photographs to match any of the vivid prose descriptions of visual sightings. Some of the purported "photographs" are patent hoaxes. Others show little detail; they could be anything. Some show a considerable amount of detail, but cannot be substantiated.

The evidence for UFO's, then, was entirely without physical proof. But were *all* of the responsible citizens who made reports mistaken or victims of hallucinations? It was an intriguing scientific question, yet I couldn't find any scientists to discuss it with.

The general view of the scientists was that UFO's couldn't exist, therefore they didn't exist, therefore let's laugh off the idea. This, of course, is a violation of scientific principles, but the history of science is filled with such instances. Some scientists refused to look through Galileo's telescope at sunspots, explaining that "since the sun was perfect, it couldn't have spots, and therefore it was no use looking for them." Other scientists refused to believe in the existence of meteorites; who would be foolish enough to think that a stone could fall from the sky?

From time to time I would urge the Air Force to make a more thorough study of the phenomenon, but nothing ever came of it. I began to feel a very real sense of frustration. As the years went by, I continued to find cases that puzzled me while I examined reports for Project Blue Book. People who were afraid that the Air Force would scoff at their reports began sending me letters that were often detailed and well written about their experiences. The Air Force never attempted to influence my view on any case, but occasionally the service would disregard my evaluations. What was more, I was not consulted on some key cases. (One of the most recent was the well-publicized incident involving two policemen in Ravenna, Ohio, last spring.)

Then, from 1958 through 1963, the UFO reports began to diminish in quality as well as quantity, and I felt that perhaps the "flying-saucer" era was at last on the wane and would soon vanish. But since 1964 there has been a sharp rally in the number of puzzling sightings. The more impressive cases seem to fit into a pattern. The UFO's had a bright red glow. They hovered a few feet off the ground, emitting a high-pitched whine. Animals in the vicinity were terrified, often before the UFO's became visible to the people who later reported the incident. When the objects at last began to disappear, they vanished in a matter of seconds.

A very real paradox was now beginning to develop. As the Air Force's consultant, I was acquiring a reputation in the public eye of being a debunker of UFO's. Yet, privately, I was becoming more and more concerned over the fact that people with good reputations, who had no possible hope of gain from reporting a UFO, continued to describe "out-of-this-world" incidents.

In July, 1965, I wrote a letter to the Air Force calling again for a systematic study of the phenomenon. "I feel it is my responsibility to point out," I said, "that enough puzzling sightings have been reported by intelligent and often technically competent people to warrant closer attention than Project Blue Book can possibly encompass at the present time."

Then, in March of this year, came the reports of the now-celebrated "swamp-gas" sightings in Michigan. On two separate nights, at spots separated by 63 miles, nearly 100 people reported seeing red, yellow, and green lights glowing over swampy areas. When I received the first accounts of the UFO's, I recognized at once that my files held far better, more coherent and more articulate reports than these. Even so, the incident was receiving such great attention in the press that I went to Michigan with the hope that here was a case that I could use to focus scientific attention on the UFO problem. I wanted the scientists to consider the phenomenon.

But when I arrived in Michigan, I soon discovered that the situation was so charged with emotion that it was impossible for me to do any really serious investigation. The Air Force left me almost completely on my own, which meant that I sometimes had to fight my way through the clusters of reporters who were surrounding the key witnesses whom I had to interview.

The entire region was gripped with near-hysteria. One night at midnight I found myself in a police car racing toward a reported sighting. We had radio contact with other squad cars in the area. "I see it" from one car, "there it is" from another, "it's east of the river near Dexter" from a third. Occasionally even *I* thought I glimpsed "it."

Finally several squad cars met at an intersection. Men spilled out and pointed excitedly at the sky. "See — there it is! It's moving!"

But it wasn't moving. "It" was the star Arcturus, undeniably identified by its position in relation to the handle of the Big Dipper. A sobering demonstration for me.

In the midst of this confusion, I got a message from the Air Force: There would be a press conference, and I would issue a statement about the cause of the sightings. It did me no good to protest, to say that as yet I had no real idea what had caused the reported sightings in the swamps. I was to have a press conference, ready or not.

Searching for a justifiable explanation of the sightings, I remembered a phone call from a botanist at the University of Michigan, who called to my attention the phenomenon of burning "swamp gas." This gas, caused by decaying vegetation, has been known to ignite spontaneously and to cast a flickering light. The glow is well-known in song and story as "jack-o'-lantern," "fox fire," and "will-o'-the-wisp." After learning more about swamp gas from other Michigan scientists, I decided that it was a "possible" explanation that I would offer to the reporters.

The press conference, however, turned out to be no place for scholarly discussion; it was a circus. The TV cameramen wanted me in one spot, the newspapermen wanted me in another, and for a while both groups were actually tugging at me. Everyone was clamoring for a single, spectacular explanation of the sightings. They wanted little green men. When I handed out a statement that discussed swamp gas, many of the men simply ignored the fact that I said it was a "possible" reason. I watched with horror as one reporter scanned the page, found the phrase "swamp gas," underlined it, and rushed for a telephone.

Too many of the stories the next day not only said that swamp gas was definitely the cause of the Michigan lights but implied that it was the cause of other UFO sightings as well. I got out of town as quickly and as quietly as I could.

I suppose that the swamp-gas incident, which has become a subject for cartoons that I greatly enjoy, was the low point of my association with UFO's. The experience was very obvious proof that public excitement had mounted to the point that it was ridiculous to expect one professor, working alone in the field, to conduct a scholarly investigation. We had quite clearly reached a new stage in the UFO problem.

Three weeks after the Michigan incident I appeared before a hearing into UFO's that was conducted by the House Committee on Armed Services. I pointed out to the committee that I had a dossier of "twenty particularly well-reported UFO cases which, despite the character, technical competence and the number of witnesses, I have not been able to explain." Ten of these reports were made by scientists or by highly trained individuals, five were made by members of the armed services or police, and five were made by other reliable people. The committee urged the Air Force to give continued attention to the subject and was assured by Air Secretary Dr. Harold Brown that it would.

A serious inquiry into the nature of UFO's would be justified, in my opinion, just on the basis of the puzzling cases that have been reported during the last two years. It seems to me that there are now four possible explanations for the phenomena:

First, they are utter nonsense, the result of hoaxes or hallucinations. This, of course, is the view that a number of my scientific colleagues have taken. I think that enough evidence has piled up to shift the burden of proof to the critics who cry fraud. And if the UFO's are merely hallucinations, they still deserve intensive study; we need to learn how the minds of so many men so widely separated can be so deluded over so many years.

Second, the UFO's are some kind of military weapon being tested in secret. This theory is easily dispensed with. Secret devices are usually tested in very limited geographical areas. Why should the United States, or any other country, test them in scores of nations? The problem of preventing a security leak would be impossible.

Third, the UFO's are really from outer space. I agree with the Air Force. There is no incontrovertible evidence, as far as I can see, to say that we have strange visitors. But it would be foolish to rule out the possibility absolutely.

Solely for the sake of argument, let me state the case in its most favorable light. We all suffer from cosmic provincialism — the notion that we on this earth are somehow unique. Why should our sun be the only star in the universe to support intelligent life, when the number of stars is a 1 followed by 20 zeros?

Stars are born, grow old, and die, and it now seems that the formation of planetary systems is part of this evolutionary process. You would expect to find planets around a star just as you find kittens around a cat or acorns around an oak. Suppose that only one star in 10 is circled by a planetary system that has life; that means that the number of life-supporting stars in the universe would be a 1 followed by 19 zeros.

We also know that some stars are many millions of years older than our sun, which means that life elsewhere in the universe may have evolved many millions of years beyond our present state. That could mean that other planets in other solar systems may have solved the problem of aging, which we are beginning to grapple with even now. If a life span reached 10,000 years, let us say, a space journey of 200 or 300 years would be relatively short. In that time it would be possible to get from some distant planetary systems to ours.

A highly advanced civilization, such as the one I am postulating, would naturally keep an eye on the progress of life elsewhere in its galaxy. Any signs of unusual scientific progress might be reason enough to send a reconnaissance vehicle to find out what was going on. It so happens that in recent years we have made a very important advance of this kind: the development of the use of nuclear energy.

This is still "science fiction," of course, but let me take the story a step further. Some skeptics who scoff at reported UFO sightings often ask why the "flying saucers" don't try to communicate with us. One answer might be: Why should they? We wouldn't try to communicate with a new species of kangaroo we might find in Australia; we would just observe the animals.

Is there any connection between the reported UFO sightings and the scientific probability of life elsewhere in our galaxy? I don't know. I find no compelling evidence for it, but I don't rule it out automatically.

The fourth possible explanation of UFO's is that we are dealing with some kind of natural phenomenon that we as yet cannot explain or even conceive of. Think how our knowledge of the universe has changed in 100 years. In 1866 we not only knew nothing about nuclear energy, we didn't even know that the atom had a nucleus. Who would have dreamed 100 years ago that television would be invented? Who can say what startling facts we will learn about our world in the next 100 years?

All of these possibilities deserve serious consideration and now, at long last, they will get it. In October the Air Force announced that a thorough investigation of UFO's will be conducted at the University of Colorado by a team of distinguished scientists, headed by Dr. Edward Condon, the former director of the National Bureau of Standards.

I cannot help but feel a small sense of personal triumph and vindication. The night the appointment was announced, my wife and I went out and had a few drinks to celebrate.

I am particularly pleased that the Condon committee will have time to work into the problem because I cannot consider anyone qualified to speak authoritatively on the total UFO phenomenon unless he has read at least a few thousand original (not summarized) reports, and is thoroughly acquainted with the global nature of reported UFO sightings. The truly puzzling and outstanding UFO reports are few in number compared to the welter of poor reports.

Recently I had dinner with several members of the Condon committee. What a pleasure it was to sit down with men who were open-minded about UFO's, who did not look at me as though I were a Martian myself. For the first time other scientists, who apparently have been wondering all along, have openly talked about the reports. One leading scientist wrote me the other day: "For some time now I have been convinced of the reality of this phenomenon based on reports in the general news media. It has seemed to me that even with a heavy discount there is a core of reliable observations which we cannot shrug off. Twice in recent weeks I have stated my views on the subject in small conversational groups of respectable, scholarly friends, and found that they were amazed that I should take these matters seriously. So I know that it took some courage for you to speak out."

I would like to suggest two more steps to help solve the UFO problem:

First, all of the valuable data that we have accumulated — good reports from all over the world — must be computerized so that we can rapidly compare new sightings with old and trace patterns of UFO behavior.

Second, we need good photographs of UFO's. Although the Air Force has probably spent less on UFO's so far than it has on wastebaskets, I realize that it is impractical to expect the service to set up a costly "flying-saucer" surveillance system across the country. When a UFO is spotted, the terrified witness usually picks up the phone at once and calls the local police, who have missed dozens of opportunities in the past to record the phenomena on film. I recommend that every police chief in the country make sure that at least one of his squad cars carries in its glove compartment a camera loaded with color film. The cameras, which could also be used for regular police work, might be furnished by civic or service groups. (I carry a camera in my briefcase at all times.)

Finally, I would like to emphasize my views on a controversial subject. During all of my years of association with the Air Force, I have never seen any evidence for the charge about UFO's most often leveled against the service: that there is deliberate cover-up of knowledge of space visitors to prevent the public from panicking. The entire history of the Air Force and the UFO's can be understood only if we realize that the Pentagon has never believed that UFO's could be anything novel, and it still doesn't. The working hypothesis of the Air Force has been that the stimulus behind every UFO report (apart from out-and-out hoaxes and a few hallucinations) is a misidentification of a conventional object or a natural phenomenon. It is just as simple as that.

Now, after a delay of 18 years, the Air Force and American science are about to try for the first time, really, to discover what, if anything, we can believe about "flying saucers."

# The
# Killian Case . . .

*The Killian case as reported by Donald Keyhoe in*
Flying Saucers: Top Secret.

The DC-6 was an hour out of Newark when the captain first saw
the UFOs.

It was February 24, 1959; the time, 8:20 P.M.

Until then, the trip had been routine. The nonstop Detroit flight,
American Airlines 713, had departed from Newark on schedule. In
command was a four-million-miler, Captain Peter W. Killian, fifteen years on the airlines. Riding the co-pilot's right-hand seat was
First Officer John Dee.

By 8:15, the two stewardesses, Edna LeGate and Beverly Pin-
gree, had finished serving dinner to the thirty-five passengers
aboard. The flight was then over Pennsylvania, the roar of its four
engines subdued to a drone in the airliner's sound-proofed cabin.

At 8:19, the plane passed over Bradford; altitude 8,500 feet, air
speed 350. Scattered clouds, more than 3,000 feet below, occasionally hid the ground. But on all sides and above the plane the
sky was perfectly clear.

Suddenly, Captain Killian noticed three brilliant lights. They
were south of the plane, higher, and in a precise line.* For an instant, he thought he was seeing Orion. Then he sat up quickly.
These were not stars. They were powerful lights on moving objects.

He could see Orion, higher up in the sky. In contrast, the strange
flying objects were huge — not only larger, but brighter. Their
color, too, was different, an intense yellowish white.

* Details confirmed in NICAP interviews with Captain Killian. Published
report on file.

*220*

Abruptly, one flying object left the formation. As it came toward the plane, Killian prepared for a hasty turn. But it slowed, some distance away, apparently observing the DC-6.

Killian knew now it was a UFO — some unknown machine, under intelligent control. He could not be sure, but it seemed at least triple the size of the plane.

As swiftly as it had approached, the UFO rejoined the formation. Not until then did Killian tell First Officer Dee about the objects. While Dee watched them, Killian cut in the intercom. It seemed wiser to warn the passengers; in case the mysterious machines came closer, there would be less chance of panic. He made a calm announcement, then had the cabin lights turned out for a better view of the UFOs. . . .

He stopped. One of the UFOs was moving toward them again.

"We'll hold course," Killian said. "I think it's just pacing us."

This time the machine seemed to come closer. Though the glow was not blinding, Killian could not see behind it. But he knew that whoever controlled the UFO must be watching them intently. It was not a comfortable feeling. He was relieved when the object raced back to join the others.

On a sudden hunch, he put out a radio call, asking if other airline flights could see the UFOs. In seconds, an answer came from an American Airlines captain flying north of Erie.

"We've been watching the formation for ten minutes," he reported. "I'll give you their bearing — you can figure their approximate speed."

When he finished, another American captain called in. His flight was near Toledo, and he had sighted the UFOs after hearing Killian's alert.

Before Killian landed, he sent a UFO report to American Airlines at Detroit. He intended to keep the story quiet, but an aviation expert aboard — Mr. N. D. Puncas, manager of a Curtiss Wright plant — tipped off the Detroit papers.

"I saw these three objects in a clear sky," he told reporters. "They were round, and in precise formation. I've never seen anything like it."

Since the news had broken, an American Airlines executive told

Killian to give out his report. Press wires quickly carried the story around the country.

Next morning, a Detroit member of NICAP called my home, near Alexandria, Virginia, and gave me the main details. I rang up the office, got our associate editor, Richard Hall. He told me an Akron member had just wired a similar report.

"Three United Airlines crews saw that formation, too," said Hall. "Captain A. D. Yates gave it out when he landed at Akron last night, and Flight Engineer L. E. Baney confirmed it. Flights 937 and 321 agreed the things weren't any known aircraft."

When the Air Force Press Desk refused to comment on the Killian story, I called a Washington news correspondent, a man with good sources in most government departments. In 1952, he had tipped me off to the famous Utah pictures — a color movie of a UFO formation, taken by a Navy photographer. To protect him and his news contacts, I'll call him Henry Brennard.

When I reached him, he had already seen the Killian story. I told him about the United Airlines confirmation.

"Six airline crews!" said Brennard. "It's really building up."

"Could you find out what the Air Force is going to say? If there's a cover-up, and we could tell certain congressmen —"

"Who you working with now?" Brennard cut in.

I told him, then added, "Also, we've promised the names of key witnesses and proof of the censorship to the Senate Preparedness Committee."

"Meaning Senator Lyndon Johnson."

"Yes. Nothing definite yet, but his staff's looking into it."

"Okay, I'll see what I can do."

When I reached the office, Hall was talking on the phone. A lean, red-haired, laconic New Englander, an honor graduate of Tulane University, he had served two years in the Air Force. Since then, he had accumulated a large file of verified UFO evidence, and eight months as NICAP's associate editor had rounded out his knowledge.

"That was Lex Mebane," Hall said as he hung up. "He'll interview Killian when he gets back to New York." Mebane, a NICAP member and an officer of Civilian Saucer Intelligence, New York, often had checked reports for us.

Hall gave me the Akron telegram. I noted the United flight numbers, then dialed the Federal Aviation Agency (formerly the CAA). An FAA press official told me, after hedging at first, that they would not investigate.

"Why not?" I asked. "It was on a Federal airway. FAA is supposed to safeguard airline passengers."

"FAA's responsibility ends when a UFO report is forwarded to the Air Force. Beyond that, no comment."

"You're not concerned about possible danger to passengers?"

"I didn't say that. But anyway, the Air Force has proved such things don't exist."

That evening I heard from Brennard.

"They're worried about Lyndon Johnson — afraid he might order hearings before they can knock down these airline reports. They can't figure any plausible answer, and they don't dare get rough with Killian — at least until they're sure those other pilots won't talk."

"I'm positive they'd back Killian," I said, "unless the Air Force puts pressure on their companies."

"Which they're probably doing right now," said Brennard.

It was not until Friday that the Air Force acted to neutralize the Killian story. Brennard had gotten the word, but I couldn't believe his source had it right until I heard the newscast:

"The Air Force tonight explained that airline pilots who reported flying saucers last Tuesday actually were seeing stars through broken clouds. Officers at the Air Technical Intelligence Center said . . ."

I turned off the radio.

It was preposterous. The sky had been cloudless; Captain Killian, First Officer Dee, the other airline crews and the Curtiss Wright man all were on record. And both Orion and the UFOs had been seen simultaneously, as Mebane's interview had confirmed.

Apparently, the censors hoped Killian would keep silent to avoid more direct ridicule. It might have worked, if they had not overplayed their hand.

On the day after the sighting, the influential New York *Herald Tribune* had asked for an explanation. Not content with the Orion answer, an Air Force spokesman had released an attack on all flying-saucer witnesses.

Some observers were sarcastically labeled as persons "who can't remember anything when they sober up next day." All the others, the spokesman implied, were either deluded, incompetent, or liars.

To many who later wrote NICAP, it seemed that Captain Killian had been purposely grouped with drunks, to discredit his testimony.

When I finally got Killian on the phone I could sense a controlled anger.

"I never drink before or during a flight," he said flatly. "The Air Force knows it's a strict airline rule."

"What do you think of the Orion answer?"

"It's not true," said Captain Killian. "In the first place, the clouds were 3,500 feet *below* us. Second, we saw the UFOs and Orion at the same time, repeatedly. Even if there had been broken clouds, no experienced airline pilot would be deceived like that."

"Would you tell all this to a Congressional committee?" I asked him.

"I certainly would!"

After I explained NICAP's purpose, Captain Killian agreed to meet me in New York on March 27. Before we finished, I asked about a statement the *Herald Tribune* said he had made:

"I am sure there are people on other planets who have solved the problem of space travel. I sincerely believe their vehicles are coming close to the earth."

"Is that correct?" I asked.

"Yes," said Killian, "that is what I believe."

The anonymous spokesman's attack, combined with the Orion explanation, brought a quick reaction. At NICAP, a flood of mail, telegrams, and calls protested the Air Force treatment of Killian. On Long Island, between trips, Killian was beseiged with requests for press and radio interviews. In one statement taped by Paul Parker, of WIP, Philadelphia, he bluntly denounced the Air Force tactics.

The Orion answer, he said, had been put out by a Pentagon group without ever hearing the evidence. Not a single Air Force representative had questioned him or Dee or the other American crews.

At that time American Airlines appeared to be backing his fight. The *Flagship,* the line's magazine, published a full report of his sighting, and a copy was sent to the Air Force.

By coincidence, a Navy statement helped to boost public interest in UFOs. On March 11, Rear Admiral George Dufek advised the public not to discount the reality of flying saucers.

"Some of the supposed meteor explosions in our atmosphere," he said, "might be saucers from Venus or other planets, driven by intelligent creatures. I think it is very stupid for human beings to think no one else in the universe is as intelligent as we are."

By the middle of March, the censors knew they were in trouble. Not only was sympathy building up for Killian, but the Orion story was being called an outright phony by many who had followed the case.

On March 19, Air Force Headquarters came to a hard decision. The Orion explanation would have to be killed.

Next day, at a Pentagon press conference, this answer was officially retracted. Then a new explanation was released:

The "mysterious objects" seen by Captain Killian and other pilots had proved to be nothing but B-47 bombers refueling in flight from a KC-97 tanker.

Whether the reporters believed it or not, most of their papers ran the story straight. A few used it to get laughs; Killian was quoted as saying he'd been chased by a "saucer with little green men."

Even before this, the ridicule had spread to Captain Killian's family. When the tanker story came out, his smoldering anger flamed.

"First they said I'd been drinking!" he told reporters. "Then I was seeing stars through clouds. Now they jump to another contradictory story.

"I don't care what the Air Force says! I know exactly what B-47's look like refueling. I know the KC-97 tanker, the number of lights it has. The objects I saw were at least three times the size of any tanker or bomber we have. They could travel at 2,000 miles an hour. And they were *not* conventional aircraft!"

Killian's hot retort was printed in New York and Long Island papers, and word swiftly reached the Pentagon. One PIO, I learned later, was about to blast back when the censors stopped him. The Air Force grimly kept silent.

Four days after this, as I was preparing material for the discussion in New York, Lou Corbin called.

"I have a Maryland congressman — Representative Sam Friedel — all set to hop onto this Killian business."

"Does the Air Force know he's working with you?"

"I don't know. He's not afraid of them, if that's what you mean. Are you going to see Captain Killian on Friday?"

"Yes, he's coming into New York."

"See if he'll come down to Washington and meet Congressman Friedel. I think Friedel will ask Senator Goldwater and some others to listen to Killian's story. It might work into a red-hot press conference."

When I flew to New York on the 27th, Corbin had arranged to tape a preliminary interview with Representative Friedel. He was to phone me afterward.

I checked into my hotel and called Killian's home. His wife answered. Then the blow fell.

"Captain Killian has been silenced by the Air Force," Mrs. Killian told me. "He's under strict orders. He can't meet you or talk with anyone about what he saw."

Then she told me how it had happened.

The demand that Killian be muzzled, after his blast at the Air Force, had been relayed through American Airlines. It was a clear violation of the pilot's civil rights, as well as the airline's. What arguments or pressure had been used, Mrs. Killian did not know. But a private citizen, in peacetime, had been summarily silenced.

An hour or so later, Lou Corbin phoned.

"I suddenly had the idea of getting Killian on this tape with Representative Friedel. I called — and his wife said the Air Force had shut him up!"

"I know. She told me, too."

"Well, whoever ordered it may get a jolt! Friedel says he'll guarantee Killian his 'day in court' if he has to start a Congressional investigation."

"Can we quote that?"

"Absolutely. It's on the tape."

"Is Representative Friedel writing Killian?"

"No, Killian has to make the first move."

"He won't do it, Lou."

"But, good heavens, a congressman —"

"If a committee subpoenaed him, he'd have to talk, but he won't dare disobey that order. He'd lose his job."

"Say, do you suppose they found out about Friedel? This could've been rushed through to stop Killian from meeting any congressmen."

"It's possible. But I think they'd have shut him up, anyway, after he lit into them."

When Killian was muzzled, I thought the censors would be satisfied. But there still was a danger, as Henry Brennard pointed out when I returned to Washington:

"Killian is on record that he knew exactly what night refueling looks like. He even gave reporters the number of lights on a KC-97's belly. So how could he have been fooled? That's what a lot of people would like to know — and they're asking questions."

As disbelief in the Air Force answer mounted, the censors took a final, incredible step.

"You won't believe this," Brennard said when he told me. "They've put out a statement Killian is supposed to have made on the night of the sighting. The Air Force claims American Airlines gave it to them. Here it is:

" 'Having never seen night refueling of jets by a tanker, I suppose that could be what we saw.' " *

"Henry, that's absolutely untrue! I talked with Captain Killian myself, and he described night refueling —"

"Well, they've fixed him now. But it's almost unbelievable — to silence a man like Killian and then call him a liar, when he can't defend himself. I wonder what kind of thinking is back of a trick like that."

It was the first time Brennard had shown such concern over the

---

* Signed Air Force statement in NICAP files.

censorship, though other newsmen I knew had been increasingly disturbed. Even some congressmen were seriously worried, suspecting that something frightening lay behind the official secrecy. One, I recalled, was Representative Ralph J. Scott. He had revealed his uneasiness in writing a NICAP member:

> I quite agree with you that the general public should be allowed information thus far known about Flying Objects, except of course in the case where they might become unduly alarmed or panicked by such a revelation. I am sure you can readily understand and appreciate the seriousness of such a reaction.
>
> If the information could be presented to the American public in such a way as to appeal to reason and not to emotion, I think it would be a good thing.*

But could the facts be presented without causing panic? Would an appeal to reason work?

There was no easy answer. To evaluate the grounds for fear, one would have to know the main points of the whole flying-saucer story, especially the important items NICAP had learned since '56:

The hushed-up Captain Ryan case, involving three government agencies . . . the truth behind the November '57 crisis, and why an Air Force major general had warned his command not to talk . . . the refusal of ATIC (Air Technical Intelligence Center) to explain its earlier admission about pilots firing on UFOs . . . and the strange script on "saucers" for closed-circuit use at Lackland Air Force Base.

There were scores of other revealing developments, all of them documented. Perhaps the most serious of all was an extract from an Intelligence report — the startling opinions of an Air Force pilot and his crew, after a peculiar encounter.

Somewhere in this hidden information were the clues to the UFO riddle and the causes of censorship.

The search for the truth, by NICAP, had begun in early '57.

It had been a sobering, sometimes incredible two years.

---

* Original in NICAP files.

# The
# Killian Case . . .

*And the same case, as reported by Lawrence Tacker*
*in* Flying Saucers and the U. S. Air Force.

. . . On 24 February 1959 at 8:45 PM the pilot of an American Airlines Flight in the vicinity of Bradford, Pennsylvania, enroute from Newark Air Field, New Jersey, to Detroit, Michigan, sighted a mysterious lighted object and called the attention of his passengers to this strange sight. This sighting was also seen by a United Airlines pilot who reported seeing the strange lights 50 miles East of Youngstown, Ohio at 8:45 PM. Ground observers also reported the strange lights over Akron, Ohio, at 9:15 PM. The pilot of the American Airlines Flight made the following statement:

"It was approximately 2045. I noticed these three lights off my left wing in the vicinity of Bradford, Pennsylvania. I was flying at 8,500 feet on top of broken clouds. Visibility was unlimited with no upper clouds observed. It was extremely difficult to ascertain the distance of the lights. The color of the lights were from a yellow to a light orange. The intensity of the lights also changed from dim to a bright brilliance. Sometimes the interval of the three lights were identical to the Belt in the Constellation Orion. Occasionally the rear lights lagged somewhat behind. Also they changed altitudes. During the 40 minutes of observation, the three lights occasionally came forward from a 9 o'clock position. Also occasionally the light extinguished completely alternating from one to another, sometimes the whole three were extinguished and during this whole operation, as I mentioned before, the lights changed in intensity. This action was not only seen by myself but four crew members and passengers on board and also by two other airplanes in the area.

"The only possible explanation other than flying saucers could be a jet tanker refueling operation. Never having witnessed a refueling operation at night, I am not aware of the lighting of the jet tanker.

"My air speed during this complete flight was 250 knots indicated. I also do not know the air speed of tankers during operation if this could be so. I contacted Air Traffic Control to find out if they had any airplanes on a clearance and no three airplanes were given.

"In summary, it was difficult for me to believe they were jets because of low speed and configuration. If they weren't jets I still don't know anymore than I did before even though I watched them for 40 minutes before. Due to the dark and strong lights I was not able to ascertain any size or shape. The altitude of the objects was 30 degrees above my horizon. Distance away is unknown."

The geographical area concerned was bordered on the North along the New York-Pennsylvania border by the route of American Airlines Flight #139, which had departed Newark, New Jersey, at 7:10 PM and was scheduled to arrive at Detroit, Michigan, at 10:52 PM. On the South the geographical area concerned was bordered by the Pittsburgh, Pennsylvania — Akron, Ohio, locale, overflown by the United Airlines flight reporting this incident. The American Airlines pilot, Captain Killian, said "sometimes the interval of the three lights were identical to the Belt in the Constellation Orion." This was initially mentioned as a possible solution by the United States Air Force, with a qualifying statement that the report as submitted had not yet been analyzed and that the findings of the Aerospace Technical Intelligence Center would be based upon a complete analysis and evaluation of the reported sighting.

The pilot's written statement suggested the possibility that he had witnessed a night aerial refueling operation. This statement was furnished to the Air Force by Mr. J. A. Maxwell, Manager of Operations, American Air Lines, Detroit, Michigan, and was taken from the pilot's flight report turned in to the airline operations office immediately after the flight.

This sighting turned out to be B-47 type aircraft accomplishing night refueling from KC-97 tanker aircraft. The pilot's report confirmed this, and Air Force records indicate that three B-47 aircraft were in the geographical area mentioned on night refueling operations. Air Force KC-97 tanker aircraft have several groups of lights which at a distance would appear to be one or more lights. The time duration of the refueling operation varies and can last well over an hour, depending on the type of operation.

The KC-97 tanker refueling a B-47 aircraft normally flies at an altitude of approximately 17,000 feet, at approximately 230 knots true air speed. This accounted for the lights seen by Captain Killian being approximately 30 degrees above his aircraft and remaining in view for approximately 40 minutes. These facts also coincide with his report of low speed and general configuration of the object or objects.

In addition, since the tanker was making a ground speed of approximately 210 knots (230 knots true air speed, with a 20 knot headwind) and the United Airlines pilot first reported seeing the lights at 8:45 PM, 50 miles East of Youngstown, Ohio, heading toward Akron, Ohio, a distance of 120 miles, this also accounts for the tanker aircraft lights being sighted over Akron at 9:15 by ground observers. The final proof was supplied by the 772nd Aircraft Control and Warning Squadron at Claysburg, Pennsylvania, which confirmed the fact that three B-47 type aircraft were conducting night refueling operations in the area. . . .

# The Florida
# Scoutmaster . . .

*Was this a hoax? asks Edward J. Ruppelt in another
selection from* The Report on Unidentified Flying
Objects.

On the morning of August 20 I was getting ready to go to work,
when one of these rare occasions occurred and the phone rang — it
was the ATIC OD. An operational immediate wire had just come
in for Blue Book. Lieutenant Flues had gone over to the message
center and gotten it. He thought that it was important and wanted
me to come right out. For some reason he didn't want to read it over
the phone, although it was not classified. I should come out, so I
left in a hurry.

The wire was from the intelligence officer at an air base in Florida. The previous night a scoutmaster and three boy scouts had
seen a UFO. The scoutmaster had been burned when he approached too close to the UFO. The wire went on to give a few
sketchy details and state that the scoutmaster was a "solid citizen."

I immediately put in a long-distance call to the intelligence officer. He confirmed the data in the wire. He had talked briefly to the
scoutmaster on the phone and from all he could gather it was no
hoax. The local police had been contacted and they verified the
story and the fact of the burns. I asked the intelligence officer to
contact the scoutmaster and ask if he would submit to a physical
examination immediately. I could imagine the rumors that could
start about the scoutmaster's condition, and I wanted proof. The
report sounded good, so I told the intelligence officer I'd get down
to see him as soon as possible.

I immediately called Colonel Dunn, then chief at ATIC, and

gave him a brief rundown. He agreed that I should go down to Florida as soon as possible and offered to try to get an Air Force B-25, which would save time over the airlines.

I told Bob Olsson to borrow a Geiger counter at Wright Field, then check out a camera. I called my wife and asked her to pack a few clothes and bring them out to me. Bob got the equipment, ran home and packed a bag, and in two hours he and I and our two pilots, Captain Bill Hoey and Captain David Douglas, were on our way to Florida to investigate one of the weirdest UFO reports that I came up against.

When we arrived, the intelligence officer arranged for the scoutmaster to come out to the air base. The latter knew we were coming, so he arrived at the base in a few minutes. He was a very pleasant chap, in his early thirties, not at all talkative but apparently willing to co-operate.

While he was giving us a brief personal history, I had the immediate impression that he was telling the truth. He'd lived in Florida all of his life. He'd gone to a private military prep school, had some college, and then had joined the Marines. He told us that he had been in the Pacific most of the war and repeated some rather hairy stories of what he'd been through. After the war he'd worked as an auto mechanic, then gone to Georgia for a while to work in a turpentine plant. After returning to Florida, he opened a gas station, but some hard luck had forced him to sell out. He was now working as a clerk in a hardware store. Some months back a local church had decided to organize a boy scout troop and he had offered to be the scoutmaster.

On the night before the weekly scout meeting had broken up early. He said that he had offered to give four of the boys a ride home. He had let one of the boys out when the conversation turned to a stock car race that was to take place soon. They talked about the condition of the track. It had been raining frequently, and they wondered if the track was flooded, so they drove out to look at it. Then they started south toward a nearby town to take another of the boys home. They took a black-top road about 10 miles inland from the heavily-traveled coastal highway that passes through sparsely settled areas of scrub pine and palmetto thickets.

They were riding along when the scoutmaster said that he noticed a light off to his left in the pines. He slowed down and asked the boys if they'd seen it; none of them had. He started to drive on, when he saw the lights again. This time all of the boys saw them too, so he stopped. He said that he wanted to go back into the woods to see what was going on, but that the boys were afraid to stay alone. Again he started to drive on, but in a few seconds decided he had to go back. So he turned the car around, went back, and parked beside the road at a point just opposite where he'd seen the lights.

I stopped him at this point to find out a little bit more about why he'd decided to go back. People normally didn't go running off into palmetto thickets infested with rattlesnakes at night. He had a logical answer. The lights looked like an airplane crashing into the woods some distance away. He didn't believe that was what he saw, but the thought that this could be a possibility bothered him. After all, he had said, he was a scoutmaster, and if somebody was in trouble, his conscience would have bothered him the rest of his life if he hadn't investigated and it had been somebody in need of help.

A fifteen-minute radio program had just started, and he told the boys that he was going to go into the woods, and that if he wasn't back by the time the program ended they should run down the road to a farmhouse that they had passed and get help. He got out and started directly into the wood, wearing a faded denim billed cap and carrying a machete and two flashlights. One of the lights was a spare he carried in his back pocket.

He had traveled about 50 yards off the road when he ran into a palmetto thicket, so he stopped and looked for a clear path. But finding none, he started pushing his way through the waist-high tangle of brush.

When he stopped, he recalled later, he had first become aware of an odd odor. He couldn't exactly describe it to us, except to say that it was "sharp" or "pungent." It was very faint, actually more like a subconscious awareness at first. Another sensation he recalled after the incident was a very slight difference in temperature, hardly perceivable, like walking by a brick building in the evening after the sun has set. He hadn't thought anything about either the

odor or the heat at the time but later, when they became important, he remembered them.

Paying no attention to these sensations then, he pushed on
through the brush, looking up occasionally to check the north star,
so that he could keep traveling straight east. After struggling
through about 30 yards of palmetto undergrowth, he noticed a
change in the shadows ahead of him and stopped to shine the flashlight farther ahead of him to find out if he was walking into a clearing or into one of the many ponds that dot that particular Florida
area. It was a clearing.

The boy scouts in the car had been watching the scoutmaster's
progress since they could see his light bobbing around. Occasionally he would shine it up at a tree or across the landscape for an
instant, so they knew where he was in relation to the trees and
thickets. They saw him stop at the edge of the open, shadowed area
and shine his light ahead of him.

The scoutmaster then told us that when he stopped this second
time he first became consciously aware of the odor and the heat.
Both became much more noticeable as he stepped into the clearing.
In fact, the heat became almost unbearable or, as he put it, "op-
pressively moist, making it hard to breathe."

He walked a few more paces and suddenly got a horrible feeling
that somebody was watching him. He took another step, stopped,
and looked up to find the north star. But he couldn't see the north
star, or any stars. Then he suddenly saw that almost the whole sky
was blanked out by a large dark shape about 30 feet above him.

He said that he had stood in this position for several seconds, or
minutes — he didn't know how long — because now the feeling of
being watched had overcome any power of reasoning he had. He
managed to step back a few paces, and apparently got out from
under the object, because he could see the edge of it silhouetted
against the sky.

As he backed up, he said, the air became much cooler and
fresher, helping him to think more clearly. He shone his light up at
the edge of the object and got a quick but good look. It was circular-shaped and slightly concave on the bottom. The surface was
smooth and a grayish color. He pointed to a gray linoleum-topped

desk in the intelligence officer's room. "Just like that," he said. The upper part had a dome in the middle, like a turret. The edge of the saucer-shaped object was thick and had vanes spaced about every foot, like buckets on a turbine wheel. Between each vane was a small opening, like a nozzle.

The next reaction that the scoutmaster recalled was one of fury. He wanted to harm or destroy whatever it was that he saw. All he had was a machete, but he wanted to try to jump up and strike at whatever he was looking at. No sooner did he get this idea than he noticed the shadows on the turret change ever so slightly and heard a sound, "like the opening of a well-oiled safe door." He froze where he stood and noticed a small ball of red fire begin to drift toward him. As it floated down it expanded into a cloud of red mist. He dropped his light and machete, and put his arms over his face. As the mist enveloped him, he passed out.

The boy scouts in the car estimated that their scoutmaster had been gone about five minutes when they saw him stop at the edge of the clearing, then walk on in. They saw him stop seconds later, hesitate a few more seconds, then shine the light up in the air. They thought he was just looking at the trees again. The next thing they said they saw was a big red ball of fire engulfing him. They saw him fall, so they spilled out of the car and took off down the road toward the farmhouse.

The farmer and his wife had a little difficulty getting the story out of the boys, they were so excited. All they could get was something about the boys' scoutmaster being in trouble down the road. The farmer called the Florida State Highway Patrol, who relayed the message to the county sheriff's office. In a few minutes a deputy sheriff and the local constable arrived. They picked up the scouts and drove to where their car was parked.

The scoutmaster had no idea of how long he had been unconscious. He vaguely remembered leaning against a tree, the feeling of wet, dew-covered grass, and suddenly regaining his consciousness. His first reaction was to get out to the highway, so he started to run. About halfway through palmetto thicket he saw a car stop on the highway. He ran toward it and found the deputy and constable with the boys.

He was so excited he could hardly get his story told coherently.

Later the deputy said that in all his years as a law-enforcement officer he had never seen anyone as scared as the scoutmaster was as he came up out of the ditch beside the road and walked into the glare of the headlights. As soon as he'd told his story, they all went back into the woods, picking their way around the palmetto thicket. The first thing they noticed was the flashlight, still burning, in a clump of grass. Next to it was a place where the grass was flattened down, as if a person had been lying there. They looked around for the extra light that the scoutmaster had been carrying, but it was gone. Later searches for this missing flashlight were equally fruitless. They marked the spot where the crushed grass was located and left. The constable took the boy scouts home and the scoutmaster followed the deputy to the sheriff's office. On the way to town the scoutmaster said he first noticed that his arms and face burned. When he arrived at the sheriff's office, he found that his arms, face, and cap *were* burned. The deputy called the Air Force.

There were six people listening to his story. Bob Olsson, the two pilots, the intelligence officer, his sergeant, and I. We each had previously agreed to pick one insignificant detail from the story and then requestion the scoutmaster when he had finished. Our theory was that if he had made up the story he would either repeat the details perfectly or not remember what he'd said. I'd used this many times before, and it was a good indicator of a lie. He passed the test with flying colors. His story sounded good to all of us.

We talked for about another hour, discussing the event and his background. He kept asking, "What did I see?" — evidently thinking that I knew. He said that the newspapers were after him, since the sheriff's office had inadvertently leaked the story, but that he had been stalling them off pending our arrival. I told him it was Air Force policy to allow people to say anything they wanted to about a UFO sighting. We had never muzzled anyone; it was his choice. With that, we thanked him, arranged to pick up the cap and machete to take back to Dayton, and sent him home in a staff car.

By this time it was getting late, but I wanted to talk to the flight surgeon who had examined the man that morning. The intelligence officer found him at the hospital and he said he would be right over. His report was very thorough. The only thing he could find out of the ordinary were minor burns on his arms and the back of his hands. There were also indications that the inside of his nostrils might be burned. The degree of burn could be compared to a light sunburn. The hair had also been singed, indicating a flash heat.

The flight surgeon had no idea how this specifically could have happened. It could have even been done with a cigarette lighter, and he took his lighter and singed a small area of his arm to demonstrate. He had been asked only to make a physical check, so that is what he'd done, but he did offer a suggestion. Check his Marine records; something didn't ring true. I didn't quite agree; the story sounded good to me.

The next morning my crew from ATIC, three people from the intelligence office, and the two law officers went out to where the incident had taken place. We found the spot where somebody had apparently been lying and the scoutmaster's path through the thicket. We checked the area with a Geiger counter, as a precautionary measure, not expecting to find anything; we didn't. We went over the area inch by inch, hoping to find a burned match with which a flare of fireworks could have been lighted, drippings from a flare, or anything that shouldn't have been in a deserted area of woods. We looked at the trees; they hadn't been hit by lightning. The blades of grass under which the UFO supposedly hovered were not burned. We found nothing to contradict the story. We took a few photos of the area and went back to town. On the way back we talked to the constable and the deputy. All they could do was to confirm what we'd heard.

We talked to the farmer and his wife, but they couldn't help. The few facts that the boy scouts had given them before they had a chance to talk to their scoutmaster correlated with his story. We talked to the scoutmaster's employer and some of his friends; he was a fine person. We questioned people who might have been in a position to also observe something; they saw nothing. The local citizens had a dozen theories, and we thoroughly checked each one.

He hadn't been struck by lightning. He hadn't run across a still. There was no indication that he'd surprised a gang of illegal turtle butchers, smugglers, or bootleggers. There was no indication of marsh gas or swamp fire. The mysterious blue lights in the area turned out to be a farmer arcwelding at night. The other flying saucers were the landing lights of airplanes landing at a nearby airport.

To be very honest, we were trying to prove that this was a hoax, but were having absolutely no success. Every new lead we dug up pointed to the same thing, a true story.

We finished our work on a Friday night and planned to leave early Saturday morning. Bob Olsson and I planned to fly back on a commercial airliner, as the B-25 was grounded for maintenance. Just after dinner that night I got a call from the sheriff's office. It was from a deputy I had talked to, not the one who met the scoutmaster coming out of the woods, but another one, who had been very interested in the incident. He had been doing a little independent checking and found that our singed UFO observer's background was not as clean as he led one to believe. He had been booted out of the Marines after a few months for being AWOL and stealing an automobile, and had spent some time in a federal reformatory in Chillicothe, Ohio. The deputy pointed out that this fact alone meant nothing but that he thought I might be interested in it. I agreed.

The next morning, early, I was awakened by a phone call from the intelligence office. The morning paper carried the UFO story on the front page. It quoted the scoutmaster as saying that "high brass" from Washington had questioned him late into the night. There was no "high brass," just four captains, a second lieutenant, and a sergeant. He knew we were from Dayton because we had discussed who we were and where we were stationed. The newspaper story went on to say that "he, the scoutmaster, and the Air Force knew what he'd seen but he couldn't tell — it would create a national panic." He'd also hired a press agent. I could understand the "high brass from the Pentagon" as literary license by the press, but this "national panic" pitch was too much. I had just about decided to give up on this incident and write it off as "Unknown" until this happened. From all appearances, our scoutmaster was going to make a fast buck on his experience. Just before leaving for Dayton, I called Major Dewey Fournet in the Pentagon and asked him to do some checking.

Monday morning the machete went to the materials lab at Wright-Patterson. The question we asked was, "Is there anything unusual about this machete? Is it magnetized? Is it radioactive? Has it been heated?" No knife was ever tested so thoroughly for so many things. As in using a Geiger counter to check the area over which the UFO had hovered in the Florida woods, our idea was to investigate every possible aspect of the sighting. They found nothing, just a plain, unmagnetized, unradioactive, unheated, common, everyday knife.

The cap was sent to a laboratory in Washington, D.C., along with the scoutmaster's story. Our question here was, "Does the cap in any way (burns, chemicals, etc.) substantiate or refute the story?"

I thought that we'd collected all the items that could be analyzed in a lab until somebody thought of one I'd missed, the most obvious of them all — soil and grass samples from under the spot where the UFO had hovered. We'd had samples, but in the last-minute rush to get back to Dayton they had been left in Florida. I called Florida and they were shipped to Dayton and turned over to an agronomy lab for analysis.

By the end of the week I received a report on our ex-Marine's military and reformatory records. They confirmed a few suspicions and added new facts. They were not complimentary. The discrepancy between what we'd heard about the scoutmaster while we were in Florida and the records was considered a major factor. I decided that we should go back to Florida and try to resolve this discrepancy.

Since it was hurricane season, we had to wait a few days, then sneak back between two hurricanes. We contacted a dozen people in the city where the scoutmaster lived. All of them had known him for some time. We traced him from his early boyhood to the time of the sighting. To be sure that the people we talked to were reliable, we checked on them. The specific things we found out cannot be told since they were given to us in confidence, but we were convinced that the whole incident was a hoax.

We didn't talk to the scoutmaster again but we did talk to all the boy scouts one night at their scout meeting, and they retold how they had seen their scoutmaster knocked down by the ball of fire. The night before, we had gone out to the area of the sighting and, under approximately the same lighting conditions as existed on the night of the sighting, had re-enacted the scene — especially the part where the boy scouts saw their scoutmaster fall, covered with red fire. We found that not even by standing *on top of the car* could you see a person silhouetted in the clearing where the scoutmaster supposedly fell. The rest of their stories fell apart to some extent too. They were not as positive of details as they had been previously.

When we returned to Dayton, the report on the cap had come back. The pattern of the scorch showed that the hat was flat when it was scorched, but the burned holes — the lab found some minute holes we had missed — had very probably been made by an electrical spark. This was all the lab could find.

During our previous visit we repeatedly asked the question, "Was the hat burned before you went into the woods?" and, "Had the cap been ironed?" We had received the same answers each time: "The hat was not burned because we [the boy scouts] were playing with it at the scout meeting and would have noticed the burns," and, "The cap was new; it had not been washed or ironed." It is rumored that the cap was never returned because it was proof of the authenticity of the sighting. The hat wasn't returned simply because the scoutmaster said that he didn't want it back. No secrets, no intrigue; it's as simple as that.

Everyone who was familiar with the incident, except a few people in the Pentagon, were convinced that this was a hoax until the lab called me about the grass samples we'd sent in. "How did the roots get charred?" Roots charred? I didn't even know what my caller was talking about. He explained that when they'd examined the grass they had knocked the dirt and sand off the roots of the grass clumps and found them charred. The blades of grass themselves were not damaged; they had never been heated, except on the extreme tips of the longer blades. These had evidently been bending over touching the ground and were also charred. The lab had duplicated the charring and had found that by placing live grass clumps in a pan of sand and dirt and heating it to about 300 degrees F. over a gas burner the charring could be duplicated. How it was actually done outside the lab they couldn't even guess.

As soon as we got the lab report, we checked a few possibilities ourselves. There were no hot underground springs to heat the earth, no chemicals in the soil, not a thing we found could explain it. The only way it could have been faked would have been to heat the earth from underneath to 300 degrees F., and how do you do this without using big and cumbersome equipment and disturbing the ground? You can't. Only a few people handled the grass specimens: the lab, the intelligence officer in Florida, and I. The lab wouldn't do it as a joke, then write an official report, and I didn't do it. This leaves the intelligence officer; I'm positive that he wouldn't do it. There may be a single answer everyone is overlooking, but as of now the charred grass roots from Florida are still a mystery.

Writing an official report on this incident was difficult. On one side of the ledger was a huge mass of circumstantial evidence very heavily weighed against the scoutmaster's story being true. On our second trip to Florida, Lieutenant Olsson and I heard story after story about the man's aptitude for dreaming up tall tales. One man told us, "If he told me the sun was shining, I'd look up to make sure." There were parts of his story and those of the boy scouts that didn't quite mesh. None of us ever believed the boy scouts were in on the hoax. They were undoubtedly so impressed by the story that they imagined a few things they didn't actually see. The scoutmaster's burns weren't proof of anything; the flight surgeon had duplicated these by burning his own arm with a cigarette lighter. But we didn't make step one in proving the incident to be a hoax. We thought up dozens of ways the man could have set up the hoax but couldn't prove one.

In the scoutmaster's favor were the two pieces of physical evidence we couldn't explain, the holes burned in the cap and the charred grass roots.

The deputy sheriff who had first told me about the scoutmaster's Marine and prison record had also said, "Maybe this is the one time in his life he's telling the truth, but I doubt it."

So did we; we wrote off the incident as a hoax. The best hoax in UFO history.

Many people have asked why we didn't give the scoutmaster a lie detector test. We seriously considered it and consulted some experts in this field. They advised against it. In some definite types of cases the lie detector will not give valid results. This, they thought, was one of those cases. Had we done it and had he passed on the faulty results, the publicity would have been a headache.

There is one way to explain the charred grass roots, the burned cap, and a few other aspects of the incident. It's pure speculation; I don't believe that it is the answer, yet it is interesting. Since the blades of the grass were not damaged and the ground had not been disturbed, this one way is the only way (nobody has thought of any other way) the soil could have been heated. It could have been done by induction heating.

To quote from a section entitled "Induction Heating" from an electrical engineering textbook:

> A rod of solid metal or any electrical conductor, when subjected to an alternating magnetic field, has electromotive forces set up in it. These electromotive forces cause what are known as "eddy currents." A rise in temperature results from "eddy currents."

Induction heating is a common method of melting metals in a foundry.

Replace the "rod of solid metal" mentioned above with damp sand, an electrical conductor, and assume that a something that was generating a powerful alternating magnetic field was hovering over the ground, and you can explain how the grass roots were charred. To get an alternating magnetic field, some type of electrical equipment was needed. Electricity — electrical sparks — the holes burned in the cap "by electric sparks."

UFO propulsion comes into the picture when one remembers Dr. Einstein's unified field theory, concerning the relationship between electro-magnetism and gravitation.

If this alternating magnetic field can heat metal, why didn't everything the scoutmaster had that was metal get hot enough to burn him? He had a flashlight, machete, coins in his pocket, etc. The answer — he wasn't under the UFO for more than a few seconds. He said that when he stopped to really look at it he had backed away from under it. He did feel some heat, possibly radiating from the ground.

To further pursue this line of speculation, the scoutmaster repeatedly mentioned the unusual odor near the UFO. He described it as being "sharp" or "pungent." Ozone gas is "sharp" or "pungent." To quote from a chemistry book: "Ozone is prepared by passing air between two plates which are charged at a high electrical potential." Electrical equipment again. Breathing too high a concentration of ozone gas will also cause you to lose consciousness.

I used to try out this induction heating theory on people to get their reaction. I tried it out one day on a scientist from Rand. He practically leaped at the idea. I laughed when I explained that I thought this theory just *happened* to tie together the unanswered aspects of the incident in Florida and was not the answer; he was slightly perturbed. "What do you want?" he said. "Does a UFO have to come in and land on your desk at ATIC?"